McCARTHY FOR PRESIDENT

McCARTHY
FOR PRESIDENT
Arthur Herzog

NEW YORK | THE VIKING PRESS

Grateful acknowledgment is made to Senator Eugene J. McCarthy
for permission to use his poem "Three Bad Signs" and
excerpts from "Lament of an Aging Politician."

If there were adequate language two by-lines would appear on the cover of this book. Nothing suffices. "As told to" is wrong; "with" has come to connote, in an age of ghost-written books, a ghost-writer; "in association with" is theatrical.

Nonetheless it is true that my wife, who as a reporter writes under the name Lael Scott and who was a sturdy McCarthy campaigner herself, was responsible for much of the research, editing, and thinking which are the foundation of this book. In short, though one author signs the work, two are represented in the single name.

ACKNOWLEDGMENTS

A great many people have helped by contributing their recollections or expertise and at the risk of forgetting a few I should like to thank Bella Abzug, Herbert E. Alexander, Carl Ally, Jim Avis, Grace Bassett, Ellen Blunt, Ben Bradlee, Robert McAfee Brown, Sam Brown, Blair Clark, Betty Comden, Don Conway, Edward N. Costikyan, Paul Counihan, William Davidson, Tom de Vries, Congressman Don Edwards, Ronnie Eldridge, Jerome Eller, Jason Epstein, David Evans, Thomas K. Finletter, Thomas Finney, Philip Freedman, Eleanor Clark French, Erich Fromm, Joseph Gabler, Francis X. Gannon, Curtis and Genie Gans, David Garth, Martin Gleason, Richard N. Goodwin, Jack Gore, Paul Gorman, John Grace, Adolph Green, Donald Green, Jerome Grossman, Barbara Handman, Senator Philip Hart, Robert Healy, Russell Hemenway, Arnold Hiatt, Gerald N. Hill, David Hoeh, G. W. (Joe) Holsinger, William Honan, Jeremy Hornsby, Emerson Hynes, Madelyn Jamieson, Eliot Janeway, William and Sandy Johnson, Erica Johnston, Francis Kelley, E. W. Kenworthy, Sarah and Victor Kovner, Werner H. Kramarsky, Jane Kronholtz, Jeremy Larner, Joshua Leinsdorf, Laurence Levine, Terry Liss, Congressman Allard K. Lowenstein, Myrna Loy, Patrick Lucey, Dr. Austin McCarthy, Mary McCarthy, Michael Maccoby, Thomas McCoy, Mary McGrory, Sister Maris Stella, Rick Merrill, Lawrence Merthan, Arthur Michelson, G. Theodore Mitau, Stephen A. Mitchell, David Mixner, Jim Moody, Mrs. Paul Moore, Howard Morgan, Thomas B. Morgan, William and Kay Nee, Charles Negaro, James O'Gara, Fred Papert, Martin Peretz, Don Peterson, Robert Pirie, Tony Podesta, Stephen Quigley, Shelley Ramsdell, Joseph Rauh, Norval Reece, Herbert Reed, Father Walter Reger, O.S.B., Maurice Rosenblatt, John Safer, Jerry Schaller, Philip Scharper, Herman Schauinger, John Schmidt, David Schoumacher, Mark Segal, Terry Segal, J. B. Shea, Dan Singal, Stephen Smith, Ben and Rosanne Stavis, Richard Stearns, Howard and Janet Stein, Martin Stone, Bob Terry, Andrew Teuber, Steve Thomas, Jessica Tuchman, Father Dunstan Tucker, O.S.B., William vanden Heuvel, Ted Warshafsky, Wayne Whelan.

Special thanks to Sandra Silverman, who scheduled the researchers like candidates; to Kitty Kelly of Senator McCarthy's Washington staff; to Maria Opie; and to Louise Fisher, whose ability to transform tangled handwriting into typewritten pages is unsurpassed.

Contents

Part I | ROOTS
   1. A Memoir   3
   2. Beginnings   15
   3. The Candidate   37

Part II | JOHNSON
   4. New Hampshire: a Pilgrimage   75
   5. On to Wisconsin   100

Part III | KENNEDY
   6. Indiana and Nebraska: Senator Who?   127
   7. The Oregon Trail   144
   8. California: a Denouement   173

Part IV | HUMPHREY
   9. McCarthy Summer   193
   10. Confrontation at Chicago   240
   11. End or Beginning?   282

   Index   299

Part I | ROOTS

1 | A Memoir

"McCarthy for President!" The words conjure up a brash, whimsical, dead-earnest, unpredicted, and unpredictable endeavor unique in American politics which, it seems inevitable, will long be of interest. Even in defeat the McCarthy "movement" scored significant successes, by its own terms at least, bringing down a President in office, moving the United States toward peace in Vietnam, pulling what sometimes seemed an entire new generation into politics, and forcing the Democratic Party to take stock of itself—an effort which is far from over.

Some salient features of this remarkable effort might be noted at the beginning. Our—Eugene McCarthy was not heard to say *my;* it was always, and necessarily, *our,* for this was truly a case where the candidate was often propelled from the bottom, like a rocket—our campaign started inauspiciously enough, damned by the Democratic Party and mocked by the press, and yet, before it was over some one hundred thousand students had canvassed in the streets, some one thousand McCarthy-for-President organizations had operated throughout the country, some half-million people had made recordable contributions, and in all probability a million people actively participated. McCarthy for President, without question, was the most broadly based preconvention campaign in American history. It was also the first or second most expensive,[1] spending between eight million and ten million dollars, if state and local efforts are added—and this with a paucity of television, the principal item in the standard campaign budget. (As one might expect in a "grass-roots" campaign, some of the largest bills came from American Telephone and Telegraph.) None of this could have been foreseen when the first bands of McCarthy volunteers straggled into New Hampshire, the first primary state.

I was fairly typical of the McCarthy irregulars who learned politics in the primaries and then braced for the confrontation at Chicago. Typical with one visible exception. Forty years old at the time of New Hampshire, I was a genuine old duffer for a campaign in which the average volunteer was pushing twenty. In general, though, I was a newspaper version of a McCarthyite—"a shaggy, rumpled amateur," as the *New York Times* described me. I was strongly against the war in Vietnam, but I had singularly failed to make a determined gesture of protest. I had not withheld income tax or stormed the Pentagon—out of caution, timidity, or pessimism about marches and demonstrations, and a suspicion of doing things which might, in the end, be more of a sop to my ego than anything else. I also had a latent desire to work within the Democratic Party. McCarthy was to remark during the campaign that society shouldn't require martyrdom from those who seek change —the burden should not be put on the individual conscience.

Even beyond the issue of Vietnam, I wanted—had long wanted —serious and sweeping reform. Contemplating the country, I had been assailed by the uncomfortable sensation of living in a Manichaean world. The platitudes of political leaders, the prevalence of what one felt to be half-truths masquerading as truths, of nonideas, nonthings, and even nonpeople pretending to exist—all contributed to an atmosphere which seemed to elevate the phony and

[1] The only primary McCarthy rival was Richard Nixon. Nixon's 1968 campaign, according to Herbert E. Alexander of the Citizens' Research Foundation, cost more, but the figures include campaign expenditures for 1966 and 1967. Which campaign spent more in 1968—Nixon's or McCarthy's—was not known at this writing.

enshrine the old patterns and attitudes.[2] There was, it seemed, almost no way to break out of the established molds and assert more imaginative solutions. Events appeared not only out of the individual's control but out of control altogether and so, as Richard Goodwin has written, "alienation, rage, desperation and a growing sense of futility increasingly mar our political life." Helpless to change anything at all, politically disembodied, I had come to feel like a noncitizen.

When the call to go to New Hampshire issued from Mrs. Sarah Kovner of the New York Coalition for a Democratic Alternative (at the time I knew neither her nor the organization), the urge was to continue being too lazy, skeptical, cynical, busy, orderly, money-minded, and mired in complexity. But frustration had reached the breaking point and, in the end, there really was no alternative. Besides, the primary election was approaching and, as Mrs. Kovner said, "It'll only be for ten days." After that, everybody said, the McCarthy campaign would be over.

A Sunday at the beginning of March. General Westmoreland was pressing for between one hundred thousand and two hundred thousand more troops for Vietnam; another Buddhist monk had made ashes of himself in a pyrotechnic prayer for peace. On the gray-snowy road to New Hampshire my wife, Lael, and I finally and seriously asked each other what we expected to accomplish in (where were we headed?) the Granite State. We didn't want to make just a gesture, that would be quixotic and farcical; we hoped to be *effective*. Chugging north in a Volkswagen—virtually the McCarthy movement's family car, while the Kennedy campaigners buzzed around in sports cars and the Humphrey people in Fords

---

[2] Of another period in American history when the national mind seemed wrapped in a "steel chain" of ideas, the late nineteenth century, from which several McCarthyesque political revolts developed, Eric F. Goldman has said, "The dominant groups in America had simply done what dominant groups usually do. They had, quite unconsciously, picked from among available theories the ones that best protected their position and had impressed these ideas on the national mind as Truth."

and Chevys—we fantasized, in a fit of high seriousness, our goal: to turn out such an overwhelming vote for this quiet Senator from Minnesota that the highhanded President of the United States would be forced to change the policy in Vietnam and possibly step down from office. That Hanoi, the Vietcong, or the Republican Party had failed to defeat the President certainly would not deter us, for the alchemy of a campaign had begun to work. The underdog must not consider defeat.

Concord, New Hampshire, housed the state headquarters. Earnest flesh was everywhere: working mimeograph machines, assembling packets of buttons and literature, sweeping the floor, writing releases, and especially talking into the telephone. Everybody, evidently, was doing *something,* although it was often difficult to determine what or, for that matter, why. I was received with calmness and eight hours later, changing positions in my chair, I still awaited instructions. The lateness of the hour did not bring any slackening in the proceedings; quite the opposite, the swirling group appeared to be increasing its velocity and would acquire peak energy, one supposed, about dawn. During this very long wait I came upon the central insight or inspiration without which no one could long function in the McCarthy movement. The campaign was the ultimate existential situation: you had to invent yourself.

To comprehend this, one must look into the heart of volunteer psychology, and volunteers *were* the heart of the McCarthy-for-President campaign, making the effort famous and providing the very model of its cry for "participatory democracy." Volunteers are not paid—indeed, the volunteer's first discovery is that one can work harder for goals than for money—and *because* they are not paid but wish to prove that their cause and ardor for it outshine crass monetary considerations they insistently work harder than paid help. Great strain is thus placed on the ingenuity of the campaign manager who must find jobs for volunteers. His newest ideas for busywork may not always come on time, and for this reason many capable folk, especially older folk, arrived eagerly at Con-

cord only to depart on the next bus in tears and disgust, feeling
unneeded. This was where the campaign separated the boys from
the men. There was plenty to do, only you had to figure out a job
description, and fill it, yourself. At that point it became your job;
and those who invented the best jobs and performed them most
capably became the leaders. The process was precisely the reverse
of corporate organization, where slots exist to be filled, and provided hope for the future of anarchy. (The campaign manager has
to be careful, of course, because volunteers in their zest can insti-
gate ruinous projects, wasting money and losing elections.)

Having scented such truths, I went to a map, studied the location
of McCarthy headquarters in the state of New Hampshire, identified by colored pins, and discovered that a portion in the south,
around the town of Salem, containing about five per cent of the
voting population, was uninhabited by McCarthy forces. There
was no campaign office in this McCarthy desert. Surprised, I asked
young Harold Ickes—the son of Roosevelt's Secretary of the In-
terior who himself tried to unseat Truman in 1948—the reason and
was given two, in his customarily salty language. First, the area was
dreadfully, hopelessly, hawkish and conservative; second, there
was nobody experienced enough to send. Ickes thought that, yes,
perhaps we should go there, being adult, that is over twenty-one,
and thus capable of gracefully absorbing certain defeat.

About midnight I was summoned to the desk of the New Hampshire campaign coordinator (a term used to designate the out-of-
state, as opposed to the indigenous, leader), a sallow fellow of
about thirty named Curtis Gans. (Gans was thin to start with but
later, after months of four hours' sleep and a diet of hamburgers
and Cokes, he was almost to disappear, leaving only hair, like a
barber's version of the Cheshire cat.) I made my proposal.

"Impossible. You can't go to Salem. You're just an amateur."

Well, anybody who had spent an hour at McCarthy headquarters
knew that a professional there was somebody with a week's experience. I persisted, indulging in self-praise: capable, adaptable,

ingenious, a winner. Also, I pointed out, there was another Me-
thuselah hanging around the place who would come along. His
name was L. Rust Hills and he possessed an incomparable campaign asset, a blue Ford pickup truck.

In some weird way Gans and I were now bargaining, following
the tradition that everything in politics is a trade-off. It was suddenly established that the Herzogs could go to Salem on the condition that L. Rust Hills could not. The judgment seemed a pity.
Hills, formerly and to be again fiction editor of *Esquire,* critic, and
anthologist (*How We Live*), and I were old, customarily devoted
friends. We were exceptionally competitive with each other on
almost every gaming field known to man: tennis, poker, chess, and
even croquet at midnight under the lights of a large, carefully
placed, Druidic circle of cars. We could be depended upon to
compete for votes. Hills went into a rage. Discontented with his
present occupation, scouting shopping centers for appearances by
actor Tony Randall, Hills made the volunteer's ultimate gesture
of defiance: he threatened to *resign.* Gans sighed and capitulated.

Early next morning Hills' truck was loaded with McCarthy buttons, bumper stickers, posters, and literature, and the campaigners
were presented with three hundred dollars in cash, carefully recorded by Jessica Tuchman, daughter of Barbara Tuchman.
(Everybody was the son or daughter of *somebody.*) We were ready
to begin the conquest of Salem.

It has been nearly forgotten that before the McCarthy movement, the "new politics" was, in the words of James M. Perry, "the
expanding technology of political manipulation." According to
Perry, there were "two essential ingredients of the new politics.
One is that appeals should be made directly to the voters through
the mass media. The other is that the techniques used to make
these appeals—polling, computers, television and direct mail—
should be sophisticated and scientific."

Before the New Hampshire primary meant anything to me personally I happened to inspect the best-laid plans of a professional group called Campaign Consultants, Inc., for the 1968 New Hampshire Republican primary campaign of Governor George Romney of Michigan. A book, some 150 pages thick, complete with colored charts and acetate overlays, had been compiled. In it, voting patterns were measured as though by calipers and the "swing vote" meticulously identified, as were "CZs" (Communication Zones), points at which media could be expected to converge for maximum exposure and through which Romney was carefully scheduled, day by day, hour by hour, minute by minute. Every Republican voter in the state was on a card at a secret computer center, and there were even figures on how many doorbells a volunteer could ring in an hour. Yet so remote and abstract was the candidate in *this* version of new politics that Romney could be appropriately referred to as "the Body" or even "the body of the candidate."

Driving south to Salem, we could not yet know that the McCarthy campaign would be based on a new politics of an entirely different sort—on issues, "grass-roots" (a misleading populist term) support, citizen participation, and a candidate whose style and manner would shock the professionals and bewilder the journalists. We could only know that our resources were next to nothing. No money (what could three hundred dollars buy?), no plan, no local supporters or "friendlies," no compilation of the swing vote—we didn't even have voter-registration lists. The situation was so ludicrous that only by remembering our principled reasons for being in New Hampshire did we leave the freeway at the right exit instead of continuing back to New York. We arrived in Salem and that same day we rented a storefront. There it was, *our* headquarters, a "McCarthy for President" poster mounted defiantly on a dirty plate-glass window. "He Stood Up Alone and Something Happened," the poster announced.

The storefront had been untenanted for several years except at Christmas, when teen-agers, for a small fee, assembled do-it-yourself gifts. The campaigners were working in a similar vein. Next door was the old Rockingham Hotel, whose sheets were rough as ballots. Its clientele, eying the campaigners suspiciously, was mostly old people and touts from the near-by track. Salem's little downtown area couldn't compete with shopping centers and Massachusetts, and the place, like other small New England towns, seemed to totter on the edge of disaster. The waitresses and the chef at the Rockingham restaurant, the first prospects for McCarthy buttons, turned rapidly away.

In all of Salem and its satellites—Atkinson, East Kingston, the metropolis of Windham, the village of Sandown—the campaigners had precisely one name of a potential friendly, an Episcopal minister who displayed anxiety when confronted that first day. "My God," he said, "come out for McCarthy? *Publicly?* Do you know what you're asking? Half my parishioners are right wing, hawk, Birch. Get the picture?" he asked gloomily. He added, "Now, as a matter of fact, I'm sympathetic toward your candidate. I'll do anything I can, just so my name doesn't go on a list." Speechless with gratitude, we accepted his offer, and a magnificent Christian lot it was—tables, chairs, even a typewriter. Senator McCarthy had himself another working office. It was Monday, March 4, 1968, eight days before election Tuesday.

From this point on time was forgotten. Or rather there was no time at all but a blur of movement and evanescent impressions as progress was measured by such indices as the change in the expressions of people or the number of high-school girls who came in the evenings to type. We had a few little newspaper ads and radio commercials; once we were graced by the appearance of actors Robert Ryan and Tony Randall (who arrived the same day and were carefully juggled at shopping centers). Above all, of course, there were the students. They drove, hitchhiked, or came by bus from every school, it seemed, in the East, in such numbers that we who had prayed for their presence began to groan at the sight of every new young face. Behind them came the newspaper reporters and the network television people.

Our office now had five telephones, at least, and we canny old campaigners shocked the young by arranging to have the office called constantly from pay phones around the corner when the crews were shooting. I wanted the public to believe that Salem was turning on. Was it?

By the first and last weekend—had it been only five days?—the McCarthy campaign was putting on a show Salem had not seen before and was not likely to see again. The little storefront throbbed with activity. Twenty out-of-state adults were now working full time—a strange assortment of scientists, newspaper reporters, a public-relations expert, an electronics engineer, a librarian, and Ph.D. candidates galore. Several hundred student volunteers combed the neighborhoods and leafleted the shopping centers and factories. There were even traffic jams on streets that had thought themselves eternally safe from such big-city menaces. No, Salem had never experienced anything like it, and neither had the campaigners, few of whom had seen in the flesh their candidate, that fellow who stood up alone and made things happen, Senator ah— sometimes one almost forgot the name.

Several days before the primary, Richard Nixon came to speak in a church hall that had been offered to McCarthy student volunteers as a dormitory, an offer that was rescinded when the churchmen learned that boys and girls would be sleeping in the same room, though fully clad. The Nixon caravan, heavy with busses and crowded with members of the press, filled the street like a smug column of tanks. In the hall a band blasted away and high-school girls in high white boots and Nixon hats twirled batons and pressed campaign literature into every hand. Talking with fervent directness into the television cameras, the candidate wore make-up so thick that it was impossible to determine where the old Nixon ended and the new began. Indeed, he seemed like a machine designed for campaign purposes, and who could say whether anyone lived beneath the creamy surface. Now the McCarthy campaigners began to want desperately a visit from their own tiger and on Monday, the day before the election, they were rewarded.

On Sunday the warnings had begun. The leader might come to Salem on Monday, but then again he might not. Just what the choice depended on, and who would make it, was not explained. Perhaps the campaigners were being tested; they would have endured any ordeal to have the candidate among them. But whatever was expected was not communicated and the insight began to solidify: the McCarthy campaign was modeled on Kafka's *The Castle*. About noon on Monday the telephone suddenly shrieked that McCarthy was not only coming but that he was already en route. We had no more than two hours to prepare for him. (The Nixon appearance, you could bet, had been prepared weeks in advance.) An itinerary was instantly worked out, posters distributed, newspapers and radio stations alerted, and student volunteers brought back from the hinterlands to make a crowd. Our candidate was said to abhor the usual campaign hoopla. Sound trucks were banned as ill suited to a dignified effort based on issues. The Salem office evaded the ban by equipping several cars with sound gear that could be plugged into the cigarette lighter. These sound *cars* circulated through town while telephoners called those now identified as friendlies to come meet the candidate.

McCarthy's caravan consisted of two cars. The travelers might have managed with one, as the party, in addition to the Senator, consisted only of a young lawyer, Charles Callanan, who acted as aide-de-camp; David Hoeh, the McCarthy state chairman, doubling as the Senator's chauffeur; one or two reporters from the national press. It was my first look at McCarthy: handsome, graygreen eyes, narrow nose, and very pale. There was about him a uniform grayness of hair, skin, and suit, blending with the snow, the gray sky, and perhaps the prospects at the polls. On the street we had a semihumorous exchange—"I hear this is the best-run office in the state"; "I bet you say that to all the campaign coordinators"—and then McCarthy went into the storefront, cheered by the volunteers, and told a radio interviewer that the United States should never have become so deeply involved in Vietnam and should seek to extricate itself. Then McCarthy set out to visit a shoe factory and shopping centers. At two of these there was no crowd and McCarthy, in his baggy suit, walked bravely, with a slight limp, from store to store to shake hands with patrons who often didn't seem to know who Eugene McCarthy was. But at one of the centers McCarthy had a crowd. It was only several hundred but they were new faces, the faces, at last, of New Hampshire. I was both proud and shocked to hear Callanan say of the little assemblage: "This is one of the best crowds we've had in New Hampshire."

McCarthy departed and election day arrived. There were good omens. The people on the street had begun to smile and talk about the students, and the waitresses next door were suddenly festooned with McCarthy buttons. The chef positively glittered with them: they covered his cap and ran in a torrent down the front of his greasy shirt. (Eventually, short of buttons, we had to ask him to return all but one.) But late in the afternoon our little hopes began softly falling. It had begun to snow. We knew that Republicans vote early, Democrats traditionally late in the day. Snow would hinder the McCarthy voters who worked in near-by Boston and might deter people in outlying areas, while it would clearly aid the regular Democratic vote which, one thought, would always turn out. We had been dispatching student volunteers to the houses of friendlies to urge them to vote, but when the snow began to clog the roads, one of the adults, properly and maturely fearful of accidents, told the students to desist. I argued that if the students could get to the houses then the voters would see that they could get to the polls, a bit of logic with which insurance companies would not have agreed. Wet and weary, the students continued the canvass.

The pollsters were still predicting that the President would squash the challenger, and the campaigners waited edgily. Then, late in the evening, slow because of a record turnout, Salem posted the results. Forty per cent of the vote for the President, fifty-three per cent for Eugene J. McCarthy! Dear Salem, hawkish, right wing, hopeless Salem, which actually gave twelve of its votes that night to Herbert Hoover. The McCarthy results, telephoned to the election-night party in Manchester, brought sounds of pandemonium back through the wire. Only dimly, amid the backslapping, did one begin to realize what small numbers were involved—the 1466 Salem Democratic votes for McCarthy might have been delivered from a couple of New York City apartment buildings. Somehow one had come to imagine Salem much bigger. And other results from our area came in—beautiful Atkinson, 82 for McCarthy, 54 for Johnson; charming East Kingston, 15 to 10; picturesque Plaistow, 18 to 18; and wonderful Windham, 190 to 89. Only backward Sandown let us down, 10 to 14. All over New Hampshire little towns like these were making the mood of the country clear. It was going to be a new day! But for all the excitement no one could yet foresee that the movement, in exhilaration and agony, would roll all the way to Chicago. Least of all did anyone (including the candidate) believe that Gene McCarthy—with luck, organization, and strategy—had a solid chance for the Democratic nomination and the Presidency. We only knew that General Westmoreland had called for 206,000 more troops for Vietnam. Perhaps, in good-hearted towns like Salem, such demands had begun to be thwarted.

2 | Beginnings

There has to be a beginning and yet there is no beginning at all. There are merely strands, endless strands, reaching back into history and forward into the future, none sufficient unto itself. Let us begin with a particular evening (though it, too, had antecedents) — a dinner party at the luxurious New York apartment of Thomas K. Finletter, on March 22, 1967 Secretary of the Air Force under Truman, U.S. Ambassador to NATO under Kennedy and Johnson, Finletter epitomizes the powerful Eastern liberal Democratic "establishment." This had been Adlai Stevenson's financial bastion and it was here that another liberal Democratic candidate, if he were not a Kennedy, would look first for funds. Two of Finletter's guests were John Shea, a lawyer and prominent New York reform Democrat, and Russell Hemenway, director of the National Committee for an Effective Congress, a handsome man who could charm, or bully, a campaign contribution from Scrooge. (Later, he was to extract a five-thousand-dollar pledge for McCarthy from a rich drunk he found wandering in a hotel hall.) Over a meal of vegetable soup, veal, and wine, these three men concentrated on the fourth man at the table, Senator Eugene Joseph McCarthy, who was talking about running for President—to the surprise and delight of the rest.

All four shared a mood of anxiety, frustration, and dislike, close to raw anger, over the condition of the United States—"There was a sense of dismay at the moral base of the U.S., which pretended to have highfalutin principles it didn't have," Finletter was to say later—but each had his own perspective, his reason for alarm. Hemenway's particular concern was the low quality of national legislators; to him the parties were peddling salable wares, not providing leadership. Shea, the reformer, was depressed about the Democratic Party, which less than three years before got 24,000,-000 more national votes than the Republicans and which now, in 1967, was, he felt, on a precipitous and disastrous decline, losing favor everywhere but especially among the young. He thought the Democrats could easily lose the White House in 1968. Finletter, then working on a book on American foreign policy (*Interim Report,* published a year later), was stung by the American intervention in Vietnam. America had lost touch, he thought, with the truth. We had blundered into a deplorable war on the mistaken notion that American combat help would not be required, but even now, with American casualties high and no end in sight, the government gave no hint of remorse, or self-blame, and showed no desire even to clarify our war aims.

To one degree or another the four men were insiders on the Washington scene, and inclined to view it not in textbook fashion, as the clash of forces and influences, but in terms of the actions of fallible individuals. And so they spoke, for example, of one member of the Administration as slow-moving and trapped in the rhetoric of the thirties, and of another, an opponent of the Vietnam policy, as essentially calculating and ambitious. But the man whose character and mentality they blamed most of all was the President of the United States.

Eugene McCarthy was known to be sarcastic, irreverent, utterly opposed to the deification of political personages. He was not famous for the gentleness of his tongue. Politicians often aim their humor at themselves to avoid antagonizing others; McCarthy had no such scruples. If Vice-President Humphrey was going to mount the head of a deer he had shot on the LBJ ranch in his den, Mc-

Carthy said, the President should at least ask the taxidermist to remove the rope burns. Another example is McCarthy's pleasure in telling of Humphrey's desire to use Air Force One, the President's plane. No, not tonight, says the President, like a father refusing his adolescent son the use of the family car.

McCarthy's stories were often signals of concern, and he was upset not by the war alone but also by the increase in Presidential power. He believed that Johnson had ruined the Democratic National Committee by taking over its money-raising functions through the President's Clubs; that he had misused the Supreme Court by making the Chief Justice chairman of the commission to investigate the Kennedy assassination and again by sending Arthur Goldberg to the United Nations. ("When the President's only half worried he calls in the Jews. When he's *really* upset he calls in the Negroes," McCarthy joked to Goldberg, who wasn't sure if he was being insulted.) In foreign affairs, the President had ignored the Senate and especially the Foreign Relations Committee, of which McCarthy was a member. McCarthy was, in short, a constitutionalist and as such worried about the flow of power to the executive and the increasing difficulty of effective opposition.

But, McCarthy said later that evening in Finletter's living room, no amount of attempted persuasion would change the President on the central issue, Vietnam. The only action that would impress Johnson was to threaten him politically by running against him. The conversation veered to the potentials of a third party. McCarthy was opposed; the President had to be battled for the nomination within his own party. McCarthy did not believe that Senator Robert Kennedy would run and offered to do the job himself. "He was putting himself on the block as a sacrificial goat," Hemenway remembers, "and I for one was flabbergasted."

Ever since 1960, when McCarthy made his famous nominating speech for Adlai Stevenson, the New York Stevensonians had had their eyes on the Minnesotan. They had become implacably anti-Johnson because of the war, but they were also hostile to the political ambitions of the Kennedys. To some extent the ex-Stevensonians saw in McCarthy a vehicle with which to stop Robert Kennedy, but they also believed he could become the successor to the liberal leadership, and during the months preceding the dinner they had talked of helping to establish the Minnesota Senator as a national figure behind whom the anti-Vietnam war forces could gather. The group intended to arrange to finance the hiring of a small staff, for press relations and scheduling. "Up to the time of the dinner," Hemenway says, "there was no concept that he'd run for President, although you must be ready for any exigency, including death or retirement. The people who can capitalize in politics are the ones who are ready to do so. McCarthy had to begin to think about unanticipated events beyond the ken of thinking at that time and to prepare for them."

Yet now McCarthy said he would make the run. He would be an active candidate, and the group was excited. So was the Senator. "I've never seen him so up," said one of the participants. "He was charming, ebullient, brilliant, cutting, and prophetic." Then, a few days later, inexplicable to the men in New York, McCarthy changed his mind. "I wonder," one of them remarked, thinking of Stevenson in 1960, "if we haven't got ourselves another phantom candidate."

Eugene McCarthy is a complicated mixture of responsibility and ambition, of poet, theologian, philosopher, and hard politician. The ambitious politician had talked, in 1958, of becoming the first Catholic President and, after trying for the Vice-Presidential nomination in 1964, he had told close friends, "Next time might be our time," meaning the Presidency. In 1966, with an associate, he had gone so far as to draw up Operation Casablanca (White House) which sketched the bones of a McCarthy Presidential try. But now, after the dinner at Finletter's which could have led to a rich fundraising event, the McCarthy pendulum began to swing back. The ambitious politician having been heard in New York, the philosopher-skeptic had doubts back in Washington. Did he really want to make the effort? He didn't mind losing but would his campaign crystallize the antiwar sentiment? Would the President be convinced of the depth of dissent? Would the American people feel the same way as the Minnesota Senator? Where would he find money and an organization? Halfway down the road McCarthy turned back. He would not strive for the Presidency, not yet, nor would he hire a staff—he saw no need for one, and besides, he felt uncomfortable with strangers, an aide said. He would wait. Yet the group in New York was perplexed, and its doubts were later to have an adverse effect on McCarthy's candidacy.

At this juncture Eugene McCarthy fades temporarily from view, to be replaced by a tiny group of embattled antiwar partisans who were not thinking in terms of a candidate yet, but of a "stop the war" movement. The seeds for such a movement were already widely scattered. In March 1965, college professors opposing the war in the South and the newly instituted bombing of North Vietnam began their much-publicized teach-ins.

That spring, Robert Lowell, the poet, refused to participate in President Johnson's White House Festival of the Arts, and twenty other writers and artists followed his lead. As a consequence, Johnson, according to Eric Goldman, the historian, wrote off the intellectuals as "sonofabitches," "fools," and close to traitors. In June, peace advocates met at Ann Arbor, Michigan. An academic strike was considered and abandoned, but the meeting led to the first major peace march on Washington. Held in the fall under the auspices of the National Committee for a Sane Nuclear Policy, it was attended by some thirty thousand well-dressed, clearly middle-class people. Nothing *seemed* to have been accomplished, but a few more minor Democratic politicians, housewife activists, professors, students, clergymen—a grab bag of dissidents—exchanged phone numbers before they went home.

The election year of 1966 included one of the first attempts of the peace movement to move from simple demonstrations directly into politics. Robert Scheer, running for Congress in Oakland, California, as a peace candidate, came astonishingly close to success and elsewhere in the country "Peace in Politics" was becoming a theme. In New York City anti-Vietnam-war sentiment had been strong early. "We organized the peace groups with the objective of channeling pressure, built up by the war, into a political process for change," says Bella Abzug, a long-time activist. "We wanted to find a way to influence the selection and nomination of candidates." A Peace Action Committee was formed, and it backed State Senator Jerome Wilson against incumbent Republican Congressman Theodore R. Kupferman in the Seventeenth ("Silk Stocking") District, which had formerly been held by Mayor John V. Lindsay. In the eyes of Democratic party politicians the peace people were too sharp and too shrill; and they concentrated on a single issue at the expense of everything else. The Democratic clubs asked the peace group to soften its approach. The peace people replied by threatening to pull out of the campaign, and the clubs discovered that they would lose many of the volunteers who manned the phones and stuffed the envelopes. Wilson lost, though he did run better than most Democrats had in the district. The peace group was encouraged. "We saw," says Mrs. Abzug, "how important to a campaign the peace people could be."

The peace movement was still very much outside the mainstream of American politics, but its importance was enhanced because an increasing number of voters and candidates had begun to question the war. Nevertheless, a split began to appear between those who were impressed by the possibility of working for change within the party system and those of the New Left, like the Students for a Democratic Society and the black militants, who rejected the system entirely. This split was seen at a meeting of the steering committee of the National Conference on the New Politics, in Chicago, in 1967, where those less militant, less hostile to the party system, uninterested in revolution or, in the end, a third party, began to eye the 1968 Presidential election. One of the men they speculated about was Robert F. Kennedy, who was already talking privately about running, although he did so in a joking, deprecating way.

The tempo of the war beat faster and the protests escalated in direct proportion. Early in 1967 the *New York Times* carried several full-page ads headed, "TEACHERS APPEAL FOR PEACE IN VIETNAM" or "MR. PRESIDENT: STOP THE BOMBING OF VIETNAM." These ads, listing the names of thousands from all over the country, reflected something besides great anxiety about events. But they were not summonses to marches or rallies; they were, rather, threats to the President himself. Translated into political terms, they said, "Mr. President, change the policy *or else.*" The "or else" meant, now, *someone* else, not someone specific yet but simply an unknown competitor.

"Who's your candidate?" Robert Kennedy, sympathetic but apparently amused, asked Allard K. Lowenstein on a plane trip to California that year. Lowenstein replied, "You need a movement before you can get a candidate." Then thirty-eight years old, Lowenstein is a dark, sturdily built, intense, superenergetic lawyer and university teacher from New York. He had been a protégé of Eleanor Roosevelt, a passionate opponent of South African apartheid, a president of the National Student Association (before its connection with the CIA), vice-chairman of Americans for Democratic Action, and, until his Congressional victory in 1968, a repeatedly unsuccessful contender for New York Democratic Congressional nominations. Lowenstein had been among the first to comprehend the President's vulnerability. He had originally believed in forming a third party, but by April 1967 he was convinced that a peace candidate could be successful within the Democratic Party and he was soon fighting a tactical battle with another prominent member of the ADA, Joseph Rauh, who considered an assault on the regular Democratic citadel hopeless and recommended that the dissidents concentrate on the adoption of a Vietnam peace plank for the platform of the 1968 Democratic Convention. Lowenstein wanted to contest the Democratic nomination itself and, stubbornly committed to action, he set out, in the spring of 1967, almost alone, to refurbish the Democratic Party.

The strategy argued by Lowenstein and a few others in those early organizational attempts was forcefully outlined in the July 1967 issue of the ADA *World* in an article, "The Issue: Vietnam; The Target: Johnson," signed by a contributor to the magazine but actually the work of the *World*'s editor, Curtis Gans, who didn't want to be identified because of his official position. There was hope after the Glassboro summit conference that spring, the article argued, that the President could de-escalate the war, but it was

> of paramount importance that it not be taken for granted that the liberal community will support the President. . . . The liberal community must work to lay the groundwork that would present the best possible alternatives to the electorate in 1968 for both foreign and domestic policies. . . . The most effective strategy must be for liberals to work within the Democratic Party for a change of policy if possible and a change of leadership if necessary. And organization should begin in preliminary form for a primary challenge to Johnson. Hopefully this can be accomplished by a national candidate of stature who might run in opposition to Johnson, but if not it could well be done through local candidates of stature who might be willing to oppose him in the primary. It must be remembered throughout that if the President . . . wanted to he could force his nomination at the convention, even if he had not won one single primary. But it should also be remembered that in 1952 in the midst of a war much less unpopular than Vietnam, Harry S. Truman chose not to run. And the true analogy of 1968 is 1952 not 1948 as is often used.

Whatever analogy, if any, was true, Lowenstein went off like an ideological Johnny Appleseed to plant a movement. Using his own money, he went heavily in debt to form a national stop-the-war, dump-Johnson-if-necessary organization. It was slow at the start, as Lowenstein, now joined by Gans and Harold Ickes, moved from state to state, but there was movement, if not *a* movement: in New York, California, Michigan, Oregon, Wisconsin, and Colorado people were talking within and across state lines, using the telephone, the medium of a modern committee of correspondence. Most of them had never met. This effort went all but unnoticed in the press, although Democratic politicians were aware of it and attacked it bitterly. An example of regular Democratic insensitivity was a remark by the President's friend, Ed Weisl, then National Committeeman from New York. When told by a group of West Side reform leaders (including Alex Rosenberg, a future Mc-Carthyite, and Ronnie Eldridge, a Kennedyite) that the dissidents could not support the President, Weisl replied, "Well, we simply must tell everyone that Johnson is a man of peace."

Such answers were utterly unsatisfactory to the rebels. Gerald N. Hill, president of the California Democratic Council, gave a much more satisfying one when he spoke to a group of them from five Eastern states in June 1967. CDC planned a convention in the fall to field a slate of delegates opposing the war in the California primary, and Hill explained,

> CDC has been told that its opposition is divisive—to the Democratic Party and the nation. That's nonsense! The *war* is dividing my party. The *war* has turned the hopes for a massive war on poverty into prolonged frustration. The *war* has divorced America from advancement of civil rights and economic opportunity for all Americans. And the *war* is killing peasants and young Americans in Southeast Asia.

Mammoth peace marches in San Francisco and New York that spring, the "Vietnam Summer" project (in some sections of New York State the dissidents found that sixty per cent favored withdrawal from Vietnam), petition drives—something far beyond ordinary protest and dissatisfaction was brewing. In August 1967,

Lowenstein could tell the National Student Association convention at College Park, Maryland, that in the fall something would be happening. The students then formed ACT, the Alternative Candidate Task Force. (One of the students, Samuel W. Brown, returned to Harvard only to collect his scholarship money. He then went on the road, visiting campus after campus. He used his father's credit card and later he presented him with a bill for fifteen hundred dollars and the words, "Thank you for your first campaign contribution.")

The "Dump Johnson" movement had formally begun. In August, too, Lowenstein and Hill formed a national umbrella organization called the Conference of Concerned Democrats, a biggish name for an outfit with a bankroll of only one thousand dollars. With it they hired a single staff member, Curtis Gans, who quit his job at ADA. For months the CCD's office was Gans' small living room in Washington, D.C. Gans and Lowenstein worked the country like a couple of con men. Gans would slip into a state with a notebook of names and organize meetings. Lowenstein would address the meetings and Gans would stay to form the organization. They did their act in twenty-two states and in all but one, Nebraska, where the lack of organization would later hurt, they were successful.

By fall, they could count, among others, on Dissenting Democrats, a California-based, antiwar petition group recently organized by Robert Vaughn, the actor; Hoosiers for a Democratic Alternative; the Coalition for a Democratic Alternative in New York; the Wisconsin Concerned Democrats, which planned to vote no to President Johnson (Wisconsin law gave them the option to vote no if only one Presidential candidate appeared on the ballot) but could easily be persuaded to vote yes for someone else. With the exception of a few, like Zoltan Ferency, former Michigan Democratic State Chairman, the dissidents—like David Hoeh, a Dartmouth official; Jack Gore, a Colorado professor; Don Peterson, the sales manager of a Wisconsin pizza company; a Minnesota state legislator, Alpha Smaby—were, nationally, completely unknown. By conventional political standards it was not an imposing assortment, but the times were not conventional. There was an issue, Vietnam and the President; lacking was a focus, a candidate.

Lowenstein had begun candidate shopping in May. "I talked to many prominent Democrats," he said, "but the only one who was willing to put his prestige on the line was John Kenneth Galbraith." Economist, professor, President of ADA, novelist, former Ambassador to India, Galbraith is clearly a man of many parts. Regarding himself "an independent operator at the guerilla level of American politics," as he once told a reporter, Galbraith was sufficiently impressed with Lowenstein's proposal to consult Constitutional lawyers, who advised him that his birth in Canada rendered him ineligible for the Presidency. ("It was too bad," Galbraith remarked. "With Romney having been born in Mexico, I could foresee a real all-American primary in New Hampshire.") In the spring, already turned down by Robert Kennedy and George McGovern, Lowenstein talked to Eugene McCarthy, who agreed that someone should run. He suggested that Kennedy had a much broader base but said nothing more. Kennedy, convinced that his entry into the race would be seen as a personal feud with the President, suggested General James Gavin, but Gavin told Lowenstein that it was idle to suppose that an incumbent President could be defeated within his own party. He could only be beaten by a Republican, and Gavin, a Republican, would not run as a Democrat. In addition to McGovern, Senators Vance Hartke and Frank Church and Representative Don Edwards of California were all approached, and while almost all seemed sympathetic none felt he could enter the race. (Edwards felt it would be presumptuous for a Congressman to run.) Still, for Lowenstein, there were hopeful signs. In the early fall McCarthy, Church, and McGovern had lunch in Washington, and it was tacitly agreed that one of the three would have to go if no one else would. But there was no eagerness among Democrats to put their heads on the block.

"Let's get a reading on it," McCarthy says frequently, and from March on he had been trying to read the country, inscrutable as always. What was really happening behind the fringe of dissent? By late summer only half the U.S. Senate and thirty-eight per cent of the people approved of Johnson's handling of the war; by November the figure had dropped to twenty-three per cent. But the public mood and the polls were volatile, and more people opposed a bombing halt than favored it. Those who favored an outright military victory remained strong. Not a single Democratic governor and only a few Democratic Senators had spoken out against the President's policy—the party seemed united behind Lyndon Johnson.

"Obviously," McCarthy says, "I did not make the decision casually." He knew he would be accused of dividing the party and called a traitor. There might be strong pressures on himself and his family in Washington. If he were demolished in the first primary, a good possibility, he would be a laughingstock—and for nothing. He would be trapped either way. If the miraculous happened and he ran well but the President still got the Democratic nomination and lost in November, McCarthy would be blamed for the defeat. Even if he unhorsed the President but yet another Democrat got the nomination, and lost, he might still be held responsible.

If he ran, and against such odds, where would he find the organization and the money for a campaign? One early prospective supporter thought so little of his chances that when he was encouraged to take McCarthy to the World Series, he replied, "I'd rather take my wife." At least one fear that deters many conventional politicians did not sit heavily on McCarthy (although it would the following summer when his campaign was a million dollars in debt): that of being burdened with enormous obligations, as Kefauver,

Stevenson, and Humphrey had been. Candidates are rarely threatened with suits but there is a moral obligation to pay the campaign debts off; this can condemn a candidate to years on the lecture circuit and endless plates of overdone roast beef at fund-raising dinners, which former enthusiasts might not attend. But the McCarthys—the Senator and his wife Abigail alike—were insouciant, almost un-American, on the subject of money: they did not think about it, and thus it was possible, after the convention, for McCarthy to discover he did not have the cash for his quarterly income tax.

A poor run in 1968 might doom McCarthy in 1970, when he was up for re-election. Unlike many Senators, he was not particularly intimidated by this consideration, but he had to think about the fate of others. In the tricky three-dimensional chess of American politics an unsuccessful insurgent candidacy might bring down with it liberal Senators and Congressmen. A beaten campaign could damage its own cause by proving massive support for the President. There could be still other possible effects. As a high Administration official warned, "If McCarthy fizzles it will kill any chance any moderate Republican has, and the right wing will put all kinds of war pressure on us."

So there were excellent reasons for abstaining, including the opposition of Abigail McCarthy to the candidacy. Intelligent, sensitive, a good reader of political tea leaves, she thought the enterprise was hopeless. Her daughter Mary argued the opposite. She pointed to the depth of student dissatisfaction and reminded her father of his own dictum: "The calling of a Christian is not to judge the world but to save it." To save it, pre eminently, from the war in Vietnam—which was heating up sharply that summer as American planes struck within ten miles of the Chinese border. Fears of a Sino-American conflict had increased and the "nervous Nellies," as the President called them, thought it was madness not to be nervous. McCarthy was also frightened by the processes that had gotten the United States mired in the war, through decisions, made in secret, by a handful of men who were by no means preternatural. If Senators were powerless to intervene, so much more were ordinary men, and the result was separation from political life.

" 'Malaise,' 'frustration,' 'alienation,' 'identity,' " said the National Committee for an Effective Congress that fall, appraising the American mood, "are now becoming part of the professional political vocabulary. At all levels of American life, people share similar fears, insecurities, and gnawing doubts to such an intense degree that the country may in fact be suffering from a kind of nervous breakdown. This breakdown is acutely visible in our political life." It was nowhere more visible than among the young who were increasingly taking their dissatisfaction to the streets. "As voters begin to look inside the political package, beneath the wrappings," the NCEC report went on, "they are searching for subtler things, for quality, for personal and national purpose. Amid the crisis, the disappointed idealism, there seems to be a sincere yearning for the restoration of the American dream."

Was such an appraisal naïve? There were those who didn't think so, such as Richard Goodwin, who argued (in *The New Yorker*, in September 1967, under the meaningful pseudonym Daley Unruh) that an unknown contender could become in that fluid situation a national figure in a month. The issue of Vietnam won't beat Johnson by itself, Goodwin wrote, but "there's this vague sense of suspicion and distrust, which is very deeply rooted. People tend to vote against someone rather than for something, and I think they could really turn on the President." The dialogue goes on: "I tell you, the big prize is hanging right there ready to be grabbed by the first man who fights his way to it. It can't just be given out by the big boys, like in the old days."

During the summer McCarthy was constantly discussing the idea of an active campaign with people who came to his gray-blue office urging him to run. He was not a man who thought in terms of the "big prize," but one who agonized over the serious choices before him. In this period of uncertainty a friend found McCarthy in his large, nicely furnished house playing records, songs of Irish rebellion like "The West's Asleep":

> But hark! a voice like thunder spake
> The West's awake, the West's awake.

It must have been the background music in his mind, songs of fiery brigands sweeping down from the hills.

In the end there were four chief components, events and non-events alike, that meshed in McCarthy's decision to attempt the absurd and run for President. The first of these, from the Senator's point of view, was the continued intransigence of the American government on Vietnam. In August, Undersecretary of State Nicholas deB. Katzenbach had come before the Senate Foreign Relations Committee to say that the President had the authority even without the Tonkin Gulf Resolution to do everything that he had done or might want to do in Vietnam without bothering with Congress at all. The testimony put McCarthy in a cold fury. In the middle he stalked out, and in the hall he ran into a reporter and said, "This is the wildest testimony I have ever heard. There is no limit to what he says the President could do. There is only one thing to do—take it to the country." But the Congress was passing the Defense Appropriations Bill, with its two billion dollars a month for Vietnam, and nobody was listening to McCarthy. On October 12, Secretary of State Rusk told a press conference that Asian communism was trying to "cut the world in two." Four days later, McCarthy responded on the Senate floor. Rusk's reference, he said, to "a billion Chinese armed with nuclear weapons" reflected the "ancient fear of the yellow peril."

> Many of our problems today are the result of our unwillingness or inability in the past to anticipate what might be the shape of the world twenty years in the future. . . . We must ask whether we are prepared to maintain from one hundred thousand to two hundred thousand troops in South Vietnam

. . . for fifteen or twenty years after the fighting stops. If we are not prepared to do so, the process must be reversed. . . . We must begin now the adjustments of attitude which will be necessary if we are to reduce or liquidate our commitments in Asia.

And, he said soon after, "There comes a time when an honorable man must raise the flag. There comes a point when you can't let people be denied a voice in a democracy. If you do, you can be pushed into complete ineffectiveness or utter submission." This was component two: McCarthy's sense, sharpened by his visits to campuses, that the young people *were* disenchanted and would take to the streets. Washington, for all its intelligence apparatus, seemed to be cut off from the currents of the country and insulated behind thick government masonry. Few prominent politicians gauged this antigovernment sentiment as well as McCarthy, and he felt a responsibility, especially to the young, to provide a channel for change or at least a medium, to use one of his campaign's central themes, for participation. But the outpouring of sentiment for a middle-aged politician surprised even the Senator. "I had the feeling," said one who accompanied McCarthy on one of the pre-campaign forays he began making in August 1967, "that the students would eat out of his hand."

The third consideration was the absence of anyone else. McCarthy's hope that fall was to encourage others to make the break with the President so that Johnson would be confronted by a whole stable of dissenters, each ready to run as a favorite son in his own state if possible but at least presenting a united front. McCarthy was aware that he might be in the best position to grab the leadership from a group of favorite sons, but in the end that wasn't really the point. For at the time, the Minnesota Senator was ready to back, and campaign for, the junior Senator from New York, and twice that fall he urged him to run, suggested that Kennedy was better known and "would make a better race." But, he said, if Kennedy would not go, McCarthy would have to, although he wanted to reassure Kennedy that his purpose was not to impede or embarrass him. Kennedy was regretful; he could not make an open break with the President. The meetings were brief, amicable, and fruitless. Through a friend, Kennedy then offered to give McCarthy the benefit of his experience in Presidential campaigns, but the Minnesotan, somewhat to Kennedy's surprise, sought no advice.

As late as October 26, in Berkeley before a student audience, Eugene McCarthy was still trying to goad or taunt Kennedy into the race, although by now it was almost an afterthought.

> I am not prepared to nominate anybody today, but I think that we have to establish that this responsibility does exist. There come certain times in politics when the individual I do not think really has the right to anticipate how things are going to be better for him in 1972. I have to be careful of what I say.

"Why won't they run?" McCarthy asked plaintively of his old friend Maurice Rosenblatt, founder of the NCEC and an experienced Washington hand. "Why won't Bobby run? Why won't McNamara run?" McCarthy himself had tried to get Senator Hartke of Indiana and Senator George McGovern of South Dakota to come out, at least as favorite sons, and he knew about others who had been approached, like Senator Joseph Clark of Pennsylvania. Said Rosenblatt: "It was a battle over reality. It was clear to him that any public figure who wanted to had a good chance to unseat the President, although there was a timetable. It had to be done quickly or the country would be committed to four more years of Johnson rule. I said, 'They don't see it, Gene. It'll have to be you.'"

The fourth factor was his knowledge that he could depend now on at least some organized support from the "Dump Johnson" group. In October, McCarthy was asking the practical questions: How many volunteers do you have? How much will it cost to campaign in your state? (He would not ask for money, or help of any kind, directly, and succeeded in alienating several prospective contributors because of his low-keyed approach to blacks and civil rights.) He gave a clear hint of his intentions to Gerald Hill of the California Democratic Council by saying, "You fellows have mentioned Church, Hartke, McGovern, and myself. I know you can cut it down to one." A clinching conversation was one between McCarthy and Dean Francis Sayre of the Washington Cathedral, who urged him to run. By October, then, the word was flashing around the primitive political organization, "We've got a candidate!" For Lowenstein, "The long nightmare was over." At the Detroit airport, in October, McCarthy was greeted by the first "McCarthy for President" signs.

Weeks before he announced, McCarthy had carefully and deliberately been creating a climate for his candidacy, and as to the actual moment of decision he has said, "It was nothing like Saint Paul being knocked off his horse, I assure you. I don't think I had any kind of a special light. I think that it is very hard to fix the exact moment of something of this kind—it's a little too soon and a little bit too late. Somewhere between those two points you pass the point of no return." The Katzenbach testimony, the Rusk press conference, the enthusiasm of the Berkeley students—these were the high points on the map of his progress toward a public declaration, and, apparently, on the plane returning from California McCarthy finally decided that he must make the test.

> I didn't think there was anyone who had better knowledge of the issues than I did, or who in the long run could be a better candidate—in all modesty I really always do these things on a comparative basis, and I looked around at the other prospects and felt that I was really not—if I became the candidate—I really wasn't offering a bad candidate.

Before making his announcement, McCarthy thought of talking with the President and, with his own potential campaign as a lever, persuading him of the depth of dissent, in hope that Johnson would

change the Vietnam policy. But Johnson, McCarthy decided, would
never listen.

Eugene McCarthy is not easily detoured, and not likely to show
very much of what he feels, although he is susceptible to high
hilarity and deep Irish gloom. November 1967 was a gloomy month
for the undeclared candidate.

On the 7th, between planes, McCarthy held his first serious
campaign meeting during a late lunch at the Golden Door Restaurant at New York's Kennedy Airport. Assembled with McCarthy
were his administrative assistant, Jerome Eller, a large man with a
big mustache, whose mocking tone was often a good mirror of the
Senator's own attitudes; John Safer, a wealthy Baltimore real-estate
man who had offered to leave his business for a year to help the
Senator; John Shea and a New York lawyer, Laurence Levine, who
represented the New York Stevensonians; and, finally, one of Mc-
Carthy's former aides. It was nonsense to set his heart on the
Presidency, McCarthy said; he could only campaign on the issues.
He was urged to enter the New Hampshire primary, to make it
plain that he would not run as a third-party candidate, and to
develop a plan for Vietnam—it was not enough to say that he was
a dove. It was clear, as well, that one immediate exigency super
seded all the rest—money.

Here the Stevensonians, with their access to big liberal money
and lists of contributors from previous campaigns, were supposed
to present optimistic estimates, but they did not. Many potential
contributors, they said, could not come forward because of con-
tracts in Washington. Others were locked in because of commitments to Johnson through the President's Club. The Stevensonians
wanted to help, but McCarthy's seemingly erratic pullback in
March and silence until November had upset them, creating uncertainty about his sincerity as a candidate. Besides, they were
given no advance notice of the meeting or its purpose. McCarthy,

finding them less than enthusiastic, was disappointed and angry; but, with characteristic disinclination to ask anybody for anything, he let the matter drop. As McCarthy went glumly to his plane, the group was estimating his chance for the nomination between a thousand and a million to one, although, they said, he had little to lose and much to gain by running: Johnson might make him Secretary of State.

The result was that McCarthy began his effort almost without funds—by the end of November only four thousand dollars had arrived at his Washington office, hardly enough to buy campaign buttons. On his early forays the press comments were not of the sort which would bring big money out in the open, either. E. W. Kenworthy of the *New York Times,* writing in the *New Republic,* laid down the themes which were to follow the campaign to its conclusion, regardless of what the candidate did.

> How is McCarthy doing on the stump? The answer—on which all reporters accompanying him agree—is, not too well. . . . He makes the same speech over and over again. . . . His speeches do not build up to a climax; they trail off and stop when he thinks he has talked long enough . . . he throws away . . . lines . . . his wit tends to be a little special . . . speeches lacked . . . fervor and eloquence . . . a bad mistake in concentrating on students, the professors, the clergy and the trade union leaders who already agree with him. . . .

A great deal else was said about the candidate, much of it unflattering. "Detached. Philosophic. Cynical. Moral. Learned. Lazy," announced the *Wall Street Journal.* "Nobody's patsy" and "formidable candidate," columnist Joseph Kraft countered. The President's friend, William S. White, considered McCarthy an "improbable Caesar" whose "fierce fire of ambition [was] fanned by the hot, fanatic thirst that now grips the throats of the American peacenik movement." Others wrote: "no national figure," "dreamy Stevensonian," "too sophisticated . . . too much of a man of formula," "sardonic humor is cynicism; his casualness, indifference," "needs emotional firing," "European Catholic worker leader whose beliefs make him an ardent supporter of government welfare schemes." A labor leader said bluntly what many believed to be true: "McCarthy's candidacy is a slight annoyance to Johnson, a major embarrassment to the Kennedys, and a boon to Nixon— maybe Nixon is behind it."

If McCarthy was berated in public, there were subtler pressures in private as the news spread around Washington that McCarthy was about to announce. A great many people were frightened of Lyndon Johnson, and the McCarthys noted without surprise a sudden slackening of telephone calls and invitations. Mrs. McCarthy no longer visited her friend Lady Bird Johnson for fear of causing embarrassment. A woman made a date to meet Mrs. McCarthy, left a ticket for her at a theater box office, and then pretended to run into her in the lobby.

Politically as well as personally, McCarthy was hurt most by the failure of nationally known Democrats to support him. A few Democrats, like Congressman Edwards, backed him, and Senator Robert Kennedy was quoted as saying that a McCarthy challenge "would be a healthy influence on the Democratic Party," but no governors or Senators showed any signs of coming out, though many, McCarthy knew, agreed with the aims of his campaign. "They pretend they don't know me," he said bitterly. "Their first principle is survival. They think they can oppose the war without opposing the President and keep the organization happy. That's all right with me."

Shortly before he announced, McCarthy returned to his alma mater, St. John's, in Minnesota, and there a friend, a priest, said to him, "Gene, you have no money and no backing. Aren't you afraid of what you'll lose?"

"No," McCarthy said. "I think I've discovered an area people haven't been aware of before—the students, the faculties. Johnson and the others don't know about this strength. I'm going to tap it."

"Well, *viriliter agite*," said the dubious priest. Act manfully.

A poll in Minnesota was then giving McCarthy two and a half per cent of the vote.

McCarthy remained detached as he stood before the cameras in the Caucus Room of the Old Senate Office Building on November 30.

> My decision to challenge the President's position, and the Administration's position, has been strengthened by recent announcements out of the Administration. . . . I am concerned that the Administration seems to have set no limits to the price that it is willing to pay for a military victory. . . . In addition there is growing evidence of a deepening moral crisis in America. . . . I am hopeful that this challenge I am making . . . may alleviate to at least some degree this sense of political helplessness and restore to many people a belief in the processes of American politics and of American government. . . . The issue of the war in Vietnam is not really a separate issue but one which must be dealt with in the configuration of other problems in which it is related. And it is within this broader context I intend to take the case to the people of the United States.

Subdued and restrained, it was not the announcement of a man who expected to end in the White House, and it was treated with no more than polite interest by the press. So little attention did the candidate expect that he told a friend that he imagined he'd be campaigning like a lone pilgrim, on foot with a wooden staff. "I don't know if it will be political suicide," he said. "It'll be more like an execution."

3 | The Candidate

By any conventional standards Eugene McCarthy was not the man to shake the Democratic Party from end to end and perhaps cost it the Presidency in 1968. By conventional standards—if there are, indeed, such standards—McCarthy should not have been a candidate for President at all.

He was born in Watkins, Minnesota, seventy miles from Minneapolis, one of a thousand Minnesota farming villages. In the summer the town is surrounded by dark-gold fields of hay, some piled in huge baled stacks; and there are the gently plodding Holsteins, the endless chain of lakes, the picnic parks, the granary, and the silver mushroom of a water tower with WATKINS stenciled on it. Towns like these love self-advertisement:

Welcome to
WATKINS
Population 760 Friendly People
Plus a Few Grouches
A TOWN OF FREE ENTERPRISE

Even the grouches, if asked, would stand up and identify themselves—people in such places pride themselves on honesty. The commercial street is, of course, Main Street, two blocks long and lined with two-story frame buildings: Brixius Market; Weber's V-Store, Dry Goods and Variety; Leander Salzi, Blacksmith and

Welder, Lawnmowers Sharpened; Leo's Cafe, Meals, Short Orders; The Farmer's State Bank. The defense line of small-town America is only one store deep; go out the back and there is nothing. Watkins is a place whose young are sucked into the vortex of the big cities, never to return. It ought, by sheer attrition, to yield to the new day when the whole of rural America will be tended by machines. And yet somehow it seems that it never will.

One day in August 1968, Main Street was a solitary blond boy engaged in several activities at once—juggling an apple, turning on a water fountain, and eying a cracked plaster wall where someone had written WERE FOR MCCARTHY. A visitor wondered whether an apostrophe had been omitted or whether the sign was a premature admission of defeat, two weeks before the Chicago convention. One McCarthy poster stood in a store window, and outside town somebody had put a simple, stenciled WATKINS, HOMETOWN OF SENATOR EUGENE MCCARTHY sign, as though not to be completely outclassed by Waverly, forty-five miles away, with its spectacular HOMETOWN OF HUBERT HUMPHREY sign in red lights. No, Watkins still had hope of wresting the big trophy from Waverly.

This was where Gene McCarthy was born on March 29, 1916; and he grew up in a small, two-story, cream-colored clapboard house with a screened front porch. When the temperature dropped to thirty below, the family would bank the foundation with tar paper and straw. There were four McCarthy children, two boys and two girls, all still living. "My grandfathers were a carpenter and a blacksmith, respectively," Dr. Austin McCarthy, a surgeon and Eugene's younger brother, told the visitor. "Our father would always say that he was a horse thief and a cattle rustler but actually he bought and sold cattle. He didn't really rustle them." Of Irish descent, Michael McCarthy, the father, was born in Forest City, Minnesota, and was ninety-three years old when his son ran for President. When Eugene tried for the Senate, Michael was asked what he thought. "Yes, Gene is doing all right," he said, "but you should ask me about my son Austin. *He's* a doctor." Mc-

Carthy's mother, born Anna Baden, was of German extraction. Watkins itself was mostly German, and the nuns spoke German at McCarthy's parochial school. The McCarthy boys dueled with laths near the grain elevator. They placed pennies on the railroad tracks and waited for speeding trains to flatten them. Gene played the clarinet in the Watkins band and later in the University Symphony orchestra. (The only Christmas present the Senator ever got that visibly pleased him, we are told, was a clarinet, given him recently by his children.) The "smartest young man in the county" read many books; he devoured the Harvard "five-foot shelf" of fifty classics in one summer. He was a little standoffish, without close friends. (Not even Austin had been informed in advance that his brother planned to run for President.) He was good at baseball and hockey but, Austin says, "when a melee started he probably had something to do with it, yet when the dust cleared *we* were banged up and he was unscathed." Hubert Humphrey might have made a similar observation in 1968.

McCarthy went to St. John's Preparatory School and then, at sixteen, to St. John's University. St. John's, thirty miles from Watkins, was where most local kids went to college. Not many Watkins boys went to college, Austin McCarthy told a reporter. "I couldn't think of more than ten—if I racked my brain—out of about a hundred that I grew up with," he said. "And if you went to school it was either St. John's or St. Thomas and that was it." For Gene McCarthy the existence of such a school was fortuitous. There were not, of course, as there are now, Marcel Breuer buildings with sweeping arcs and angles, but then, as now, James O'Gara, editor of *Commonweal,* points out, "the Midwest Catholic community has for a long time been more ecumenical and liberal than the East, and St. John's is one of its principal centers." The famous Father Vergil Michel was there preaching revolutionary ideas of liturgical reform and, beyond that, the necessity of Catholic involvement in social action. Late into the night the priests discussed reforms needed to bring Minnesota out of the agricultural depression. Social action was blended with "Benedictine cynicism," expressed by one monk as "Be kind to people but keep your doors locked at night." It was a good place to be, McCarthy has said, for the alert and the curious.

It was the kind of place where the faculty knew all the students, and Gene McCarthy would be remembered now even if he had not become a luminary and planted a tree recently in front of the new library. (There is also a tree that Humphrey planted, which still stands although it is dead: like Castor and Pollux, the two are forever bound together in their Minnesota constellation.) Good-natured, gentle, athletic, correct, a neat writer though not a stylist, especially competitive—these are some of the remembrances. "He enjoyed it when someone made a fool of himself in class," recalls Father Dunstan Tucker, who taught English literature and doubled as baseball coach, "and he was a rough competitor on the ice." He majored in literature and got A's in every course but trigonometry, including a science course which McCarthy took for the sole purpose, says an old friend, of testing his mettle against his roommate —a science major, who got a B. McCarthy was bright and poor, a combination which saw him graduate *summa cum laude* in three years. "Gene didn't have a lot of drive, not like he does now," recollects Father Walter Reger, fifty-two years at St. John's and known there as Mr. Chips, "but he was always an exceptionally independent-minded young man." His parents wanted him to become a priest, but instead McCarthy went to the University of Minnesota, where he started work on a master's in sociology and economics (a degree that no longer exists). He could not afford school full time—he did not receive his master's for a few years— and at nineteen he began teaching in Minnesota high schools, where he stayed for several years before moving on to Mandan, North Dakota, and another high school.

Here he met a schoolteacher named Abigail Quigley. A year older than himself, she, too, was from a small Minnesota town, Wabasha. Her father, among other things including some political activity, had owned and edited one of the oldest weeklies in the Midwest before the Depression forced him to sell out. She was the oldest of four children. Her mother had died of cancer when she was nine and she had been brought up mainly by relatives. An aunt, Abigail O'Leary, who taught high-school creative writing in Minneapolis, was the chief influence on her life during this period. Abigail became a writer herself and twice won national contests for the best short stories written at Catholic women's colleges. Her themes were by no means provincial Catholic but had to do with the Depression, the dust bowl, and German farmers in the Midwest. She was later to write about the role of religion in the modern world, including a chapter of a book she edited, *First Steps in Christian Renewal,* a collection of essays on ecumenism. Because Eugene McCarthy's admiration for Thomas More was invariably mentioned in newspaper articles, it is worth noting a term paper of Abigail's written at St. Catherine's College in 1936, titled "Thomas More, Knight," which tells something about her. "His tender understanding of a woman's heart is unique," she says girlishly, and goes on: "It was not only a realization but an understanding and appreciation of a woman's problems that few men have ever equalled. . . . Modern, indeed, was Sir Thomas More, the first man to believe in intellectual equality for women."

Abigail graduated Phi Beta Kappa from St. Catherine's, in St. Paul, in 1936, and feeling lucky to find a job during the Depression, took one at Mandan. The requirement was for someone who could teach English and German, and, accepted, she arrived to find the principal worried because she looked so young. She was, though, a good if demanding teacher and remained in Mandan three years. During the third year Eugene McCarthy arrived, and by Christmas Miss Quigley was pronouncing herself in love. "He was too handsome to be true," she said, "and I don't think I ever met anybody who was so unconscious of it." The couple became engaged.

But they could not marry. They were too poor and each had brothers and sisters to help put through school. Abigail got a better job in Minnesota, while McCarthy stayed at Mandan one more year. Then he went back to St. John's, to teach, working for his Ph.D. in the summers. They were each trying to eat on a dollar a day to save money to get married, but somehow never made it— they were too hungry at the end of the day. In his second year back at St. John's, McCarthy began to think he had a vocation as a monk, and broke the engagement. Mrs. McCarthy told Sister Maris Stella, her good friend and mentor at St. Catherine's College, "If I love him I can't come between him and the things God wants him to do."

McCarthy became a theology student in 1941 and was deferred from the draft. He needed a year of Latin in order to begin his novitiate. He continued to see Abigail, although, by then, she was dating other men and getting a graduate degree in English. An old friend of the McCarthys' suggests that when Eugene met Abigail he became a little frightened of marriage because it meant abandoning the priesthood altogether, which was something he had never quite gotten out of his system. It was a dramatic time, although McCarthy describes it casually: "Oh, I don't know, it was a mixed sort of case. I was inclined to give it a test. On the other hand, if it didn't prove out, it doesn't really hurt to spend nine or ten months drawn away from it all." He suggested quite seriously that Abigail get her to a nunnery, but she replied that she did not have the vocation. She was teaching school at St. Catherine's, and McCarthy retired to St. John's Abbey.

St. John's Abbey is the largest Benedictine monastery in the world. *"Ora et Labora"*—worship and work—is the order's motto.

For a year and a day the novice prays and meditates, and then he decides whether to become a monk. He rises at four-thirty a.m., retires at nine or ten. He does manual labor, beautifying the cemetery, for example, and translates a textbook from Latin to English, in line with St. John's ideas of liturgical reform. There are no radios and few visitors. Seven times a day he prays, and he studies, deeply, St. Benedict's Rules for the Monasteries. Father Walter is convinced that these rules, written in A.D. 529, were the making of Gene McCarthy, and their influence upon the man became more and more apparent during the campaign. "They are the key to Gene perhaps without his realizing it. He has absorbed them. He talks about moral issues, and he is conscious of moral and spiritual values. He wants to achieve these values. He conceives of them for others as well as for himself." Of course, a priest might say this.

These are a few of the rules:

WHAT KIND OF MAN THE ABBOT OUGHT TO BE

Only for one reason are we preferred in His sight: if we be found better than others in good works and humility.

In his teaching the Abbot should always follow the Apostle's formula: "Reprove, entreat, rebuke"; threatening at one time and coaxing at another as the occasion may require, showing now the stern countenance of a master, now the loving affection of a father. That is to say, it is the undisciplined and restless whom he must reprove rather sharply; it is the obedient, meek and patient whom he must entreat to advance in virtue; while as for the negligent and disdainful, these we charge him to rebuke and correct.

ON HUMILITY

The sixth degree of humility is that a monk be content with the poorest and worst of everything. . . .

The seventh degree of humility is that he consider himself lower and of less account than anyone else.

The eleventh degree of humility is that when a monk speaks he do so gently and without laughter, humbly and seriously, in few and sensible words, and that he be not noisy in his speech. It is written, "A wise man is known for the fewness of his words."

The twelfth degree of humility is that a monk not only have

humility in his heart but also by his very appearance make it always manifest to those who see him. . . .

Frater Novice Conan, as McCarthy was called at the monastery, pondered such precepts. Eventually he saw that the monastic life was not for him. The forms were perhaps too rigid; he wanted a secular involvement. He left the abbey after nine months, finishing out the year in a Milwaukee seminary, thinking perhaps he was better suited to be a secular priest than a monk. Then he was on his own.

As if sensing that McCarthy was only transiently in the religious life, the Abbot of St. John's, contrary to custom, had permitted Abigail and Eugene to correspond. "I really hope I had something to do with his coming out," she said later. "I think he missed me." Her instinct, nonetheless, told her that it was not wise for McCarthy to plunge directly from the monastery into marriage, and each continued in his own way, though Abigail's roommate remembers special-delivery letters arriving almost every morning. Abigail went on teaching school while Eugene went to Washington, D.C. He had developed an acute case of bursitis in both feet—at one time he could not walk around the block—which also threatened his back, and X-ray treatments and injections were ineffective. It was to clear up, eventually, leaving McCarthy with only a slight limp, but he was classified 4-F. Though sympathetic toward conscientious objectors, he was not a pacifist. He became a civilian employee in the War Department, where he worked on breaking the Japanese code. (The experience may partly relate to McCarthy's subsequent interest in intelligence and the CIA.) In 1945 he taught school in Grand Rapids, Minnesota, and that same year he and Abigail were finally married in Abigail's parish in Minneapolis by a priest who was Eugene's cousin. The couple then bought a farm near Watkins to put some of their reformist-religious ideas into practice.

The farm was a culmination of various influences playing upon the McCarthys and their response to them. "It's hard to know, isn't it," a close friend of the McCarthys reflected, "what's personal and what comes out of a cultural matrix. People always think of Gene in terms of an Irish Catholic from the East, but of course he isn't that at all.[1] What you see in Gene is a coming together of various traditions, of Christian thought as well as the forms that American democracy took in the Midwest."

To cast a large cultural net, one might go back to 1848 and the arrival in Minnesota of German revolutionaries, and proceed from there to the Populists of the late 1900s who railed against the excesses of the Gilded Age, hated Wall Street, baited Eastern intellectuals and sometimes Jews, and were deadly suspicious of power in any form, especially Washington authority. The Populists, with free silver, their anodyne, and after them the Progressives, were responsible for direct election of Senators, farm programs, Federal regulation of railroads, the initiative, the referendum, postal savings banks, credit unions, and other reforms. The whole tradition was especially aimed at helping the farmer and the small businessman. In the forties, this tradition was connected with the McCarthys' interest in a book, *Sweden: The Middle Way*, by Marquis Childs. Published in 1936, it explored the middle ground between socialism and capitalism through cooperative societies, state monopolies of tobacco and liquor, and nationalized utilities. Like many other Midwesterners, the McCarthys believed that political democracy should be extended to become economic democracy as well, with producers owning the instrumentalities which affected them most. The McCarthys were also Catholic activists, followers of the Catholic Worker movement, which held that social reform was a religious responsibility and direct involvement necessary. The concepts of scholar-workers and the rural-life movement in-

[1] Speaking of Irishmen and misconceptions, see Norman Mailer's *Miami Beach and the Siege of Chicago*. Mailer tells of encountering McCarthy "by chance" at a restaurant. McCarthy, says Mailer, was surrounded by "big Irishmen like himself . . . some were big genial Irishmen with horn-rimmed glasses and some were lean Irishmen with craggy faces. . . ." Eller, Gabler, Carlson, Davidson, Merthan—Irishmen all! In fact, there were one and one-half Irish there, a hotel man from Limerick and the half-Irish McCarthy.

fluenced the McCarthys. Their farm, then, was meant to be the beginning of a cooperative community to help farmers in the area. It failed because the McCarthys couldn't do it alone.

McCarthy then took a $2750-a-year job teaching economics at the College of St. Thomas in St. Paul, and his students observed, not always approvingly, that he was more concerned with the distribution than the consumption or production of wealth. Abigail had her second child, Ellen, here. (The first had died immediately after birth and been buried in the small Watkins cemetery.) The family lived in one of the on-campus converted barracks heated by a temperamental oil burner. There was a shower but no tub; the floors were cement.

McCarthy's old friend Herman Schauinger, professor of American history at St. Thomas and author of *Profiles in Action: American Catholics in Political Life,* which he dedicated to McCarthy, recalls, "The frost would cover the electric outlets and the pillows. The lights often went out about five-thirty in the afternoon when everyone turned on his auxiliary heater—you had to have one at Tomville, as we called it. All the barracks had pious names in alphabetical order—I broke the order when I insisted on calling mine after a married saint, Sir Thomas More. I moved in directly from a siege at the hospital, and there was Gene hammering weather stripping around the front door and all the windows of Sir Thomas More. Every morning during my convalescence Gene would leave a five-gallon oil can at my front door filled—you had to get your own stove oil from a big outside drum. When Abby was pregnant Gene did the cooking, but not when they had guests. They were a disorganized couple and they still are. Gene went to chapel every day. I organized the village council and Gene and I were both council members—it was his first political job. I remember him sitting in the college office we shared, typically, his feet up on a desk, and he was reading the Pope's Christmas Allocution, which talked about democracy and the need for Christian involvement. 'Herman,' he said, 'the Pope says we should get into politics. Instead of griping we should act.' "

Minnesota has a long and rather schizophrenic political tradition. Usually a staid Republican dowager, she would sometimes produce or nurture radical third parties. "Especially in periods of economic depression," writes a Minnesota historian, G. Theodore Mitau,

> voices of agrarian and urban protest, often discordant and intense, have risen from the mining pits of the Mesabi Range, from the slaughterhouses and railroad shops of the cities, and from the debt-ridden farms of the Red River Valley to find expression in the platforms and conventions of Minnesota's third and minor parties. Through the Anti-Monopolists and the Greenback party of the 1870's, and the Nonpartisan League and the Farmer-Labor party of the present century, this tradition of protest has continued to exert pressure on state politics. Thus the fervor for social justice and economic opportunity has long had organizational expression in Minnesota, even though success in national elections has been rare and erratic.

When McCarthy got into politics in 1947, a Republican-run administration had been in control of the state for nine years. Harold Stassen, an unknown country attorney, had won the governorship in 1938 in a campaign with strong currents of anti-Communism and, say local observers, some anti-Semitism. The state went for Roosevelt, but Democrats could not win local offices because of feuding with the Farmer-Labor Party, as Hubert Humphrey, then a young professor, discovered when he ran for mayor of Minneapolis in 1943 and lost. Largely because of Humphrey's efforts the two factions were fused into the Democratic-Farmer-Labor Party, which proved strong enough to elect Humphrey mayor in 1945. The unification was a requiem for Farmer-Labor; the party had rapidly been losing supporters. The ideology of the Farmer-Laborites had a radical ancestry—a strange combination of Marxism, agrarian egalitarianism, and Utopianism—and its adherents joined with left-wingers within the Democratic Party so that there was a built-in split within the new party. (This division corresponded to a national one at the time: the Americans-for-Democratic-Action liberals on the one side against the left-leaning, anti-Truman Independent Citizens Committee of the Arts, Sciences and Professions on the other, which left the Democratic Party to support the Presidential candidacy of Henry A. Wallace.) The Minnesota anti-Communist liberals returned from the war determined to wrest the party both from the radicals and from the machine Democrats. Their means was to rally enough popular support to dominate the precinct caucuses by sheer numbers. There was talk, of the sort now commonplace, of renewing the party and democratizing the process of nomination for office. During his Presidential campaign the talk of participatory democracy would seem perfectly natural to McCarthy. Indeed, in 1968, the McCarthys were somewhat surprised to see that people had never heard of such things as precinct caucuses.

Joining the anti-Communist, back-to-the-people Democrats headed by Humphrey and Orville Freeman (later the Kennedy-Johnson Secretary of Agriculture), McCarthy had no thought of holding office himself. He was an organizer in St. Paul, where the liberals were holding state-wide caucus schools to instruct partisans on how to take control of the machinery on a precinct level. Their success impressed him deeply—from this point on, through his campaign in 1968, McCarthy would prefer volunteers to professionals. He proved to have a genius for party organization, working tirelessly in Ramsay County—which includes St. Paul—precinct by precinct, so that he was well known at the county convention and was elected county chairman.

Only one Democrat had ever been elected to Congress in Minnesota's Fourth Congressional District (he had lasted only one term), but McCarthy believed it could be done again in 1948. He had narrowly won the D-FL endorsement at its state convention and then he found himself confronted in the state primary by a candidate from organized labor. "They're both good men," Hubert Humphrey said, a remark that rankled with the McCarthys: "The whole idea of our work was that the party, the grass-roots party as we had organized it, would make its own nominations. That's what we had fought for. And there was Humphrey saying, 'They're both good men.'" McCarthy's secret weapon was the mimeograph room at St. Thomas, which helped keep his primary campaign costs down to six hundred dollars. "As I look back on it," says one of the men associated with the first campaign effort, "he had some things money couldn't buy—a very apparent goodness and sincerity, and the courage of his convictions. He was obviously a truthful man people felt they could trust." His speaking style, slow and deliberate, was the same as it is now. His notion of "standing," rather than "running," for office was shown by his distaste for the energetic stumping made famous by Humphrey. To McCarthy's opposition, his campaign was an amateur's effrontery, a poor unknown against a well-financed labor candidate. ("Where does the *professor* think he can get the money?" one labor man scoffed.) The professor found his support among the more conservative Democratic voters, white-collar workers, businessmen, the Catholics, and even some labor. The primary election was so close that McCarthy thought he had lost until a retabulation showed he had won by 380 votes.

"Gene loved the business from the start," says an old friend. "He found exactly what he'd been missing as an intellectual and teacher—political action." His Congressional campaign cost about seventy-five hundred dollars. He had a 1937 Chevrolet, and he would drive down the street passing out his mimeographed literature to friends on either side of the car, who would deliver it to the houses. Given almost no chance of winning at the start, he won the general election by 25,000 votes. McCarthy recalls,

At that time I looked at the record of the Congress, particularly of the incumbent, and I thought that there were five or six things that had to be done in this country. The only way they could get done would be to get people elected to Congress who could do them. The chances of my winning were said to be very scant, especially in the primary, where I was opposed by organized labor, or part of it, anyway, in the city of St. Paul. And it was a very strong segment of the labor movement then. I had opposition from the old party and what was considered to be an unbeatable incumbent Republican. Nonetheless, I did run and won in the primary and also won the general election; and proceeded to try to get enacted into law the things that I as a teacher had thought were necessary.

In Congress, where he began on the Post Office Committee—an assignment he disliked—McCarthy voted almost the straight liberal-internationalist ticket, winning the plaudits of labor and the ADA. (The ADA was to give him a 92-per-cent rating over 19 years; labor's COPE 69 out of 70 over 20 years; and the Rural Electrification Co-op Association 37 good marks to a single bad one over 19 years.) Labor, and migrant labor—whose condition McCarthy was calling a "national disgrace" in 1951 as he introduced pioneering legislation—taxation, education, open housing: there was little if anything in the McCarthy legislative record that liberals could fault, though he also displayed a high degree of party regularity, including a vote for the Communist Control Act of 1954. (He also voted in 1967 in support of the Subversive Activities Control Board.) He worked hard enough in Congress to win the respect of Sam Rayburn and was promoted, in 1955, to the House Ways and Means Committee. This was an important move for a younger Congressman, and while McCarthy's being a Midwestern Catholic had something to do with it, he was clearly being groomed. Dedicated to the Democratic Party platform of 1948, which corresponded to his own campaign promises, he was a "dream liberal," intelligent, cultivated, well-informed, though not quite exciting or dramatic. His private self corresponded to the public one. "I've known Gene since 1948," said Mary McGrory, the columnist, "and he was very nice and quiet with little to say. At parties he read books. You hardly noticed him except he did say funny things sometimes. And yet he also did the marvelously improbable, like taking on Joe McCarthy or the CIA."

These two acts did mark McCarthy as extraordinary. Beginning in 1954, four times in the House and five in the Senate, he introduced bills and resolutions to establish watchdogs over U.S. intelligence and the sacrosanct CIA. In 1952, with his own election only a few months off, he confronted Joe McCarthy in a radio debate. He was the first member of either House or Senate to oppose him face to face. "We begged him not to do it," an old Minnesota friend remembers, "but his answer was typical—'They couldn't get anyone with a big name so they got someone with the same name.' I don't know of anyone who was in favor of it. It wasn't a monumental debate but Gene came out looking a lot better than anyone had anticipated. He has always surprised the experts since he entered politics."

The radio program, called "American Forum of the Air," was sponsored by the Bohn Aluminum and Brass Corporation, whose noncommercials themselves told a good deal about what Eugene McCarthy risked in the confrontation. "To keep America the way it is, freedom must be protected from the weeds of socialism," went the Bohn plug. Joe McCarthy seized about two-thirds of the time, interrupting frequently.

After the discussion, Joe said, "It's hard to debate him. He's so nice." Gene McCarthy's opponent in the Congressional election in 1952 was not so graciously inclined. McCarthy was attacked as being "soft on Communism" and partial toward people of "doubtful loyalties," which brought out the Minnesota academic defense in force. McCarthy, angry for himself and for his wife, who was accused of being the hard-line Red of the family, campaigned hard and won by a large margin. (Just before the election, some of McCarthy's supporters collected money to pay for a newspaper ad with charges against his opponent. When McCarthy read the proposed material, which his friend, theologian Robert McAfee Brown, describes as "devastating," he said, "No. It is not worth winning, to have to win in that fashion.") His opponent, Roger Kennedy, is now a St. Paul banker. He said of McCarthy during the 1968 campaign, "He is resolute—certainly in the mid-fifties, when I had occasion to know him, it was a pretty cold season for liberals. Many of them scuttled for cover. . . ."

McCarthy's most important contribution in the House was in 1957, when he provided a rallying point for what was known as McCarthy's Marauders or McCarthy's Mavericks, a group of liberal Congressmen who organized around a set of principles called the McCarthy Manifesto. This group devised a strategy for passing liberal legislation. In 1959, after McCarthy had left the House, it became known as the Democratic Study Group—a name deliberately chosen because it was innocuous—and it fought successfully for enlarging the House Rules Committee so that legislation could be wrested out of the conservative committee. It is generally credited today for the surprising number of liberal laws passed in the Eighty-ninth and Ninetieth Congresses. The same behind-the-scenes style was continued throughout McCarthy's legislative career.

In 1958, against the advice of almost everyone close to him, McCarthy determined to run for the Senate. "The House is not a home," he said. "I will either go to the Senate or back to teaching." Most of Minnesota's Democratic luminaries, who were approached in order of seniority, wouldn't run against Edward Thye, the two-term Republican Senator, but McCarthy wanted to make the run. He was on the phone with a talkative constituent when he suddenly put his hand over the receiver and said to a close friend, "I'm going to go for the Senate. Thye can be beaten. I'm tired of the House. I've done my duty." McCarthy quickly discovered that he had an opponent, Eugenie Anderson, a well-known Democrat and former Ambassador to Denmark. The outcome was to be decided at the state convention. Mrs. Anderson had good support from suburbanites and the universities; it was now McCarthy who was heavily backed by organized labor and a number of practical politicians. A deciding factor in getting McCarthy the endorsement on the vital first ballot was Coya Knudsen, the Congresswoman whose husband took out ads ("Coya, come home") saying that a woman's place was at home. Mrs. Knudsen previously had been unable to get the endorsement of her own district, and a McCarthy negotiator agreed to get her the nomination from the state convention in exchange for her support for his man. It proved to be the swing vote for McCarthy, although Mrs. Knudsen herself lost in the general election.

One of McCarthy's principal problems in 1958 was his Catholicism, and for this reason his supporters stressed his German, rather than Irish, ancestry. An anti-Catholic whispering campaign proved ineffective because Thye himself was married to a Catholic. For obvious reasons, the race attracted the interest of the Kennedys. At one point McCarthy understood that John F. Kennedy had offered financial support, but nothing came until after the election and then it was only $1500. (Some of McCarthy's friends believe his animosity toward the Kennedys began at this point.) Generally, though, the style of campaigning McCarthy developed in 1958 was to remain characteristic. It was a low-budget Senate race, costing between $100,000 and $125,000, with little stress on paid television and radio. As usual, McCarthy discounted organization— there was a difference, he said, between an organization campaign and a candidate campaign, and he believed in the latter. The organization, as a result, was chaotic, with different people tackling the same project, the candidate—sometimes forgetfully and sometimes on the theory that the more people assigned the better—having duplicated assignments. No McCarthy campaigner was ever fired for incompetence—the candidate was too kind for that. (A few years later a political expert suggested that McCarthy fire some of his Washington Senate staff, saying, "They're nice but they're no damn good." "I know," McCarthy said, "but who else would hire them?") Besides, McCarthy viewed a campaign staff as generally unnecessary, and his campaign managers were mostly figureheads. If pushed, he would perform the campaign rituals but not always in expected ways. An early media adviser, Minneapolis advertising man and good friend of the candidate William Nee, urged McCarthy to compliment a popular Minnesota sport by posing for pictures as a fisherman. McCarthy finally assented and went out with a photographer. A few days later, with a small smile, he handed Nee an envelope full of photographs. They showed McCarthy in a boat with a fishing rod, sure enough, but he was wearing a business suit and shirt, with cufflinks, suspenders, and a hat. His press releases have been described as tracts, almost unusable by reporters, and McCarthy liked to write his own ad copy. Once he gave Nee copy for a farm advertisement, and Nee, testing it against the Rudolph Flesch reader scale, returned it to McCarthy with the verdict that the ad could be understood only by Ph.D.s. The candidate allowed Nee to rewrite the copy.

McCarthy did not believe in the committees of supporters, often racial or ethnic in make-up, which populate the usual campaign. Mrs. McCarthy, however, formed Women-for-McCarthy clubs with two thousand active members (there were to be fifteen thousand in 1964), who worked separately from the regular campaign. Speech writers, constantly thrust upon him, would soon find themselves engaged in a different campaign activity, and the candidate, though appreciative, was not receptive to outside suggestions. Some of his speeches were so dull the staff called them the "blue sky" speeches. The eccentricities and leisure of the McCarthy campaign brought accusations that McCarthy was weak and lazy, compared to Humphrey's unflagging, unending zeal. (The McCarthy people, for their part, did not believe that Senator Humphrey was doing much to help their candidate.)

McCarthy relied on a sober presentation of the issues, eager volunteers, timing, and himself. He would flood a locality with literature just before he knew polltakers were scheduled to arrive and thus managed always to keep Thye's lead in the polls within reasonable limits. The campaign photography relied heavily on the candidate's hard, clean-lined face, his distinct look of manliness and statesmanship. And he was at his best before large informal audiences, as at the State Fair, where his essential seriousness and concern for principles were effective. McCarthy, counter to predictions, defeated Thye by almost 100,000 votes, and those close to him, aware of the oddities of his campaign, began to credit him with faultless political judgment and timing.

McCarthy had various reasons for wanting the Senate seat in 1958; something of a political missionary, ambitious, cramped in the House, he felt he needed a bigger audience for his views. Beyond this, he had begun to think he might be the first Catholic President of the United States, and the Senate was the logical place to start. McCarthy was not alone in this view; the Catholic intellectual community looked to Gene McCarthy and not to John F. Kennedy. McCarthy himself was distrustful of Kennedy, and his suspicions deepened in 1959, when Senator Kennedy encouraged him in a debate on the Landrum-Griffin labor bill to take an exposed position and then backed off himself. Since then, he told a reporter, "I've had my guard up against the Kennedys." He was not overly impressed with John Kennedy as Congressman or Senator and said privately that he didn't think Kennedy was a good Catholic. McCarthy irritated Kennedy by making sophisticated theological jokes, and Robert Kennedy would say later, "McCarthy doesn't respect anyone who can't quote as much Aquinas as he." The politicians McCarthy liked were those he regarded as unpretentious and straightforward, like Harry S. Truman. It was McCarthy, not a Republican, who inserted President Eisenhower's Farewell Address into the Congressional Record, only partly because it contained Ike's famous passage about the "military-industrial complex." In 1960, when McCarthy was assisting Humphrey's Presidential campaign in the Wisconsin primary, he was warned by one of the Kennedys that Humphrey would be smothered if he campaigned in West Virginia. Tell Humphrey, he was told, that the Kennedys would use Humphrey's war record against him. Annoyed by the pressure, McCarthy snapped, "Tell him yourself."

McCarthy's preoccupation with the Kennedys was to become an important fact of his political life. The Kennedys, McCarthy seems to have felt, were overrated, achieving their goals through an adroit use of public relations rather than by distinguished effort. Glamour, not ability, was paying off. McCarthy also resented, he told friends, the Kennedy assumption that there was only one game in town—theirs. In 1960, McCarthy became a stop-Kennedy man at the Democratic National Convention. Since his first choice, Humphrey, had been effectively eliminated in the primaries, he was for Stevenson or Lyndon Johnson, although, as he later said, he had reservations about Johnson. Toward the Majority Leader his attitude was at least officially correct, but McCarthy doubted Johnson's ability to inspire or "move the nation on to new or greater achievements." Johnson, he later said, would have made a fine "prime minister [who] is much more subject to party directions and restraint under the British parliamentary system than a President of the United States." But in 1960, when arriving at Los Angeles for the convention, he said that Johnson was the best qualified candidate. He was aware that Stevenson's chances were remote, depending on a deadlock between Johnson and Kennedy, just as he would see his own chances for the nomination in 1968 dependent on a Humphrey-Kennedy deadlock. Both McCarthy and Humphrey thought that Kennedy might be stopped at the 1960 convention, and both were interested in the Vice-Presidency under either Johnson or Stevenson. Stevenson's first choice to place his name in nomination was Humphrey, not McCarthy, but Humphrey could not because his good Minnesota friend Governor Orville Freeman was to give the Kennedy nominating speech—and an obvious split in the Minnesota delegation might hurt Freeman's chances for his

upcoming fourth term. McCarthy was not enthralled by the prospect of making the nominating speech either and wanted to decline
but finally assented. Thomas B. Morgan, a free-lance writer and
then Stevenson's press secretary (he helped McCarthy in 1968 and
is now press secretary for Mayor John V. Lindsay), remembers
that a speech for McCarthy had been written by a magazine editor
and was ready for release, but McCarthy, as always, insisted on
giving his own speech. It was put together in note form on hotel
stationery moments before he walked out to the convention podium.
It was and still is a moving speech, especially the famous paragraph
beginning "Do not reject this man," but looked at closely it con-
tains many strangely flat sentences, such as: "There's demagoguery
abroad in the land at all times, and demagoguery, I say to you,
takes many forms. There's that which says 'here is wealth, and
here is material comfort.' We suffer a little from that in the United
States." If a great speech it was, raising high the crowd and prompting Norman Mailer to call it "the best nominating speech" he had
ever heard, its secret was in the delivery. Eight years later, Mrs.
McCarthy was asked why her husband could not make fighting
speeches like that for himself. She answered, "He always finds it
easier to ask in behalf of others."

Despite his reservations, McCarthy campaigned hard for Kennedy in 1960. He was angry enough about the introduction of the
religious issue that, using his own money, he bought TV time for
a debate with three ministers on Kennedy's Catholicism and the
Presidency. He could remark about one of Kennedy's speeches that
it "was like a meal at the Hot Shoppes. It wouldn't poison you, but
it wouldn't nourish you either," but he traveled 50,000 miles in
fifteen states, campaigning for Kennedy as a former Stevensonian,
and exhausting himself so that when it was over he was hospitalized
for several weeks with pneumonia. Relations between the two men
were now somewhat better and, besides, McCarthy had probably
raised more money for the party than any other liberal Democrat.
McCarthy could now suggest Orville Freeman for Secretary of

Agriculture, and the President sent McCarthy as an unofficial observer to a conference of Christian Democrats in Santiago. McCarthy gradually developed respect for Kennedy, and after the assassination McCarthy wrote a moving elegy. He said, in part:

John Fitzgerald Kennedy demonstrated in action his realization that there must be a judgment of nations, as well as of persons. He demonstrated his awareness of the two great facts of contemporary history—first, that the mass or the volume of current history, of the things which demand some judgment and some commitment from our Nation and from us, is greater than ever before; second, that the movement of history itself is now at a rate more rapid than ever before known—and that in the face of these two ultimate facts, we are called upon to exercise, as best we can, and to the fullest possible measure, the power of human reason in attempting to control and give direction to life and to history.

John F. Kennedy's entire efforts demonstrated a confidence in the future, a hope that the world of men could and would be improved, a belief in the universality of mankind and, in these far-reaching searches, a belief that there was no satisfaction except in the intensification and perfection of the life of every person.

Empty words of politicians of the past are echoed again: "The country will survive," and "the Government will stand." These are true statements, but for some days Americans will not walk as certainly or as straight as they did in the past. The quick step is gone. A strong heart has stopped. A mind that sought the truth, a will ready for commitment, and a voice to challenge and to move are ended for this age and time of ours.

This is, therefore, a time of truth for all, a time for resolution and for strong hope that what we say today may be supplemented and perfected in the future by honest historians who will trace and define the public service of John F. Kennedy, and by good poets, who, speaking—as poets must—for each man alone, will do justice to John F. Kennedy.

These good words told much about the writer. McCarthy was a politician pitting himself against the traditionally empty words of politicians, and when he looked around, trying to penetrate to the moving center of things, what he saw was change, change so rapid, so dense in its existence, as to be a mass, a volume. How dramatic this must have been for a man schooled in the unchanging ways of the Catholic medieval world! His education, his turn of mind, his predilection for the universal and general rather than the particular and specific led him to a conception of his role as Senator similar to Edmund Burke's, who believed that the responsibility of a legislator was primarily national rather than toward his particular constituency.

Some feel that in his first term in the Senate McCarthy underwent an important change. He had been "a fine legislative mechanic, with great technical ability," as one Washington expert says of him, but now, more and more, he detached himself from daily routine. He hated hearings where, he said, everyone droned on. Minnesota patronage he usually left to the office of Senator Humphrey. He called lobbyists "rainmakers." He couldn't bear roll calls—"You get into this silly stuff about what your attendance record is, about the percentage of the roll calls you've missed, and stuff like that. Margaret Chase Smith had to get arthritis before she stopped answering roll calls," he said—and there were times when he simply forgot, as, later, his absence for the vote confirming Clark Clifford as Secretary of Defense. He regarded the Senate seniority system as cumbersome and outmoded, and long before his surprising departure from the Foreign Relations Committee early in 1969, McCarthy was a committee jumper. His aloofness from the system led some to call him Eugene Cardinal McCarthy. One of his former assistants said, "He was frustrated by the tedium and the rigidity of the Senate routine and he wouldn't play the game. He wouldn't bow to the feudal lords." He was, however, "a very effective if unconventional Senator," according to Grace Bassett, a prize-winning Capitol Hill reporter who worked in his 1968 campaign.

One of McCarthy's fellow Senators, a man well known and respected for his assiduous work for civil-rights legislation, was asked by this reporter why he had not supported Eugene McCarthy for President. The Senator became sincerely emotional, red in the face. He made the reporter promise that his remarks would not be attributed to him, and then said, "Why didn't I come out? Well, first it appeared inevitable that Johnson would be the nominee, and, except for Vietnam, I had a strong conviction that Johnson would be better than Nixon, who looked certain to be the Republican choice. The important thing was what kind of a Congress a President would bring in. It never occurred to me that McCarthy had a prayer. Later I started using an alibi—that Vietnam would be a footnote to history and the important matters would still be the race issue and the cities. But let me tell you the truth. Out of one hundred liberals, McCarthy would be ninety-nine on my list. He is not worth a damn. These civil-rights fights have been miserable fights. They took work and commitment and a lot of calls. I never saw McCarthy from one month to the next."

On the other hand, Eliot Janeway, the economist, a man knowledgeable about the government, says, "McCarthy is as creative and has as shrewd an instinct for political analysis as any Senator in the country's history. It's a commonplace of the Senate that Senators who run efficient offices or who are astute about getting their names on bills don't necessarily have a perceptive sense of how things work in the present or how they will work in the future." And Russell Hemenway—whose job as head of the National Committee for an Effective Congress is precisely to appraise the worth of individual legislators—says that "McCarthy has as much integrity as any public figure I've known. He was clearly the star of his class in both the House and Senate and could have taken the leadership of the liberal caucus in Congress any time he wanted to."

How to solve the discrepancies among these observations even puzzled McCarthy supporters, and the answer seems to be, paradoxical as it sounds, that all sides are right. McCarthy was not particularly an activist, nor was he interested in the minutiae of specific legislation. Many Senators do not do legwork or sponsor bills, and the latter-day McCarthy felt his job to be both long-range and behind-the-scenes. Like most Senators, he supported various special interests at times, particularly Minnesota interests, when the issues did not seem overwhelmingly important, and in some areas of liberal concern he was less aggressive than in others. He was, if no flaming radical, a studious national Senator with an influence on larger issues. "I think I am a good legislator," an angry McCarthy said on television at the close of the California campaign against Robert Kennedy, in which his legislative record had been strongly attacked. "I think I am probably better informed in the broad legislative field than, I think, probably anybody in the Senate, if you want it straight."

As a Senator and a member at one time or another of the Senate Finance Committee, the Committee on Agriculture, the Committee on Public Works and Forestry, and the Foreign Relations Committee, McCarthy could list many accomplishments and firsts.

In the Senate he continued to press the issue of the CIA's autonomy and ultimately achieved some success when members of the Foreign Relations Committee got greater access to reports of CIA activities. He was among the first to criticize American arms sales abroad and to call for regulation. He was the only member of the Senate to call for legal conscientious draft objection to particular wars on moral grounds. He initiated the successful effort to block the confirmation of Admiral Lewis B. Strauss as Secretary of Commerce in 1959. He worked on farm bills to reduce surpluses. He was a major architect of the Revenue Act of 1964, the most important tax reform bill of recent years, and he was prominent in attempts to end the filibuster. He was cosponsor of the 1966 Model Cities Act and supported extension of Social Security benefits as well as being a cosponsor of the Social Security Medicare proposal of 1965. In 1959 Johnson had made him chairman of the Special

Committee on Unemployment Problems, and the 9000-page "Mc-Carthy Report," as it was known, made the first comprehensive, detailed statement on the nation's unemployment and poverty. It laid the basis for much of the social legislation of the New Frontier and the Great Society programs and anticipated many of the recommendations of the Kerner Report of 1967.

Despite this solid legislative record, there were several persistent criticisms he could not seem to live down. One charge used heavily by the Kennedy forces in the Oregon and California primary campaigns was that McCarthy had voted with the majority against a proposal for a constitutional amendment, introduced by Edward Kennedy, to ban the poll tax. McCarthy's vote was at the urging of Attorney General Katzenbach, who was waiting for a court decision on the poll tax and believed that Congressional action might nullify the court test, which would have had the effect of making the poll tax illegal but not unconstitutional, as the Supreme Court went on to declare it. Some of McCarthy's chief spokesmen were not entirely satisfied with this explanation, though they used it during the campaign. The fact was that part of the civil-rights movement was against the Attorney General's advice. It wanted the Kennedy bill as insurance in case the Supreme Court failed to make the poll tax unconstitutional. Both the majority (the Mansfield-Dirksen) provision and the Kennedy proposal were aimed at abolishing the poll tax. The debate was over procedure, not substance, but even so McCarthy's position was portrayed in 1968 as a vote for the poll tax.

Another example of how an unpleasant light can be made to shine on almost any corner of a Senatorial voting record can be found in a postelection article in *Harper's* magazine by Jeremy Larner, one of McCarthy's 1968 speech writers. Larner felt that McCarthy had never been the crusader his campaign made him out to be and cited, among other examples, McCarthy's vote for federally assisted rifle practice. This was another Kennedy amendment, in 1967, to reduce the rifle practice budget by some two hundred thousand dollars. Not just McCarthy, but many Senate liberals, voted against the amendment, McCarthy's position being consistent with one he followed elsewhere—that reforms ought to be substantive and wholesale and not come in the form of amendments tacked to larger bills, in this case a defense appropriation of more than seventy billion dollars.

But the most persistent of the anti-McCarthy allegations—one which also troubled many McCarthy supporters—was that he had taken the side of the oil industry by voting for the depletion tax allowance. Writing in *Ramparts* magazine, Andrew Kopkind charged that McCarthy voted for the "allowances in 1964 and has generally been considered a friend of the oil and gas industries, with only a few regrets, mostly on the Senate floor where they are for public consumption, and not in Committee, where they count."

The same accusation, and even the implication that McCarthy was offered money for his votes, appeared in Drew Pearson's column just before the Democratic Convention in 1964. (Pearson openly backed Humphrey in 1968, while his wife's name appeared on several McCarthy campaign committees.) McCarthy answered Pearson as follows:

August 21, 1964

Dear Drew:

. . . I must take issue with your statement that I have consistently voted for the big oil companies, and challenge your assumption or implication in your column that my assignment to the Finance Committee was dependent upon an indication of my future support for oil and gas.

In my first five years in the Senate, I voted four times in the Finance Committee on motions to reduce the oil depletion allowance. . . .

In these years Senator Douglas offered his amendment on the floor of the Senate three times. On June 25, 1959, I was not present for the vote (I may have been having coffee, as you said), but I was listed as a co-sponsor of the four amendments offered that day, including the Douglas amendment. . . . On June 20, 1960, I voted with Senator Douglas for his amendment. We lost, 30-56. On September 5, 1962, Senator Douglas again offered his amendment and I voted with him. We lost, 23-50.

My votes on the 1964 tax bill are another matter. The House bill, which was being considered by our Committee, included changes in the law which, by changes in the oil depletion rules, would have brought an additional $40 million a year into the Treasury. It was my judgment that this was the best that could be done. This was the position taken by Secretary Dillon. . . . And it was, perhaps, as much as should have been done unless we were to have revised the whole Tax Code for depletion allowance for all other minerals. I therefore voted against the Douglas amendment in Committee . . . and on the floor . . . I also voted against the Douglas oil depletion amendment to the excise tax extension bill in Committee . . . as not being relevant to the tax provisions under consideration.

Whoever was offering $10,000 in 1958 did not stop to see me either on the way to Utah or on the way back.

Sincerely yours,

Eugene McCarthy

Such complicated charges, once on the record, are difficult to refute in a way even an informed electorate can understand. (Anything stated three times in the press, McCarthy remarked later on, automatically becomes a fact.) "There are those," he said, "who think tax reform is finding an inequity, making it universal, and calling it justice." In all, McCarthy voted seven times for reducing the depletion allowance, but his view was that while he favored a review of depletion allowances for the whole minerals industry, to single out oil was a purely political gesture, important for making liberal debater's points but not for real reform. He was, it seemed, prepared to live with imperfect justice or relative injustice rather than further the illusion that an amendment here or there would bring justice immediately. The key words in the McCarthy voting vocabulary were "appropriate" and "fair." He felt he should not be judged on the basis of individual points but rather on the basis of his over-all performance.

McCarthy was not yet opposed to the war in Vietnam despite, perhaps, private reservations—early in August 1964, he as well as Senator Fulbright and all but two Senators (Morse and Gruening) had voted for the loosely worded Gulf of Tonkin resolution— and was willing to run as Johnson's Vice-President, at the suggestion of the President, who urged him to become better known. McCarthy did not think an active campaign for the Vice-Presidency was appropriate, but he did assemble a small staff for the Atlantic City convention. He used a booklet meant for his upcoming Senatorial campaign. The first run had to be scrapped because a secretary, as a joke, wrote under one of the glowing endorsements "written by Sen. Eugene J. McCarthy" and it got into print. McCarthy's 1964 effort, indeed, had a comic-opera flavor, and the candidate did not view the outcome as a matter of life and death. He did, though, ask mutual friends to call the President on his behalf, and from the White House he continued to receive signals of encouragement. Just before the convention McCarthy and Humphrey, at Johnson's request, made a joint appearance on television, and afterward both of the hopeful candidates received calls from the President saying how much he liked it. Then Lady Bird Johnson got on the phone to tell McCarthy, "You're *my* candidate."

McCarthy had the support of Governor John Connally of Texas, and for a time, Mayor Richard J. Daley of Chicago, who apparently wanted a Catholic on the ticket. One Minnesota wheel horse close to both McCarthy and Humphrey said that Johnson favored McCarthy over Humphrey—he admired McCarthy's political acumen and his ability to keep silent—and would have chosen McCarthy if the two had come from different states. Humphrey's party seniority in Minnesota was a factor in forcing McCarthy out. Humphrey also did a far better job rounding up preconvention support, especially from organized labor, compelling Johnson to choose him. And despite McCarthy's excellent labor record, union leaders, Walter Reuther among them, favored Humphrey, whom they considered more reliable and more militant.

The week before the convention a good friend of McCarthy's learned on the highest authority that Johnson had definitely decided on Humphrey. But, he later said, "I felt so unhappy about it that I couldn't bring myself to tell Gene."

The President characteristically kept up the suspense. McCarthy held a long press conference in Atlantic City which was meant to dramatize the fact that he had nothing to say, and mostly he told jokes, although he did trick the press a little. He said he was going to Washington to meet his children, but the press soon discovered that his children were already in Atlantic City, adding to the rumors that McCarthy was going to Washington for a tête-à-tête with Johnson. But it was not the kind of game McCarthy would play very long. The greatest error for Humphrey and himself, he remarked later, was that they did not jointly refuse to participate in the manufactured drama.

The signal had still not arrived from the White House, and late Tuesday night of convention week McCarthy, listening to Al Hirt on television in his hotel suite with his wife, suddenly turned to her and said, "I've made up my mind." He wrote out a telegram withdrawing from the race and announcing his support for Humphrey. ("I don't care if Gene doesn't get it, but I'd feel terrible if Hubert doesn't," Abigail told a friend.)

If McCarthy felt misused in a Presidential publicity play, he could mount a little drama of his own. At six the next morning he got an aide out of bed. McCarthy was scheduled for an eight-o'clock breakfast with fellow Senators, and he told the aide to go to the restaurant in advance and scout out an escape route. McCarthy then called Jerome Eller and told him to send the withdrawal wire to the President and also release it to the press while McCarthy was at breakfast. The reporters were waiting in front of the restaurant. McCarthy excused himself during the meal, went to the men's room,

clambered out the window and into a waiting car, and was driven
to his hideaway, the Carousel Motel on the south side of town.

There, with some of his friends and associates—Herman
Schauinger, Joe Gabler, Bill Carlson, Maurice Rosenblatt, Emerson
Hynes, and John Safer—he was unreachable to anyone. His aide
meanwhile was calling Johnson's assistant, Walter Jenkins, to read
him the text of the telegram. "Stop the telegram," Jenkins said, "If
you haven't sent it, don't." McCarthy's aide said it was too late:
McCarthy was withdrawing from the race. The President was furious; the puppet strings had been snatched away.

Later that day Johnson called McCarthy at the Carousel. Mc-
Carthy was swimming in the ocean, and when he came back he returned the call. "I thought I'd leave you free at the salt lick," he
said to the President, explaining his withdrawal. Johnson said what
McCarthy already knew—that Humphrey was the choice, and the
group at the motel saw, via television, Humphrey and Senator
Thomas Dodd, hastily picked by the President as McCarthy's re-
placement in the mock drama, board a plane for Washington. Mc-
Carthy was at his caustic best, but still annoyed, humiliated, and,
perhaps, a little exhilarated by his own near approach.

McCarthy said afterward:

> I was not altogether naïve about what this game was all about.
> I don't quite feel that I was led down the garden path. Yes, there
> were White House people who said: "Keep in it." But it was
> helping my own Senatorial campaign back home in Minnesota.
> The kind of publicity I got couldn't be bought. . . . There was,
> as I have said before, a point at which they should have given
> me the scenario for the last act. I didn't mind that second act—
> that's always confused. But the third act is the point at which
> you want to know if the end is going to be happy or sad; whether
> you get out or get killed.

Atlantic City found its way into a McCarthy poem called "Lament
of an Aging Politician," which ends:

I have left Act I, for involution
And Act II. There mired in complexity
I cannot write Act III.

"People who write Act III," he said, "write tragedy."

Despite a small rumor campaign—he was said to have been in a mental hospital or suffering from cancer (after a reception McCarthy said, "They didn't want to shake my hand. They wanted to feel my pulse")—McCarthy did not have to work very hard for re-election in Minnesota in 1964. In the middle of his Senate campaign he was seen in a Washington department store by a woman who asked him what he was doing away from his home state. McCarthy replied that he was waiting for his daughters. He had flown in from Minnesota because he had promised to go shopping with them for coats. McCarthy won by over 350,000 votes, the largest popular majority of any Democratic candidate in the state's history.

McCarthy's 1964 campaign book is the standard formula for an incumbent Senator: an endorsement from the President ("I served with him in the Senate. He's the kind of man—as we say in the ranch country in Texas—who will go to the well with you . . . my counselor, my colleague and my friend"), and photographs of the candidate—in his long-sleeved suits, with the Washington monument in the background, in a baseball outfit, on the phone, in committee hearings, with Cabinet members, with Johnson, John Kennedy, Stevenson, Humphrey, McCarthy's wife and his four children. One prophetic photo—used in the 1968 campaign as a poster—shows the candidate standing forlornly alone in a cobblestone courtyard.

It is difficult to date or gauge the intensity of McCarthy's rupture with the Johnson Administration. If McCarthy was not precisely embittered by Atlantic City, he does appear to have gathered what he felt were fresh insights. He thought that Johnson's decision to pick Humphrey because of his labor support was "cowardly," says a close associate, but more important he now felt that Johnson had tarnished the Vice-Presidency, revealing less than clear respect for the Constitutional system. The Vietnam war had not played a role in the Vice-Presidential contest, but as the President began to escalate the war, contrary to his 1964 campaign pledges, the issues began to be drawn more clearly and the contrast between the attitudes of the two men sharpened. "Johnson," writes Tom Wicker in his book, *JFK and LBJ: The Influence of Personality upon Politics*:

> was a middle-aged man of smalltown America, both a Westerner and a Southerner, and except where politics had demonstrably forced his growth—as on the question of civil rights—he functioned like most men, as a product of his background. There is little to suggest that at this time he saw the world moving away from the stereotype he had accepted in the Fifties—the notion of the "Communist bloc" monolithically seeking to bury "the free world." Like any Rotarian or state legislator and many members of Congress, he saw the world conflict in terms of good and evil and if he was by no means a right-winger who spied a Communist under every bed and believed in holy war against them, he still was at the time of his accession to the Presidency one of those millions of Americans who were nationalist almost to the point of nativism; impressed by the lesson of World War II that aggression unchecked was aggression unleashed, and whose years of greatest activity had coincided with the frustrations and passions of the Cold War.

If Wicker's analysis of Johnson is correct, McCarthy's outlook is starkly different. As a man who takes a long view of history he is inclined to ask how necessary or vital to national interests a war being fought today would seem tomorrow. As a Catholic steeped in medievalism he is a universalist; as a Niebuhrian he might wonder how much self-interest influences men's judgment of events; as a deeply Christian man he questions, on moral grounds, war and killing; as an optimist he leans toward taking risks; as an intellectual he is suspicious of national mythology; as a practical student of foreign affairs he is inclined to think that insofar as there are American vital interests to be protected, they are in Europe, not in Southeast Asia; and as a rather rebellious individual he is ready in general to challenge the consensus of establishment thought.

McCarthy did not publicly attack the President on Vietnam until 1966, long after some of his Senate colleagues, including Robert Kennedy. He has said that he did not have enough information and therefore accepted the Administration's statement that the war would soon be over. "I don't think he paid too much attention to it, to be frank," one of his aides has said. "We didn't talk about it very much, although he was always critical of McNamara. He found his explanations glib." Indeed, the evidence is that in his second term in the Senate McCarthy's "essence," as he would refer to it, crystallized and hardened, and his role as a critic and opposition leader began to emerge, just as the Catholic Church was veering toward social action in the same period. One important element, certainly, was his exposure to foreign policy after he became a member of the Senate Foreign Relations Committee in 1965.

McCarthy broke first with the Johnson Administration in the fall of 1965, after emerging from the hospital where he had been because of a kidney infection. The issue was American intervention in the Dominican Republic. "Our function in the Senate," he said then, "is not merely to find out what the Administration's policy is and then say yes or no to it—it is sometimes too late. We have a definite responsibility to develop policy ourselves." In January 1966, he was one of sixteen Senators who asked the President to continue the bombing suspension then in effect, and he began to urge that the United States accept the idea of negotiating with the Vietcong. From then on he criticized and excoriated American participation in the Vietnam war at every turn, on moral and practical grounds, until, despairing of finding another way, he declared for President.

To many it was an odd and uncharacteristic action for a man who seemed to prefer theory to practice. He was a man who cared nothing for money or possessions, who put himself through the Senate on thousand-dollar honoraria for speeches (after the 1960 Stevenson nominating speech he received an average of a hundred speaking invitations a week), who liked his privacy and long lunches, loved poetry and his jokes, who had few intimate friends but a warm attachment for the human race. Later, questions as to whether he wanted to be President would become increasingly meaningless to him—his thrust, his role as a professional politician, drove him into the race whether he wanted the office or not. "It is a question of whether there is any purpose in politics beyond yourself," he said, just before he announced. He was not in what is generally considered a Presidential contender's mold. In his high notions of personal responsibility, his desire to connect political and religious aspirations, he was perhaps nearer to a Christian Democrat, European style, than an American politician. Yet he was ambitious enough to have considered the Presidency before, and, in his own way, he would run hard now. His very eccentricities would serve him well, his detachment from the liberal rhetoric turn out to be a boundless asset. More than was realized at the time, the people were in terror of their powerlessness and sought change and new directions. By the solitary act of risking Johnson's wrath, McCarthy seemed to offer a way out.

Part II | JOHNSON

Part II.

4 | New Hampshire: a Pilgrimage

It had happened before that a President had been successfully denied the renomination of his party, but it had not happened that a challenger, having knocked out the President, was then confronted by two more adversaries as Eugene McCarthy was in 1968. The movement, then, was forced to wage three campaigns against Johnson, against Kennedy, and against Humphrey and the party regulars, each requiring different weight gloves and a different style of attack. Each of the three campaigns had novel traits of its own.

The first, the campaign against President Johnson, began slowly, quietly. The McCarthy button was a talisman. It had not been specially designed for 1968; it was just *the* button, the one McCarthy had always used, and someone had doubtlessly decided that it would be good again. On top was a bar, then McCARTHY (the star beneath the "c" standing for the North Star State), and the fishtail of a banner. The standard colors were light and dark blue. In 1968, in states where the McCarthy Presidential campaign was rich the bar would be red; elsewhere all the markings would be dark blue, at a saving so infinitesimal that only an impoverished campaign would have considered it. In the early days of the campaign the button met responses like, "Sure good to have General McCarthy back." In New York a special button was prepared saying GENE MCCARTHY FOR PRESIDENT because no one knew who plain McCarthy was.

The candidate had originally thought of declaring his intentions to run at the Conference of Concerned Democrats in Chicago, but some of his more cautious supporters were concerned that the tone of the meeting might be too shrill, too strongly anti-Johnsonian; thus McCarthy had declared in Washington and chose Chicago for his maiden campaign speech on December 2. The audience of several thousand in the ballroom at the Conrad Hilton was seated as delegations, with a sign for every one of the forty-five states represented, as though the conference were a dress rehearsal for the take-over of the convention in August. They wanted to be roused, to leave the ballroom with spirits raised and hopes ignited by a fighting candidate. McCarthy's was a good speech, the same one which had been delighting college students:

> Instead of the language of promise and of hope, we have in politics today a new vocabulary in which the critical word is *war*: war on poverty, war on ignorance, war on crime, war on pollution. None of these problems can be solved by war but only by persistent, dedicated, and thoughtful attention.

In Chicago it filled much of the audience with inner groans. For them it was the speech of a college professor, not a candidate.

There were two influences at work on the speaker. The first was his conviction that he must campaign on the issues, that he must not attack the President, at least not yet. It was Johnson's errors or miscalculations in policy that he opposed. One of the peculiarities which distinguished McCarthy's campaign was that it was always being judged by the press, enemies and friends alike, exactly by the standards he had pitted himself against. He did not think that the President had to be a man of action, decisive, domineering. He had disliked the deification of the Kennedys; and he had found in the prevalent notion that the President and the men around him knew best, and in the excessive deference awarded to people in power, the seeds of just that alienation of the masses, helpless by comparison, which he was trying to combat. McCarthy had criticized Johnson for saying *my* Presidency, *my* White House, *my* Vice-President, *my* Presidential helicopter, and the candidate felt that he in turn had to avoid an overpersonalized style.

The second influence, this time of temperament, was also revealing. McCarthy had come down from his room at the Conrad Hilton to find himself being introduced by Allard Lowenstein, one of the conference organizers, and he had stood and listened. Lowenstein, believing McCarthy to be still in his room, and afterward embarrassed about the incident, talked for ten minutes to fill up time, making an emotional attack on the President, while McCarthy, fuming, kicked around a Dixie cup at the back of the hall. He could not hope to top the incendiary quality of Lowenstein's speech. He did not even try. Indeed, to those who heard him he seemed almost deliberately to throw his lines away, mumbling monotonously, trampling on paragraph stops. "We're making progress," McCarthy said later in the campaign. "The introductions are getting shorter and shorter."

The Chicago conference struck McCarthy as amateurish and he decided that future meetings in his behalf would be under his control. At Chicago it had been said publicly—to bolster hopes—that the campaign had a million dollars, which was far from true. Reports from the delegates were not only gloomy but showed that the real interest of many conferees was the re-election of dovish Senators, like Joe Clark of Pennsylvania or Frank Church of Idaho, neither of whom, to McCarthy's irritation, had come out for him. More and more it began to look as though the "Dump Johnson" movement, while valuable as a platform, was not going to provide a solid base for a Presidential campaign. Success would have to depend almost entirely on the candidate's ability to pull votes in the primaries.

What line to pursue? He was out of patience with the President and his policy in Vietnam, yet he chose in his early speeches to be indirect, soft, even a little corny. "Let us again hear America singing. In place of disunity, let us have dedication of purpose. In place of near despair, let us have hope." He invokes youth: "The 1968 campaign, I anticipate, will be one in which the youth of America should and will have more influence and more at stake than in any campaign in the history of the United States." He criticizes the poverty program as a handout and believes in rights, not welfare. His own recommendations for a Secretary of State—Douglas Dillon, Mike Mansfield, John Sherman Cooper—do not reveal a radical turn of mind. He has a plan for Vietnam—Gavin-type military enclaves, a readiness to negotiate, the exploration at least of a coalition government, stopping the bombing of the North, although he might continue to bomb supply lines in the South (almost exactly the terms agreed to by President Johnson in the fall of 1968) —but he stresses general solutions, not specifics, and he talks about reconciliation, regeneration, hope. He mocks Democrats who won't take a stand

> because of ambition to hold office in a party or because of some kind of permanent involvement, maybe, that they have gotten one of those invitations to a White House dinner, you know, and they have had it enclosed in permanent plastic and once a person has done that with a pen or with a White House invitation, he seems to have given up some of his political freedom. I am beginning to think that the permanent, transparent plastic was a bad invention so far as free politics is concerned.

He was clearly urbane and witty but not what the left was looking for: he "seems to lack guts. . . . We enlist in McCarthy's army but we intend to keep stirring up mutiny until the general stops yawning," said a perceptive journalist, I. F. Stone; his speeches are "dull, vague, and without either balls or poetry. . . . Make Bobby Kennedy run," said Jack Newfield in the *Village Voice* (which Ethel Kennedy, who wanted her husband to run, cheered). These critics were concerned that McCarthy would not excite the public and thus neutralize the antiwar sentiments. Reporters from middle-of-the-road papers like the *New York Times* were critical too. Apparently "half-hearted," McCarthy was not making news.

From the candidate's viewpoint, things looked somewhat different. He had learned from long experience to separate serious errors from the snipings of reporters and editors who needed stories, and he knew that news was often negative. He did not want to "pound the pulpit," he said, for "people don't want to be shouted at." If he were to satisfy the peace advocates by sharper attacks on the war, he would have no chance with the great middle spread of voters—from liberal Democrats to liberal Republicans and even conservatives from both parties who wanted change. And he would not lose the extreme doves even if he didn't satisfy them completely.

How to organize?

There was no money—the entire treasury consisted of five thousand dollars given by a generous San Francisco woman, June Degnan (who would later make other substantial contributions), and there was little coming in. There was almost no staff. (The campaign's first employee was also to be the last. In surviving the *coups d'état* of the McCarthy finance division, she was to change offices seven times and be fired on four occasions—though not by McCarthy. She also quit once.) Unlike Robert Kennedy, McCarthy could not simply revive an existing but dormant political organization. He had to build one. And here, in the opinion of many people close to his remarkable campaign, he made some understandable but highly serious mistakes.

McCarthy's ideas on organization and planning were distinctly at odds with the conventional wisdom which held that both were needed for victory. Indeed his own administrative assistant, Jerome Eller, had written, "A campaign centered on issues requires organization to an even greater extent than a personality contest." A capable staff, it is usually said, is worth between five and ten percentage points at the polls, often enough to win. "Look here," the candidate was told, "you've done a very unorthodox thing. You've ridden into the courtyard and challenged the king in full view of the court. The penalty is death. You've got to have troops of your own." That meant a press secretary, public-relations people, schedulers, advance men—in short, a full-fledged campaign organization with adequate funds. McCarthy's answer was, "No, we'll live off the land."

"He really believed that if he stood up people would come to him," remarked an old friend. As he spread the word among the people, volunteer groups would spring up behind him, he hoped, so that he would not need extensive help. Early, for example, he estimated that a New Hampshire campaign would cost fifty thousand dollars; the actual bill was six times that. A national effort for the six states he had announced for, he thought, would cost a million dollars, but his guess was eight or ten times too low. "In most campaigns," he said, "people spend two-thirds of their time talking about their opponent. We won't need to do that."

He was to end with a major campaign, but at first he did not think in such terms. For a guide he drew from his experience in Minnesota politics, where he had received record votes in campaigns run largely by himself. When it came to campaigning he had something of the mentality of a nineteenth-century capitalist—he would make the decisions and do everything almost alone. He wasn't used to consultation, nine-a.m. staff meetings, or long-range planning for contingencies. "The foot soldiers," he would say, "get in the way of the cavalry." Curtis Gans, who had as much as anyone to do with putting together the band of foot soldiers known as the McCarthy movement, believed that "the movement worried the Senator. He didn't want other spokesmen." This was the principal reason why the campaign rolled on month after month without the usual position papers, for if McCarthy would not let others develop them he did not seem to have time to do so himself.

It was true that there was nobody with professional experience to assist McCarthy even if he wanted help. McCarthy disliked making telephone calls, especially calls in his own behalf; he did not like to put others on the spot—or be beholden to them. At the beginning of his campaign he did call two prominent politicians he thought might help him. He was turned down so abruptly that he did not try again. But if McCarthy would not go to the mountain, it was difficult for the mountain to come to him.

"Anybody civilized enough to try to come through the front door always got turned down," recalls Arnold Hiatt—then executive vice-president and now president of the Green Shoe Manufacturing Company in Massachusetts—who, at forty, was to become the campaign treasurer. ("I'll be right back, right after the New Hampshire primary," he told the company president on taking a temporary leave of absence. "I'll be right back, right after Wisconsin," he said again later, and he went on saying it through Chicago. One of his first gestures was to ask people who owed him money to repay it to the campaign.) McCarthy, by design or not, surrounded himself with a well-meaning but protective Senate staff which appeared to resent new people. Letters from those wanting to work in the campaign as volunteers went unanswered. Phone calls were unreturned.

A typical instance was that of Howard Stein. He had no political experience—he was not even a registered member of any party—but he was in a wonderful position to raise money. A tall, thin, quiet man in his early forties, famous in the financial world for his acumen, Stein is president of a large mutual fund—the Dreyfus Fund—which had made great gains by buying a large quantity of Polaroid at a low price. Stein thought that McCarthy was the "Polaroid of politicians," and he related the rising spring 1968 stock market to McCarthy's surge in the polls and thus the increased prospects for peace. For him it was the "McCarthy market." He was ultimately responsible, with Hiatt, for raising several million dollars, much of it from large contributors. "McCarthy's war position impressed me," Stein said. "I had met him once or twice and he was the only politician my wife, Janet, and I had met who didn't remember our name. We rather liked that. I later told McCarthy this and he said, as a joke, 'I thought you'd be the types who would like it if I forgot your name, and that's why I forgot it.' "

Having decided to help, Stein did not anticipate that he would be forced to undergo a trial of endurance. It was the ritual for almost anybody who wanted to climb aboard the McCarthy wagon. Stein called McCarthy's office to volunteer and waited. He called again, this time giving not just his name but "President of the Dreyfus Fund." No response. Stein now called another McCarthy supporter, Eliot Janeway, an old friend of the Senator's. Janeway called McCarthy, who once more did not call Stein. Stein again called McCarthy and again called Janeway, who again called McCarthy, repeating that Stein was a good fund-raiser. This time McCarthy did call Stein, but only to thank Stein for being a supporter. Stein could not bring himself to raise the subject of fund-raising, since McCarthy did not, and he hung up the phone, perplexed. Again he called Janeway and this time, getting no call back from McCarthy, he turned to still a different friend of McCarthy—John Cogley, formerly religious editor of the *New York Times* and now with the Center for the Study of Democratic Institutions—who called the Senator. Still nothing happened. Again Stein tried both routes and finally he found himself at lunch with McCarthy, who thought it would be perfectly fine if Stein raised money for him. One had to be truly committed to persist after such treatment.

The evening of the December 1967 Chicago speech, McCarthy had a visit from a lanky, red-cheeked, pipe-smoking man named Blair Clark. Later known in the campaign as Blair Pipe, or Blark, he had written McCarthy from London offering to help if McCarthy ran. He got no answer. Returning from Europe, Clark flew to Chicago to make his offer in person. He was fifty years old, and his credentials, especially to a candidate with virtually no staff at all, were glittering: a former vice-president of CBS News and former assistant publisher of the *New York Post*. A Harvard classmate and friend of John Kennedy's, he had good connections in the world of society and money. ("We're a little too Ivy League for the campaign," he later told a friend.) Despite his lack of political experience—he had worked briefly in only one campaign before—Clark became McCarthy's campaign manager, to his own surprise, though even today there is doubt as to whether the candidate gave him an explicit charter. Things just happened in the campaign, beyond the exact understanding of anybody. Clark, early on, was partly responsible for a key decision—he was among the few who urged McCarthy to enter New Hampshire—but some found he was too gentle to exert authority over an unruly campaign and an independent candidate.

If all this were not enough to guarantee an unconventional campaign, there were also the candidate's idiosyncrasies or strengths—depending on who judged them. A visitor to his New York hotel suite in early January 1968 was surprised to see him ignore attempts of local politicians to see him; they were referred to his assistant while McCarthy went on talking about poetry. He was too tired, he said, to grant a few minutes even to a contributor who had given ten thousand dollars. At fund-raising cocktail parties he would make the barest genuflection to potential donors, in the belief that they were giving not to him but to a cause, and should expect no special thanks or favors. "He can turn contributors off," remarked his friend Erich Fromm during the campaign, "because they expect politicians to be a certain way. McCarthy has no greed. People want a candidate to be a certain way—their way. They want him to be hungry for power because then they can have power over him. If a person shows he is not greedy for power they have no power over him. It is very difficult for a full-fledged mature human being to play the role of a candidate. It is almost absurd."

The candidate did not make concessions easily. He would not give personal thank-yous for support. He would merely congratulate a McCarthy partisan for being in the right place, at the right time, on the right issue.

Where to campaign?

In his announcement of candidacy in Washington he had mentioned four state primaries for certain—Wisconsin (April 2), a liberal state where he was known; Nebraska (May 14), in which he would be entered automatically by state law; Oregon (May 28), which had been good to doves and insurgent candidates before; and California (June 4), eerily unpredictable but considered receptive and, in any case, with its great cache of delegates, indispensable. In two other states—New Hampshire (March 12) and Massachusetts (April 30)—his supporters, eager now to challenge the President, were pressing him hard. Both represented delicate political judgments.

The Massachusetts problem was multileveled. Edward and Robert Kennedy had each asked McCarthy not to enter the Massachusetts primary. A McCarthy candidacy there would have been more than a simple political embarrassment; it put the Kennedys, as it put many other politicians, in the position of having to say clearly whether they would support the President—both Kennedys, indeed, pledged fealty to Johnson immediately after McCarthy entered the Massachusetts race. (But Johnson himself, it was said, was reluctant to enter Massachusetts for fear of being booby-trapped by the Kennedys with nonsupport.) There was, too, the question of McCarthy's Massachusetts supporters, who were thought by some near to the Senator to be too left wing, too associated with the peace movement, to do anything but hurt McCarthy with party politicians and voters from the middle of the road.

But there were pulls from the other side. As a candidate, he had to be independent, not a "stalking-horse" or "Judas goat" for Kennedy. And there had been trouble in the Massachusetts delegation to the Chicago meeting. Jerome Grossman, a wealthy envelope manufacturer who had subsidized the Massachusetts group's trip, was angry because McCarthy had still not said if he would enter the Massachusetts primary. Grossman was also head of the New England Peace Action Committee (PAX) and had been active in Harvard professor Stuart Hughes' Senate campaign. Burning for action, he now feared that McCarthy was more intent on talking than fighting. The Massachusetts delegation, he claimed, would pull its people and money power out of Chicago if McCarthy did not enter Massachusetts, and McCarthy suddenly capitulated. There was, though, another reason. Ted Kennedy had assured McCarthy, in asking him to stay out of Massachusetts, that he would receive a fair share of the delegates, but a few days before the Chicago conference the Massachusetts State Democratic Committee produced a resolution overwhelmingly favorable to President Johnson. McCarthy thought it was the work of the Kennedys to keep him out and he reacted with annoyance by going in.

New Hampshire was a problem in sense perception. Would McCarthy be butchered there? The arguments against a dove candidate's entering New Hampshire were compelling and later borne out by the fate of the Romney campaign. "If George Romney had stayed in Michigan and kept quiet he would have been the next President," Robert Kennedy remarked. Though McCarthy's broad unconventional style and enthusiastic campaigners evoked a response among the New Hampshirites that Romney and his professional political managers failed to arouse, New Hampshire was considered a hawk state with many conservative voters among its 89,000 registered Democrats, and a sufficiently high concentration of defense industries to provide an economic motive for opposition to peace candidates. Its principal newspaper, the Manchester *Union-Leader,* was ultraconservative and its publisher, William Loeb, so eager to present his views that the editorials appeared on the front page. ("Nobody in New Hampshire believes the *Union-Leader*'s editorials, taken one at a time," a political expert has remarked. "But drilled in steadily, day after day, they do have an effect.") The state Democratic organization seemed unified behind Johnson and, with a small number of voters concentrated in a few cities like Manchester, it would be hard to crack. Johnson could have his name taken off the ballot (which in December he did), leaving McCarthy dangling on the periphery, a sort of Democratic Harold Stassen, while Nixon and Romney boxed manfully in the center of the ring and the country watched.

The educational level was not as high as in some of the other primary states; the McCarthy organization was primitive; and a loss in New Hampshire, the first primary, would hurt in the next, Wisconsin, and might kill the campaign, spoiling any chance to register protest. McCarthy had said in the beginning that his purpose was only to give people a chance to make a "reasoned judgment" about the war, to conduct a sort of "referendum on Vietnam." The President's men were openly challenging McCarthy to enter, certain he would be swamped. New Hampshire's Governor King predicted he would get five per cent of the vote.

Few in his entourage were in favor of New Hampshire, and McCarthy did not relish trudging around in the cold, but there were impelling reasons for going in. If he was to be a serious candidate he had to prove it in all sections of the country. The New Hampshire supporters were urging (even threatening to join a Bobby Kennedy movement if McCarthy stayed out). Most important, his campaign was losing force, with the Wisconsin primary still months away, and his press coverage almost nil. He even thought of a trip to Europe in the slack time. So, in part, McCarthy listened to Clark's urgings to enter New Hampshire because he had few other effective political choices. Clark, who had once owned a newspaper in New Hampshire before he sold it to William Loeb, thought the state would be more receptive to McCarthy than most people believed. On January 2, McCarthy called David Hoeh, the young New Hampshire state chairman for McCarthy, and said he would make up his mind in forty-eight hours. A half hour later Hoeh was paged at a restaurant. It was McCarthy again, who said, "Dave, I want to enter the New Hampshire primary."

McCarthy made several short swings into New Hampshire. He delighted his followers by refusing to take a poll. "We don't want to get discouraged," he said, which they took as a sign of fortitude; but he annoyed them too by telling the press he would get thirty per cent of the vote when no one could see it. Now he would have to do that well or look the fool. After delays, at last he settled down, in February, to serious campaigning. Gradually, his small staff learned about the candidate. He would not push himself beyond endurance but would permit only a certain number of appearances a day. (Too heavy a calendar was at the scheduler's peril; a tired McCarthy simply might not show up.) He had his own campaign chemistry—strong in the morning, progressively weaker in the afternoon, good again in the evening. He wanted his rest periods and his martini, even if he had to bootleg it in the motel kitchen while his wife was being interviewed in the living room by the *Christian Science Monitor*. The accusations that he was halfhearted, that he did not address himself to specific solutions ("His audiences," wrote Andrew Kopkind, "know the war is wrong and that black men are oppressed. What they want to know is *why* and what can be done.") were simply ignored by the candidate, who went his own way, "passion gap," as his staff called it, or not. To them he was both a difficult and a lovable candidate who would drive his campaigners wild by refusing to pose seriously for TV commercials for a professional crew sent up from New York; only his old Minnesota adman friend, Bill Nee, could get him to do it. But he would go out on the ice to play an exhausting game with semi-professional hockey players (he had thought them amateurs) and he would always redeem himself with remarks which were not only unusual for a politician but which displayed the sort of intelligence and whimsy which the campaigners dreamed might one day come to the White House. He told a ballpoint-pen manufacturer, "The ballpoint pen ruins character. In the old days a fountain pen was something. You really wrote your name. It was an event." Or, "Maybe we should abandon gold as a basis of the world monetary system and substitute S & H Green Stamps."

He was to be found—unheard of for a Presidential candidate—eating breakfast alone. A photographer hired to take shots of McCarthy surrounded by New Hampshirites gave up after five days —the only crowds were out-of-state volunteers and always the same ones. Because the people would not come to him, McCarthy had to go to them, which led to numberless visits to high schools, in the hope the students would persuade parents, or to factories. McCarthy's lack of staff work began to hurt: there was a six-a.m. visit to a plant which did not open till eight; a four-thirty visit to another which had closed at three.

Sometimes, in private, he admitted discouragement. Once, with some of his family, McCarthy was being driven to a night's lodging when the car suddenly skidded and turned a complete circle. ("The real problem," he would later say, "is to get a good man to drive your car in the campaign.") He drove the rest of the way himself. The McCarthys were being lodged in an empty house, but the heat did not work and, as they discovered when they built a fire, neither did the chimney. Sitting in the cold, smoky room, huddled in coats, McCarthy and his family asked themselves what had possessed them to come to New Hampshire in dead winter. New Hampshire was "bad," a disaster. McCarthy would lose—if he didn't freeze first.

Indeed, the portents were dreary. NEW HAMPSHIRE CAN HELP BRING THE NATION BACK TO ITS SENSES, said a McCarthy slogan, but Governor King continued to predict McCarthy would get only a few thousand votes, and Administration officials in Washington and many peace people also were saying McCarthy would lose. A survey showed that sixty per cent of the New Hampshire voters did not know who McCarthy was; the lack of media coverage didn't help. The managing editor of the *New York Times* during this period was said to have given out an order that McCarthy, not a serious contender, was to be ignored by the *Times*. In those days, you could place a bet at twelve-to-one odds that McCarthy would not get thirty per cent of the vote in New Hampshire or prevent the President's renomination. Apparently, such a bet, of more than ten thousand dollars, was placed with a bookie by a McCarthy backer and the money later given to the campaign.

Yet the candidate showed no sign of giving up. "He looked better than he had in years," recalled his eighteen-year-old daughter, Mary, who had dropped out of college to help. "It was good for him to get out of sedentary Washington and he found psychological liberation in being able to say what he had wanted to say for a long time." The candidate said, "You fight from a low crouch. You wait for events. You let it come to you."

The first break for McCarthy was the ineptness of the regular Democratic organization. It was supposed to be experienced politically, being headed by Governor King, Senator Thomas McIntyre, and Bernard Boutin, a businessman with considerable campaign experience who was directing the Johnson campaign. The President was a write-in candidate, which gave him the favorable psychological position of being able to win without actually having to expose himself in a campaign. Boutin announced the organization of two thousand neighborhood coordinators for the write-in drive, and the regular Democrats were also able to stifle dissidence through promises of jobs or favors. The organization was well financed and seemed formidable, although its neighborhood coordinators were slow to take to the streets because it was "cold and dark outside."

The regular Democrats committed an error they later conceded might have cost them up to ten thousand votes. Copying a device used successfully in the write-in drive for Henry Cabot Lodge in New Hampshire in 1964, signed pledge cards, the high-handed, overconfident Democrats took the idea a step further. The pledges for Johnson were in three parts and they were numbered. One signed section was kept by the voter, one sent to the Democratic state committee, and one forwarded to the White House. In return the voter got a thank-you note from King and McIntyre and a signed photograph of LBJ and Lady Bird on the steps of Air Force One.

Local newspapers at once began muttering that the numbers meant retaliation for those who refused to sign, and McCarthy swept to the offense. Accusing Boutin, McIntyre, and King of "coercive tactics," he denounced the cards as infringements on the secret ballot. The use of the cards had already been fought by his local supporters, who felt the state Democratic committee had no business taking a position in the race at all. Now there was a poster: YOU DON'T HAVE TO SIGN ANYTHING TO VOTE FOR GENE MCCARTHY, and McCarthy headquarters sprouted giant trash cans for the disposal of the cards. For McCarthy, campaigning quietly, it was perfect. He was given an opportunity to do what he had refrained from doing—attacking the President without even appearing to.

The poor publicity given the pledge cards rattled the regular Democrats and they reacted harshly. McCarthy was now accused, in advocating peace in Vietnam, of causing "joy in Hanoi." This hypnotic line was followed by other accusations. Governor King said a vote for McCarthy "would be greeted with great cheers in Hanoi," and there were radio spots saying, "Don't vote for fuzzy thinking and surrender—support our fighting men" or "Listen: we can all thank our lucky stars he's [Johnson] sticking with men like General Westmoreland and not listening to those peace-at-any-price fuzzy thinkers, who say give up the goal, burn your draft card, and surrender. Look, he's carrying a terrific burden. For my money, he's really doing a great job." McCarthy, continued the ads, was an "advocate of appeasement and surrender," an "apostle of retreat."

The regular Democrats in New Hampshire badly misjudged the voters there in assuming a receptivity to appeals reminiscent of Joe McCarthy's line of the 1950s or, as Governor King was to call it, "hard sell." Their charges instead accentuated what was already the underlying campaign issue—not McCarthy's peace proposals but the enormous desire for change and the character and credibility of the President who, one might assume, was masterminding his New Hampshire strategy. The result was to further damage the man in the White House. In late January the Vietcong winter-spring, or Tet, offensive was carried to thirty-eight South Vietnamese cities, the *Pueblo* was captured by North Korea, and the siege of Khe Sanh was under way. At home, the draft had been increased, graduate deferments ended. The reserve was about to be called up, and the President was requesting a ten-per-cent surtax and a cutback in Great Society programs, like pollution controls, affecting New Hampshire. It was impossible, for the time being, to gauge the impact of these events, whether they would evoke the scream of the hawk or the coo of the dove, but one section of the population responded immediately, the students.

It might be assumed that a political campaign straining under enormous difficulties with money and lack of exposure would welcome a friendly student invasion and visualize, in all those bright, beardless faces, the greatest publicity weapon in modern political history. Instead, the McCarthy campaigners were initially terrified and kept the students under wraps like military secrets.

Some months earlier, Gans, Lowenstein, and Brown had set up campus coordinators to bring out students to campaign, but they had expected platoons, not an army. There was a question, too, of using students in New Hampshire, for no one knew how to measure xenophobia. The McCarthyites shared the conventional view of New Hampshire as essentially a rural state full of taciturn farmers, stolid, withdrawn, suspicious of outsiders, especially outsiders with quick tongues, horn-rimmed glasses, and Ph.D.s. The truer understanding of New Hampshire as a modern industrial state with the usual complex of cities and suburbs did not emerge until later.

So the first students who came were subjected to three-hour briefings on local customs and usages ("*Ber*lin not Ber*lin*"), told to shave and wash (or retreat to the campaign basement), and above all not to be noisy and aggressive. They were asked to be as inconspicuous as possible, and, please, to avoid reporters.

Far from slamming doors, the Granite Staters said to the young campaigners, "You came all this way to see *us?*"

It was a good clue, and it was not missed. The New Hampshirites enjoyed the company, found the students stimulating, and seemed to suffer from the feelings of atomization and meaninglessness to which the campaign itself was a response. The students were now sent in force from house to house and the reporters followed. "Get Clean for Gene," "the children's crusade," "bridging the generation gap"—here at last was something new.

It was new, certainly, in the sense that canvassing of this dimension had never before been tried in a Presidential primary, but the techniques themselves were fairly standard in reform politics. I once asked a youthful originator of the McCarthy canvassing system whether he knew this, and, looking at me as though I were crazy, he said, "What does it matter?" with the pride of him who has just devised the wheel or umbrella. "*We* did it ourselves." Under the guidance of Ben Stavis, a Ph.D. candidate in Chinese studies at Columbia, and Joel Feigenbaum and Matty Bornstein, two brilliant young scientists from Cornell, a technique was worked out. A town would be divided into routes, each marked on a photostatic copy of a map section. The students usually worked in pairs, one on each side of the street. With the maps they carried cards on which had been typed the name and address of a Democrat, taken from voter-registration lists. They left literature at the homes of "n.a."s—no answers—but when people were home they stood and talked. Under no circumstances were they to ask the political preference of a person, for this would have seemed too forward and an obvious attempt to influence. Wisely, the approach was soft sell.

VOLUNTEER: I've come all the way up here to see you and answer any questions you might have about Senator McCarthy, who is running for President.

VOTER: All this way just to see *us?* Well, I'm mighty favorable to your man. Yes, I approved the way he handled the Commies back in the fifties.

VOLUNTEER: No, no, sir, Senator *Eugene* McCarthy . . .

Or, as happened once:

VOLUNTEER: Your dog just bit me.

VOTER: I'm really sorry. I was going to vote for LBJ, but I'll vote for McCarthy if it makes you feel better.

Leaving the porch, his back turned so that the voter couldn't see him, the volunteer would then make a rating on the card. "1" meant a person utterly favorable to McCarthy, a "2" definitely leaning in his direction, and "3" resisting every entreaty or ruse of the volunteer to discover where he stood: he was a cipher. A "4" was backward leaning, toward Johnson, and a "5" was a hopelessly dyed-in-the-wool Johnson supporter. The cards were returned to the storefront, where they were sorted and counted. The "4"s and "5"s landed in the wastebasket, and the "n.a."s were marked for contact by the telephone bank, also manned by student volunteers. Sometimes the "3"s were called again. By election day massive lists of "1"s and "2"s had been compiled and routed again on maps, and again the students went to the houses to urge them to vote. In this way an attempt, at least, was made to contact personally every Democratic voter in the state, and by the last weekend before the election there was one volunteer for every twenty-five voters. Radio ads preceded the canvassers to announce their advent, and sometimes there were ads to thank the voters for talking with them.

Nobody who saw the McCarthy student-volunteers in action—clean-cut, cool, alert, sensitive—could say the country was going to pot or fail to be impressed with a candidate who aroused this fervid outpouring. A policeman stopped a carful of canvassers for speeding, saw the McCarthy buttons, laughed, and strode off, saying, "I'm a 'one.' " The country learned that the students were coming from one hundred colleges as far away as Michigan and Virginia, sitting up all night on busses, that they slept in living rooms, on church floors, gymnasiums, garages. (They sometimes arrived at the wrong houses and popped into startled bedrooms.) The newspapers and television covered the sacrifice of beards in the McCarthy headquarters' back room, the Yale graduate students in French working in the French-speaking communities, the response of the New Hampshire people to this new life. Still more students came. One weekend there were three thousand students canvassing in New Hampshire and it was thought to be enough. Urgent calls went out to stop further busses of volunteers, including threats of barricading the highways.

The New Hampshire campaign, from the middle of February, was under the leadership of Curtis Gans, who, never having run a campaign before, was understandably nervous about the assignment. Gans had taken over from the indigenous state group, which was too small—the out-of-staters were amazed at the ever-better showings McCarthy was making in the New Hampshire polls, in contrast to his pitiful base of active local support—to handle what was rapidly becoming an operation involving thousands of people and hundreds of thousands of dollars. "It was like building a corporation in three weeks," one campaigner remarked.

Gans, rarely sleeping, his words badly slurred from fatigue, succeeded in fashioning something that at least resembled a campaign organization whose focus (apart from McCarthy) was students and whose thrust was toward a multi-issue campaign, a point McCarthy tried to make in the beginning by delivering his first speech on housing, not the war. Everything was done, including the burning of printed literature showing pictures of the Vietnam war, to take the emphasis off the war and place it on the need for new leadership and change in general. The New York advertising agency,

Papert, Koenig and Lois (later to handle Kennedy), which volunteered its services, was dropped because its ads were too stridently antiwar. STRANGE POLITICS MAKES BEDFELLOWS, said a sign in the headquarters. The campaign was responsible but it was not pure. It could protect students within its ranks hiding from draft boards but it wanted the votes of the middle class. It could declare that it would not form special racial or ethnic groups but it had Women for McCarthy, which campaigned quietly and effectively with its "Operation Penetration" among nonpolitical, especially women's and church groups, and was an important factor in the Senator's showing.

The contradictions bothered no one and as the campaign progressed toward its denouement, McCarthy began collecting help from every side. Almost anybody, it seemed, who came near the candidate's Sheraton Wayfarer headquarters in Manchester caught the McCarthy bug, an illness which was to linger, month after month. The editor of the Harvard *Crimson* doing a story on the campaign dropped out of school; a *Newsweek* reporter covering McCarthy took a leave of absence. Howard Stein made calls from under a table in the pressroom as his elegant wife, Janet, cooked meals for the Senator and his family, while Robert Lowell talked verse with him and Mary Travers, of Peter, Paul, and Mary, sang songs. There were never enough rooms. People slept on floors, six to a room, in the hallways, anywhere, if they slept at all.

The star political recruit was Richard N. Goodwin, invariably to be found holding a cigar and wearing a dark suit. Swarthy, intense, Goodwin had had a considerable career in his thirty-six years. Graduating *summa cum laude* from Tufts and first in his class at Harvard Law, he had been law clerk to Supreme Court Justice Felix Frankfurter and Counsel to the House committee then investigating the fixing of television shows. He had been a speech writer and Presidential assistant to Kennedy, a State Department official and a Peace Corps administrator, as well as an assistant to Johnson. He had softened his position on Vietnam until he had become a full-fledged dove, and he had been among the first of the new political theoreticians. He had tried, vainly, to convince Robert Kennedy to run, and on his way to New Hampshire he had dined with Kennedy, who took a mocking view of McCarthy's chances.

Goodwin was an "idea man" who saw at once the political value of the pledge cards or the need for a McCarthy position paper on civil rights. He reacted quickly without having to ponder, and in a crisis—it was always a crisis—he kept his head.

For the younger volunteers Goodwin was an inspiration; if he vanished, as he was likely to do, they panicked and cried, "Where's Goodwin?" frightened that he had returned to Kennedy. Goodwin was to discover that McCarthy was not an easy man for a speech writer—McCarthy felt Goodwin's material sounded too much like Jack Kennedy—but a friendly alliance grew up between the two.

Confidence was too strong a word to describe the campaign mood as it headed into its final week, but at least there were some small signs of what any politician likes to see, movement. In Minnesota, McCarthy had won some important precinct caucuses. Johnson had decided less than half an hour before the deadline not to allow his name on the Massachusetts ballot, giving McCarthy a certain thirty-five convention votes. Emboldened, he declared he would run in Pennsylvania. In New Hampshire, George Romney had suddenly quit, putting the focus on McCarthy as the underdog contender. Nearly finishing the one thousand miles he was to travel in New Hampshire in twenty-three days of campaigning, he was beginning to achieve some measure of familiarity for the voters. They recognized the lean, straightforward face from the posters, shook his hand on the street, and thought of him invariably as "sincere." He told the Senate during that last week:

As political leaders, it is our responsibility to summon forth the more generous impulses of the American people. This is also what the people want, for my campaigning has reaffirmed the conviction that our people will look to leadership which will remind them of responsibilities as well as rights, of the need for sacrifice as well as the blessings of abundance; and which will substitute success in the pursuit of peace for failure in the pursuit of war.

Two days before the election the emphasis of the campaign shifted almost entirely to the public's disaffection from Administration policies even beyond Vietnam. Television was used only during the last four days—Howard Stein having raised $35,000 to pay for it—and during the last two days a new radio spot was placed every half hour on every radio station in the state. A calm voice spoke to the people: "Think how you would feel to wake up Wednesday morning to find out that Gene McCarthy had won the New Hampshire primary—to find out that New Hampshire had changed the course of American politics."

The press was still deriding both campaign and candidate—as though to insure that its dire predictions of December would come true—and Governor King, as election day came, was still saying that McCarthy would be held to less than a quarter of the vote. The magic number was thirty per cent—a figure apparently derived from McCarthy's own predictions. Anything more was a victory and anything much less a defeat. A CBS poll released election night said that McCarthy would get twenty-nine per cent of the vote. If McCarthy was suffering he did not show it, but seemed gay, almost frivolous, on election day. A press aide came running in with the news that poll watchers had discovered three dead men to have been recorded as voters in one New Hampshire city. He wanted to get out a release. "Don't release it," McCarthy said. "It was the resurrection. They came back to vote for us."

McCarthy displayed that day his intransigence in the face of pressure, even from television. NBC had an elaborate studio set to cover the New Hampshire primary night which McCarthy found ostentatious. Huntley-Brinkley, he said, were in their "throne." NBC struck the candidate as too demanding when it asked him to come to the studio and, instead, McCarthy vanished. He went across to the other side of Manchester, to an unheated garage where CBS had set up shop with a seventy-seven-dollar set made of knotty-pine panels decorated with a picture. The control room was in a truck. CBS had decided not to cover the New Hampshire primary until the last minute, thinking there was no contest, and McCarthy went to the hastily constructed studio and chatted amiably with CBS reporter David Schoumacher for a long period. Schoumacher, hotly competitive with NBC, was delighted, but NBC stewed until the Senator finally arrived.

He also had a long interview for British television that evening, and emerged to get the first results. The small towns were going for him! It was feared the big cities would not, but by eleven-forty p.m. it was clear that McCarthy had exceeded most expectations. He was to get forty-two per cent of the vote, and if the Republican write-ins were counted, only 230 votes less than the President. On the way from his room to the ballroom of the Sheraton for the party, a reporter asked him, "Have you talked with Robert Kennedy?" "No," McCarthy said, "but I've talked with Robert Lowell." When he arrived in the ballroom the volunteers were shouting, "Chi-ca-go, Chi-ca-go." "We've really bridged the generation gap," he said to Ned Kenworthy of the *New York Times*. (Kenworthy, who had been dubious at first about the McCarthy campaign, was to become the campaign's private choice for Vice-President.) "If we come to Chicago with this strength," McCarthy told the audience enthusiastically, "there will be no violence and no demonstrations but a great victory celebration. If I had failed, it would have been a great personal failure because I had the most intelligent campaign staff in the history of American politics, in the history of the world!"

He returned to his suite and at twelve-thirty Robert Kennedy called. McCarthy was heard saying, "Oh, hi, Bobby. Yes, it was great. Thanks. It was rough. Those factories—I tell you, I went through more factories than I've been through in twenty years of politics." He told Kennedy that he would be in touch with him the following day in Washington. (On the plane, meeting Senator Mc-

Intyre by accident, McCarthy said, "You shouldn't be traveling first class.") Soon after, McCarthy went to bed.

Snow had fallen that evening on New Hampshire, blanketing the towns and cities, blocking the roads, but at the eighteen McCarthy headquarters there was more than simple happiness. The effects of the elections could already be seen as the regular Democrats came to the headquarters to talk with the few local people—like Richard Martin in Salem—who had fought for McCarthy and were to become new forces in state politics. (The overconfident Johnsonians had put up the names of forty-five nominees for delegates on the ballot in an election with only twenty-four openings, and McCarthy, who had just the requisite number of delegates running, won twenty of them.) There was a feeling that history was being made by a mild man and the ragged body of amateurs who had supported him. The President and his Vietnam policy had been shaken. A cause had become a candidacy, a referendum was now a movement.

5 | On to Wisconsin

The most important political catalyst in the winter of 1968 was the Vietcong's Tet offensive with its trail of death and suffering and its revelation that a military victory, short of atomic holocaust, was not to be. Tet drew Robert Kennedy into the race and it was an important if not decisive factor in the moral victory of McCarthy in New Hampshire.

And by almost any reading, the tiny New Hampshire electorate had given a momentous verdict in a vote heard 'round the world. No politician—least of all Lyndon Baines Johnson or Robert Francis Kennedy—could avoid the conclusion that the people in the secret heart of the voting booth had expressed a deep, abiding dissatisfaction with the President, and in a "hawk" state.

Yet it was tantalizingly uncertain, behind the rows of election returns, what the voters were trying to say. Change yes, but to whom or toward what? Did the people know its own mind? In a poll of New Hampshire Democrats (though one was learning to distrust the poll results) more than half of those interviewed did not know where McCarthy stood on Vietnam and the better aware they were of his dovishness the less likely to vote for him. Nor had the hawks capitulated. Here was the anguished cry of the Manchester *Union-Leader*:

MURDERERS!

. . . Moscow and Hanoi WERE watching and now they are determined that, because of the votes of the foolish people in New Hampshire who voted for McCarthy, this nation is bitterly split over its commitment to resist Communist aggression in Vietnam.

AS A RESULT OF THIS DECISION, THEY WILL NOW CONTINUE THIS WAR, KILLING MORE NEW HAMPSHIRE BOYS AND YOUNG AMERICANS FROM ALL OVER THE COUNTRY. EVERY TIME THEY LOOK AT A CASUALTY LIST, THOSE WHO VOTED FOR MCCARTHY CAN JUST REMEMBER THAT THEIR VOTES WERE IN LARGE PART RESPONSIBLE. . . .

YOU CAN COMMIT MURDER WITH A BALLOT JUST AS YOU CAN WITH A BULLET—AND THAT IS WHAT THESE VOTERS IN NEW HAMPSHIRE HAVE DONE.

William Loeb
Publisher

Now, hawks and doves differ not so much in their desired destination but in their flight patterns and the readings they make about the ground. Both wanted peace in Vietnam; the difference lay in what accommodations or compromises they were willing to make with the enemy and in their over-all appraisal of complicated questions on such issues as the nature of communist countries and American national interest, on the efficacy of applied military power, the probability of ultimate war with China, and the dangers or benefits of time.

McCarthy had begun his campaign as an "educational" venture —to convince the public that the dovish flight plan offered the best hope for a successful landing. If he could not "educate" the President he could apply the political pressure of the polling place. The President, McCarthy could reason, was not a dictator but an elected official responsive to majority judgment. He was also a politician, mind and ego connected umbilically to the national mood. If that mood could be shown for peace, perhaps his thoughts could be imperceptibly shifted to different preferences and expectations. And if majority opinion ran counter to his beliefs he might have to yield to be re-elected.

In fact, the government was more responsive to the people's preference than the people realized. Known only to those with access to the Pentagon's secrets, immediately following the New Hampshire primary the additional troop requests for the Pentagon were scaled down sharply. They would continue to be reduced, until no further requests for more soldiers in Vietnam would be made. Partly, at least, this was a fruit of the McCarthy campaign.

And, for the first time in many years, it was possible for ordinary people to conceive of citizen-government relations quite differently than they had—to hope for some visible impact of their view on the government's thinking and to see some efficacy in the popular will. That, said McCarthy, was "perhaps the most important result of my campaign so far."

McCarthy planned for Wisconsin, as he had for New Hampshire, a limited effort based on issues. But two events were beginning to force his campaign to become more personal and massive. The first was that he had come a miraculous few votes short of beating the President in New Hampshire—some thought that with a better organization he might have won outright. The showing had brought forth something too early yet to analyze but describable as a disparate following of suburbanites, academics, Rockefeller Republicans, students, peace people, left-wingers, and anarchists, a crazily juxtaposed but significant part of the population. They gave him at least some small chance of becoming President. Did he want it? "Oh, I don't suppose you want it that way," he said. "If you're in politics fifteen or twenty years you kind of respond to circumstances. Do I want it for myself? No. There's no personal need driving me toward it. But if the situation compels you and you're in politics, you go."

The other event was the entry of Robert Kennedy into the race.

Kennedy and McCarthy, if not friends, were both in opposition to the war. Each understood the reasoning of the other and each had tried to make the other move. Kennedy did not think he should run against the President. He knew that a confrontation would bury the issues he wanted to raise in the politics of personality, dooming his prospects. There was every prospect of losing—in February he had seen a private Wisconsin poll with McCarthy getting only twelve per cent of the vote against the President, seemingly invincible—and, then, like any politician, Kennedy hated to be at the mercy of events beyond his control. On January 30 he told a background breakfast meeting in Washington that he would not run against Lyndon Johnson "under any foreseeable circumstances." On the thirty-first he announced, "I would not oppose Lyndon Johnson under any circumstances. . . ." The seizure of the *Pueblo* by North Korea a few days later reaffirmed for him that he was right; political events were indeed too unpredictable.

McCarthy's feelings about Kennedy's noncandidacy and the reasons for it are recorded in an interview, surprisingly candid not merely about Kennedy but also others who swirled onto the stage of 1968. McCarthy later explained that he thought he was off the record—on several key occasions he made important revelations to reporters and then, seeing the material in print, complained that he thought he had been talking for background. Could an experienced politician be so naïve? No, says a close associate. "Gene finds it hard to lie under questioning. He knows he's on the record, then to get himself off the hook he later says he thought he wasn't."

The interview, appearing in mid-February in the *Miami Herald,* seems to have escaped attention. (The remarks in quotes are McCarthy's; those unquoted are the newspaper reporter's summaries of the candidate's remarks.)

AN INVESTIGATION into the real facts of the Gulf of Tonkin Resolution would destroy any remaining credibility in the Johnson administration.

DEFENSE SECRETARY Robert McNamara realized about six months ago that the war was "wrong," gave up, and handed it over to the generals.

"A Democrat can be elected who disowns Lyndon Johnson.

There's no loyalty to him. Who would be loyal to him? The palace guard? All he's got are slaves around him. Their loyalty is not very deep.

"Larry O'Brien, you think? Hell, Larry's served under five flags already. [Clark] Clifford has served under at least five flags. He runs them up every morning. He's got a whole locker full of flags."

About dove Senators who had not come out for him: "They rationalize that if they commit themselves to me, they'll probably lose, and then they won't be in a position to be the great dissenters. This is Bobby's rationale, too."

BOBBY KENNEDY has been overly cautious in opposing the administration's policies because he takes himself and his political future too seriously.

Bobby "hasn't been very helpful. He's like Enoch Arden. He won't go away from the window. He just comes back and taps on the window or scratches on the door.

"Every time I think he's gone to sea, he's back again the next morning. I thought he was gone, and he's back again.

"He's in a tough spot. In a way I feel kinda sorry for him. His age and his political commitment. And some sense of having to carry on for Jack. This makes it tough. It makes him too careful, I think.

"He's never been quite as free to shoot the works, the way Jack was. When Jack Kennedy ran for President, he figured if he didn't make it, life would go on somehow. It wouldn't be the great personal failure of his life.

"With Bobby, I think there is the sense that he's got, somehow, to do this thing."

Even before the New Hampshire primary, Kennedy was reconsidering—McCarthy's campaign was making his own aloofness from the struggle untenable and chipping away at his own youthful pedestal of support. "Kennedy thinks," said Mary McGrory in her column, "that American youth belongs to him at the bequest of his brother. Seeing the romance flower between them and McCarthy, he moved with the ruthlessness of a Victorian father whose daughter has fallen in love with a dustman." On March 13, the day after the New Hampshire primary, Kennedy said that he was reassessing the situation. McCarthy's New Hampshire victory had made it possible for a Democrat to campaign on "issues" rather than "personality." Robert Kennedy was forty-two, the same as Jack had been when he declared.

On the 13th McCarthy flew to Washington and he talked by phone and in person with Kennedy for about twenty minutes. To escape the press McCarthy went first to the Capitol gym and then doubled back to Ted Kennedy's office, where Bob Kennedy was waiting. Kennedy reviewed his reasons for reconsidering his decision not to run. McCarthy had presented the issues in New Hampshire in a brilliant way, he said, and the election results had shown a deep division within the Democratic Party, and that was reason one. Two was an appearance by Dean Rusk before the Senate Foreign Relations Committee indicating to Kennedy that the Administration would not change its policy in Southeast Asia— Kennedy had also tested the President with his proposal for a blue-ribbon investigative committee on Vietnam. Three, because there had been no action on the crisis in American cities and, finally, four: New Hampshire had made it clear to Kennedy that Richard Nixon would be the Republican nominee.

The talk quickly turned to practical matters, and what emerged must have sounded to McCarthy as though Bobby were saying, "You've served your function, you've made your point. Now I'll do it because I can win." As to Kennedy's attitude, one of his inner circle has commented, "Bobby underestimated McCarthy as a political entity but nobody in the group took him seriously as a candidate. We thought his personality would stop him from pushing all the way." McCarthy had never quite said that he was running for the Presidency but only to change the policy. Kennedy, quite naturally, rationalized that he was taking a burden off McCarthy's shoulders. But now McCarthy bridled.

It was O.K., he said, for Kennedy to enter, but it would have no effect on his own plans, although, he remarked, it was a crowded field. Inwardly he was furious, saying later that "Kennedy was fattening me up for the kill." He had expected Kennedy to run but not until the convention or close to it, at which time McCarthy might well have tried to throw his support to Kennedy. Kennedy's entry at this point was not only surprising but devastating. It threatened to break up McCarthy's just-forming coalition of supporters and it meant the possible drying up of the money which might have flowed into the campaign after New Hampshire. McCarthy suggested that Kennedy wait, or, if he had to campaign, to confine himself to Pennsylvania, West Virginia, and Florida. McCarthy went so far as to say that if nominated and elected he would serve only one term, and then Kennedy could have it. Kennedy's private reaction was that McCarthy was too weak to make that kind of statement.

The least that McCarthy appears to have wanted was time to get across the basic themes that his campaign was developing. There was the question of pride, the comprehensible pride of a man who had begun alone and achieved a resounding triumph; he did not like to be upstaged and overshadowed, especially on the morning after the New Hampshire election, when the headlines might have belonged to him and his campaign. He then rejected Kennedy's offer of help in Wisconsin, where it was too late for Kennedy to file.

If McCarthy wanted no part of an accommodation with Kennedy, others did, as soon as there was no real doubt that Kennedy would run. McCarthy flew to Wisconsin, and in the next few days, apparently without his knowledge, the McCarthy forces talked with the Kennedys about an arrangement of some kind. The intention was to divide the primary states so that the two armies need not tear themselves to bits in futile contests with each other. There were several other schemes. Richard Goodwin, still with McCarthy but in touch with the Kennedy camp (he was to write at least one speech for Kennedy while still serving McCarthy), suggested that

McCarthy take Nebraska, Massachusetts, and Florida, while Kennedy got Indiana, West Virginia, and Oregon. To Kennedy, Curtis Gans would have offered Indiana, South Dakota, Florida, West Virginia, and New Jersey, with Nebraska and Oregon reserved for McCarthy. In both schemes—exploratory ideas only—the contenders would have met in California head on. At the very least the Kennedys hoped to get an agreement for cooperation which Bobby could use in his statement of candidacy on Saturday, March 16.

On Friday evening, a contingent consisting of Ted Kennedy, Richard Goodwin, Blair Clark, Curtis Gans, and his assistant, Jessica Tuchman, left Washington by commercial airliner on a trip later billed as Ted Kennedy's courtesy call to tell McCarthy that Bobby had decided. Ted Kennedy had been late getting to the airport and they missed an earlier flight with a connection to Green Bay, Wisconsin, where McCarthy was. The group deplaned at Chicago, where Clark chartered a Lear jet which took them to Green Bay, where a small comic drama was unfolding.

McCarthy headquarters in Washington called to say Ted was coming and McCarthy went from Sheboygan to Green Bay to meet Kennedy, free of the press—the pretext was that he wanted to see Mrs. McCarthy, who was there. The press would pick him up the next day. One reporter who went to Green Bay, even though nothing was supposed to happen there, was David Schoumacher, and he overheard McCarthy say there were "strange vibrations in the night." He was able to learn that a Kennedy was coming—Robert, he believed. (The news, in fact, reached Schoumacher through a McCarthy aide who decided, unfairly, that the Kennedys would try to exploit the visit for publicity, and decided to get there first.) Schoumacher, with great secrecy, sequestered his camera crew in a broom closet on McCarthy's floor at the Northland Hotel. He was standing in the hall with another CBS man when two policemen arrived, instructed by the management to find and evict reporters who had been seen on the floor. Thinking Schoumacher and his partner were part of the staff, the police asked about the reporters and Schoumacher answered, Yes, they were in the lobby. The other CBS man went down with the cops to flush the reporters out and, finding none, accompanied the police to their car.

Meantime, the freight elevator had opened and Schoumacher was looking into the face of Ted Kennedy. "You might as well come out," Schoumacher yelled, but the door shut and Schoumacher and his crew raced down the stairs to the lobby. But the elevator went down only one floor before going back up. By the time the breathless CBS men had raced up the stairs, Ted Kennedy was inside McCarthy's suite.

There, the news of Kennedy's arrival in Green Bay had not been greeted with cheers. When no word came and the airport showed no scheduled arrivals, McCarthy had gone to bed. The group called from the airport about midnight and McCarthy had been awakened by his daughter Mary. He had not wanted to get up. "I didn't ask him to come," he said. Kennedy wanted to meet McCarthy at a motel, but McCarthy refused, and the group came to the Northland.

If Kennedy had been expecting to talk with McCarthy alone he must have been disappointed, for by this time there were five or six people in the suite, including Abigail and Mary McCarthy, Jerry Eller, and Susan Perry, who had been with McCarthy's Washington office. Everyone was extremely uncomfortable. Kennedy said something about the Green Bay Packers. They joked about the St. Patrick's Day parade, the drivers of candidates' cars, and at one point, trying to be funny, McCarthy referred to Goodwin as a "smuggler." People began leaving the room, and finally only four were left, McCarthy, Kennedy, Eller, and Goodwin. It was tense. Ted Kennedy said that he had come to confirm that Bob would run. The two camps should get together, he said, and spoke of harmony. He asked if McCarthy would like information on Vietnam for his campaign from a Congressional committee on which Kennedy served. McCarthy did not give him time to say much more. He said later that Teddy had been "shy."

McCarthy said something like: I have to go ahead. I'm committed. I don't much care what they ask me, I'm going to stay in all the way, and in any case it's too late at night to discuss.

Kennedy had opened the briefcase containing the statement of reconciliation, but McCarthy never gave him a chance to remove it. At the door, trying to put a light face on things, McCarthy said, "You'd better close that. They'll think you took something out."

In the hall forty-five minutes after he had entered McCarthy's suite, Ted Kennedy was met by an incredulous Schoumacher who demanded, "You flew here just to make a courtesy call?" Ted Kennedy said yes and departed. He had not looked angry but, after flying all night and arriving at Bobby's home, Hickory Hill, at six a.m., he was fuming. Kennedy was awakened and the group assembled there—William vanden Heuvel, Ted Sorensen, Al Lowenstein, among others—had what was described as a "significant meeting." Most of the group had opposed Robert Kennedy's plan to run, and now, in view of the established fact that McCarthy would continue in the race, they once more urged Kennedy to desist. Failing, they worked on his statement for that morning, Lowenstein adding phrases which would be conciliatory to McCarthy.

"Bob felt he had to run," says one of the group. "He couldn't let someone else fight his battles. I had a feeling of doom."

In the wisdom of retrospect, it looks as if Goodwin's proposal, however well meant—McCarthy, after all, would have been spared the expense and exertion of several primaries—would have ruined McCarthy by depriving him of Oregon. Gans still believes his scheme would have aided McCarthy, and, as for the Kennedys, they may have thought they were offering McCarthy a graceful way out. But McCarthy's reasoning in refusing to make any accommodation with Kennedy appears to have been correct. He needed the exposure of the primaries, the build-up from state to state. Without it, he would have had no chance for any sizable vote in the ultimate confrontation in California. His central asset was independence and sincerity, and the mere hint of a deal with Kennedy, toward whom great public hostility existed, would have instantly withered his support. He had begun on a question of principle. Only one in McCarthy's entourage, Jerry Eller, stood firm against an accommodation, and the candidate began to have doubts about the judgment of his staff members who accompanied Kennedy on the plane to Green Bay.

The bill for the Lear, $1600, was paid for by the McCarthy campaign, and Clark, believing that the Kennedys should share it, intended to send them a note. He was still searching for an appropriate form when the news came that Robert Kennedy had been shot. The bill was never sent.

It was deep winter in Wisconsin when the troops began "crossing the river" into the state, as the candidate romantically put it, since they generally came by air. Now known as the "national staff," they arrived immediately after the New Hampshire primary—some two hundred by election day in Wisconsin and growing with every primary. These were the campaign gypsies who preceded the candidate's "traveling circus" or "magical mystery tour" as it moved west. The gypsies could perform miracles and were a political asset of incalculable value—the supervolunteers candidates dream about. The McCarthy national staffer worked outside his own state and usually in two or more state primaries. Typically, he was in his mid-twenties, a graduate student who had dropped out for the semester, for the campaign. There were older exceptions, of course: like the head of a small advertising agency who let his business crumble rather than leave the movement; or Midge Miller, who joined the campaign in Wisconsin and traveled on, leaving nine children at home to be cared for by a father who approved of the venture. Young and older, they liked the smell, feel, and action of a campaign and probably the break from routine. They were "true believers" in the ideas of the movement, but skeptics, too, often critical of the candidate. A more intelligent, inventive crew would have been hard to find. They were also quarrelsome and deeply suspicious of outsiders.

In return for a per-diem stipend of five dollars a day—when and if he could collect it—and a room, either in a private house or in a hotel, which he shared with others, the national staffer ate irregularly, never slept, and worked incessantly. There was much to be done, for the McCarthy campaign, in reality, was a dozen campaigns in one. Inexperienced politically before the New Hampshire campaign, the national staffer learned a discipline or trade, and from then on that was his "thing."

The students convey the enormity of the effort. In Wisconsin, largely in three weekends, some ten thousand students canvassed for McCarthy. Any quartermaster will recognize immediately the logistical difficulties in handling that many people. The students did not simply materialize: they were recruited. Transportation, often in busses, had to be arranged for them. Someone had to decide how the student canvassers were to be distributed over the state, depending on where they came from. (A bus from southern Illinois, for example, would be sent to southern Wisconsin to make the trip shorter.) The students had to be housed, fed, entertained, inspected for beards, and briefed. Literature had to be there. The maps of canvass routes and cards with the names of voters had to be ready—and a friendly doctor, just in case. That the inexperienced McCarthy forces managed to run an effort of such magnitude was a feat something like building the pyramids.

And students were by no means the whole campaign. The stars had to be recruited, their plane tickets bought, appearances scheduled and publicized. There were specialists in crowd-gathering and car rentals; in labor unions and farms; in the telephone canvass; in mobile canvass units, minibusses with literature, sound equipment, and pretty girls; in the traffic of money; in press relations; in factory and shopping-center leafleting. And overshadowing all, there was the candidate's own campaign, which required speeches, transcripts, hotel rooms, scheduling, advancing everything down to knowing that he liked a martini or a Scotch before dinner. (The handbook for McCarthy advance men confidently named a brand of Scotch, but those close to the candidate doubted whether he knew one Scotch from another. He was not much of a drinker.)

The national staff was the group that handled the inglorious campaign mechanics. It swelled constantly with new arrivals who went to man the thirty-eight storefronts in Wisconsin. (One newcomer, for some reason suspected of being a CIA man, was dispatched to a remote spear of Wisconsin sticking out into Lake Michigan.) Ted Warshafsky, the Wisconsin chairman, was given a fifty-three-year-old dentist from New Mexico as an office boy. The national staff had its own sense of being—indeed, it had to have, for there was little contact with the candidate. He did not often mingle with the volunteers, and the staff person was too busy to attend the many rallies—the staff was only supposed to win the election.

To win, the campaign needed the help of local people, and yet it sometimes spurned them, too. In New Hampshire conflicts had existed between in-state and out-of-state McCarthy people but they had been submerged. In Wisconsin they became serious and finally got in the papers.

Though the local people were "grass roots," they were usually mature and college-educated and often had homes in wealthy suburbs. Nor, in Wisconsin, were the locals new to the politics of protest. Led by mature professional men like Don Peterson, Jay Sykes, and Warshafsky, they had been organized even before McCarthy announced. Many had been Democratic Party activists and knew the ropes. Descending upon them were young invaders who seemed to listen little and who, upon occasion, could be unbearably rude. The wife of a prominent local judge was washing the floors of the headquarters on her hands and knees. A miniskirted national-staff girl came up and said, "Listen, will you hurry? You've got to do the floors of the women's john."

One of the first decisions of the out-of-staters was to move the state headquarters from Madison to Milwaukee. McCarthy would have beaten the President easily in New Hampshire if he had carried the industrial city of Manchester. Now a major effort would be made in Milwaukee—the location of the major television stations—where the Senator was also weak. But the placing of the headquarters at the Hotel Wisconsin served to put the state campaign under the domination of the McCarthy national staff.

If the Wisconsinites had reservations about the national staff, so the staffers worried about the local people, too. They seemed to want praise and credit which the hardened members of the movement knew would not be forthcoming. Horror of horrors, they would stop work to go hear the candidate when there was no time for that. They were undependable because of children, unavailable because of jobs, inexperienced in handling a new style campaign like this, and, worst of all, they did not see a project through to the last grimy detail. "NTTL" went a quiet slogan at the Wisconsin headquarters—Never Trust the Locals.

Into the second floor of the hotel pumped the implacable, youthful energies of the movement. A small room off the main lobby existed for coats, sleeping bags, guitars, and coffee for newcomers. Up a flight of steps, a mimeo machine is pulsing in the background. People shout and run. Press conference in the ballroom; briefing in this room; meeting in that. Phones shriek. No wonder the good-hearted local people turned away in discouragement.

The splendid confusion resulted in two different arms of the campaign buying a heavy schedule of commercials for McCarthy on the same radio station the same day. The listener heard McCarthy commercials every thirty seconds from morning till night. Herbert Reed, a Negro professor of Constitutional law at Howard University and an important figure in the National Association for the Advancement of Colored People, came to Milwaukee and waited an entire weekend for Gans without being able to see him. He left in disgust and, as a result, did not join the campaign for some time—in a campaign crying for black support. Without proper sleep or food, the campaigners showed the signs of combat fatigue. Tempers flared, judgments failed. In high alarm, a press aide awakened the candidate at six a.m. over nothing. An important male member of the staff socked an important female member in the face. One of the local chairmen quit the campaign in a fury with the out-of-staters. A press secretary and his assistant resigned, charging McCarthy with neglect of the ghettos. A reporter, up from a visit to the Kennedy camp in Indiana, was shocked at the difference. "But after all," he said, "it isn't the horse that counts, it's the jockey."

The candidate took the same view. Reorganization, constantly rumored, never arrived. In fact he seemed pleased with the workings of the machine created in his name. "We're organized where we ought to be organized," he said, "and free where we ought to be free."

Among those who liked to be free was the candidate himself. His staff had problems getting him into Indiana and keeping him there. He was often late for rallies and occasionally did not show up, and he continued to require time for writing poetry, a knowledge of which McCarthy made virtually a requisite for the good leader. "No one who's insensitive to poetry and song can have respect for learning," he remarked, "and no one who has no respect for learning can have real respect for justice, and no one who does not respect justice can, in fact, manifest a true love for his country." He wrote some of his best poems during the campaign.

The poet, however, was an extremely skillful politician as well, a fact that only gradually was realized by his campaigners. He knew how to appeal to vastly different audiences, for instance, without violating his own beliefs. He could quote Cadoc the Wise to Rotarians or advocate to conservatives the dismissal of J. Edgar Hoover, General Louis B. Hershey, and Dean Rusk. After one such speech a lady was heard to murmur, "One thing you can say about him. He's sure no radical." The audiences seemed often to respond less to his specific words and more to his manner which conveyed that he represented change of a responsible kind. Something, he seemed to say, could be done, and that was what the audiences wanted to hear.

His major support was in the colleges, the thriving suburbs around Milwaukee and other large cities, and the exurbs, places where education and prosperity had not been accompanied by a rise in political power, which remained with the Democratic organizations centered in the large cities.

His campaign was singular for a Democrat in that he did not work the black ghettos. "I think," he said, "one of the difficulties we have has been in consequence of a kind of fragmentation in which each minority group was called upon to consider its minority status more than its part in the general whole, and opposite to that I think we have begun to make progress in this campaign." The decision corresponded to the racial composition of Wisconsin, where Negroes made up two per cent of the vote. Still, had McCarthy been able to begin attracting black support early it might have had a critical effect later, for in California the minority vote saved Robert Kennedy from defeat.

Otherwise, it was a conventional campaign in Wisconsin. With a smile displaying a notch of gold on one front tooth, he went to the schools and factories. He played the clarinet and listened attentively to songs like "Make the Scene with Gene." He demonstrated that he knew the names of trees and flowers or how to summon pigs and cattle. He invaded cafeterias, hand out, patted dogs, kidded people carrying hostile posters, mingled solemnly with three-year-olds, predicted victory at Chicago, and said the same thing over and over. "It almost drives you to say something irresponsible, just to say something different," he said—and yet the criticisms of his style were fading. "If you've been in the theater you get tense the first time you hear him speak," remarked the lyricist Betty Comden, who—with her partner, Adolph Green, and his wife, Phyllis Newman—campaigned hard for McCarthy. "You wish he'd come to a resounding conclusion. You'd like to get him aside and coach him. But the second time you find yourself listening for the underplaying, the understatement."

McCarthy believed that his campaign had to be low keyed—Vietnam was far too serious to be approached in any other way. He appeared to be doing better than the Cabinet members and government officials sent by the President to campaign against him. Hubert Humphrey campaigned for Johnson in Wisconsin too. Ominously for him, he was able to attract only a few hundred people, even in regular Democratic areas, while McCarthy drew 15,000 at Madison, the largest crowd of his campaign so far. A national poll was giving McCarthy only thirteen per cent of the Democratic vote, but the President had dropped to a new low in popularity, and in Wisconsin polls McCarthy topped Johnson, two to one. For the first time in the campaign a poll was showing the candidate ahead when, at the end of March, he headed for a speech at Carroll College in Waukesha. The President was scheduled to make an important address the same evening at the same time.

In Waukesha County, just west of Milwaukee, the ice on the lakes was melting and the season on walleyes and northern pike about to begin. The county comprised most of the swing-voting Ninth Congressional District, which the McCarthy forces ranked fourth as a possible winner out of the ten Congressional Districts in the state, but the outcome was by no means assured. Much appeared to depend on the Republican crossover vote, as indeed it did in the state at large, where, observers predicted, between 100,-000 and 200,000 Republicans might provide McCarthy with a winning margin.

Gans had dispatched as his Waukesha County coordinators myself and Dan Singal, a young graduate student at Columbia University, both having served with distinction in Salem, New

Hampshire. Almost the entire Salem team came to Waukesha. Singal's briefings of students were famous to watchers of Huntley-Brinkley; I, more jaundiced, was inclined to take a hoary attitude toward the idealistic young—it was *their* generation gap, not mine. Realizing that the house-to-house canvassing was indispensable in making McCarthy known, I was equally disposed toward the local volunteers, headed by an advertising man, Tom Miglautsch. Renegades from the Democratic Party for the most part, there were Republicans as well. Here was the nexus on which to build.

In a fine display of confidence, the local committee had opened a McCarthy office well before the New Hampshire primary, and now it was to give me my first taste of a serious citizens' movement. The local committee helped open five branch offices and staff them; held fund-raising parties and coffees; made piles of sandwiches and cakes and barrels of coffee; canvassed the blocks. One local lady was so impressed with the operation that she suddenly sat down and wrote a check for five thousand dollars.

The McCarthy campaign had, at its best, a mood and tone of collective action. One never knew who would pop in next—a bemedaled Vietnam hero; a doctor from New York who announced he represented Physicians for McCarthy; John Boyle, the assistant chaplain at Yale; or a plain-spoken young woman who entered and said, since no one recognized the candidate's daughter, "I'm Mary McCarthy." It was learned with great excitement that Alfred Lunt and Lynn Fontanne lived in the county. Called, Lunt and Fontanne said they didn't engage in politics, but Phyllis Newman was there, and Paul Newman, who drew such masses of adoring people that the campaigners had to be careful of riots. Poor fellow! He could not sit down to so much as a hamburger because of his admirers and finally resorted to sticking a matchbook under his upper lip as a disguise.

A small delegation of students arrived from the East and said, "We're from Harvard. We do things better." They did things not better, perhaps, but well, and there was much to do, with the busses of students from Midwestern colleges pouring in silver streams from the night. They were not always well received by the people —at Elm Grove, reputedly John Birch country, a woman in the first house on a block set off a siren at the approach of the canvassers and the canvassers fled. But as the campaign grew to a close it was evident that McCarthy was making giant strides in Waukesha County, though the candidate had not set foot there. The *Waukesha Freeman,* which had not endorsed a Democratic Presidential candidate in all its 108 years, gave Republicans apoplexy by coming out for McCarthy.

March 31 was an ordinary campaign Sunday. McCarthy, with his family, had gone to church. Then he taped some last-minute television commercials which could also be used in Indiana. After some phone calls and lunch, the candidate flew to Whitewater, where 2500 students had come to cheer him. "I don't mean to sound overconfident," he said, "but I think the test now is between Mr. Nixon and myself." Kennedy? "Oh, Senator Kennedy is an intermediate problem along the way. Nixon and myself are beyond that." It was the sort of bemused comment the crowd was not supposed to take absolutely seriously. The press, however, was in no mood to be amused. On the whole, the national press had been remarkably patient with the McCarthy campaign. Rarely were advance texts of speeches ready, and stories couldn't be filed in time. Coming in late at night, the reporters would discover no preparation had been made for food and perhaps their baggage had been lost. Even the wayward press bus sometimes got lost. At Whitewater on the thirty-first, an irate press corps realized that scheduling errors would make it impossible to cover both the next stop, Racine, and Carroll College. The result was that few national pressmen arrived at Waukesha.

This did not seem so serious at the time, because the President, expected to announce a policy switch on Vietnam, would make the news, not McCarthy, and indeed among the campaigners at Waukesha there was gloom as McCarthy's two-engine plane appeared in the gray afternoon sky. The people, they feared, would stay home to watch the President on television. The fears were groundless: the crowd that evening overflowed the large auditorium into a gymnasium equipped with speakers.

McCarthy usually preferred to enter an auditorium from the back, marching down the center aisle to the podium. A college band had been hastily assembled, and, hearing this, Charlie Callanan, the Senator's aide, remarked that McCarthy did not like bands. The call went out to disassemble the band, but I, learning about this, hurriedly collected the band again; they had come some distance and bedecked themselves in their orchestral finery: plumes, braid, and visored caps. It seemed ungracious to send them away unplayed—and, besides, *I* liked bands. However, I said distinctly, "Do not play 'Happy Days Are Here Again.' The Senator does not like the song and it is not appropriate to the campaign." Visors and plumes nodded. McCarthy, having caught the first minutes of Johnson on television in a room off the auditorium, now appeared in the center aisle. The band started up with "Happy Days Are Here Again."

It was the dullest of McCarthy's "blue sky" speeches. If a listener heard one more reference to slogging through the snows of New Hampshire he must surely scream. A million Wisconsin homes, the candidate said, had been visited by the students. The audience was on the edge of the seats, not because of McCarthy's speech, but from curiosity as to what the President would say and what McCarthy would say about the President. He finished, however, with no reference to Johnson.

It started with yelps from the rear of the auditorium, where a few people had transistor radios pressed to their ears. Then the press corps, swelled by local reporters, thundered down the aisle, screaming like a pack of Eumenides. Alarmed, the campaigners began jumping on the stage to protect the candidate, who was twisting his face this way and that as he tried to determine what had happened. "What is it? What is it?" he cried. Completely surrounded by reporters, he was now invisible to the audience. On stage it was still impossible to hear. Finally it got through. "Johnson's out! He's not running. He's not running. Johnson's out!"

McCarthy's mouth dropped open, but only for an instant. "It's a surprise to me," he said, and smiled once. The overwhelming impression one had of him was of a complete self-possession probably bred out of years in politics. He moved to the microphone and said to the audience, "Things have gotten rather complicated."

"Johnson's not running!" someone shouted again. This time the audience understood and the whole place went off. Young Michael McCarthy was trying to get in the side door while twelve-year-old Margaret McCarthy was in tears in the side balcony. McCarthy seemed to want only to leave that stage. Outside he commented, "I think it must have come as a surprise to the members of the President's Cabinet who were campaigning here for him. It changes the political picture in the United States in 1968." The candidate had frowned on police escorts; collecting his family, he was grateful now as his car moved off, cordoned by blinking red lights. Someone had instant placard capability, for a sign could be seen: BYE BYE BIRDIES. In the car he said, oracularly, "Bobby will have to run against Jack now. Before, he could run against Lyndon."

At Waukesha headquarters that night there was a party with beer and tremendous applause for the out-of-state campaigners, as though they had driven Johnson from the field. And yet, behind the hilarity, one felt a kind of hollowness. We had been campaigning against Johnson and the war for so long and now, having, it seemed, partially achieved our goals, we felt a little useless and alone.

In McCarthy's suite at the Sheraton Schroeder in Milwaukee, the implications of Johnson's withdrawal had been quickly understood. The mood was somber, almost glacial, until someone said, "The king is dead, long live the king," which relaxed things a bit. Abigail McCarthy telephoned her good friend Lady Bird Johnson to offer sympathy, and McCarthy read a short, dignified statement to the television cameras. He had refrained from making harsh personal attacks on Johnson during the campaign and so he was free to praise him. "I look upon this as a personally sad and difficult moment for a man who has given so many years to the service of his country. With this generous judgment, President Johnson has cleared the way for the reconciliation of our people."

The next day, in a prepared statement, the candidate reiterated his intention to stay in the race and under the same mandate as before:

> . . . I would in those campaigns do as much as I could within the limits of my power and the time which was available to me to stand as their candidate, not aspiring to the Presidency directly and by my own determination and by my own desire but rather because I thought there had to be some kind of personification. . . . But once one raises issues that touch upon the Presidency of the United States . . . [and] attempts to carry that kind of burden or carry those issues to the people [one] does in fact become a candidate for the Presidency of the United States.
>
> And so this is my role today. This is what I am—a candidate for the nomination of the Democratic Party for the Presidency of the United States of America.

On this day, for the first time, he sounded like a convincing aspirant. He had been surprised at the President's timing, thinking that if Johnson did withdraw it would have come much later, and in this judgment he simply shared the general underestimation of his impact. For while Johnson may have seen Kennedy's challenge as greater and more fearsome, it had been McCarthy's showing in New Hampshire that had forced Kennedy into contention and Mc-Carthy's strength in Wisconsin read in private White House polls which had compelled the President to withdraw when he did. Having achieved these things, McCarthy must indeed go on. He made some political calls—to Mayor Richard Daley of Chicago and

Governor Warren Hearnes of Missouri—to say he was still in the race. Typically, he would not ask their support.

On Wisconsin election eve, McCarthy delivered what to this observer was the best television speech given by anyone in the 1968 campaign, pre- or postconvention. There were differences, though, on how to stage it. Goodwin wanted a rally, but McCarthy's old friends, Bill and Kay Nee, thought that a "hot" performance, showing fervid crowds, would hurt McCarthy in Wisconsin, though it might help him nationally. McCarthy, they argued, would seem, to the Wisconsinites, to be dancing on Johnson's grave. McCarthy agreed with them. As staged by the Nees, the program showed to a national audience rows and rows of silent faces, a mixture of young and old, with the candidate talking to them quietly as he sat on a corner of a desk—he was always better with a live audience. McCarthy spoke from hastily scrawled notes on folded pieces of paper which read as follows:

(I)

Honesty (Truth)
Time of Truth
1. Not raising an issue
2. Not conducting ed.
3. Children's Crusade
4. Challenge for Presidency

(II)

Not a boyhood dream
White House
Inheritance of successor
Not sought out by Party
Smoke-filled room
Encouraged by early press
1966—Power comes
Well exercised

(III)

Milwaukee
Apologize Voters
1968
President
Service to Nation
De-escalate
Seek settlement
If alone—political spirit I have *seen*
End killing

(IV)

Role to unite . . .
To Unify—*Inspire*
Organic whole
Common Purpose
Shared Ideals
In *name* of Justice *to Act* . . .
Need now—Reconciliation
   Young and old
   labor and management
   farmers and consumers
   academic and community
   thought and action
   race and race
   Congress and Presidency
Begun in New Hampshire—Wisconsin *continues*
President's action

Out of this he was able to construct a simple, moving address.
As the clock raced toward the end of the half hour, he said:

And then he [Whitman] writes, speaking of the future, and
speaking of all of us when he wrote this, and we speak now to
the youngest among us and to those who will come after us:
"Poets to come, and orators to come, and singers, all of you who

are to come, come not today when you come, not to justify me."
He said: "Or answer what I am for, but you, a new brood:
native, athletic, continental, greater than any before known." He
was speaking of us. And then he said—and this must be our
theme—he said: "Arouse, arouse for you must justify me, you
must answer."

On election day, he campaigned in Nebraska, returning to Milwaukee in the evening. His staff estimated that a sympathy vote
for the President would cost McCarthy 5 percentage points; even
so, he got 56.2 per cent of the vote compared to 35 per cent for the
President, even with a less-than-predicted Republican crossover.
In Waukesha County, for instance, McCarthy and Johnson together polled a percentage of the total vote almost precisely equal
to that of Johnson-Humphrey over Goldwater-Miller in 1964,
and the state-wide results were similar. This fact should have
destroyed the idea that McCarthy's strength lay in Republican
votes that he couldn't receive in a general election.

Part III | KENNEDY

6 | Indiana and Nebraska: Senator Who?

In political campaigns the ultimate outcome may turn on a handful of key decisions made in the dead of night, or during the rush of events, by exhausted, fallible men whose knowledge of the future is fragmentary. If the McCarthy campaign is seen as a serious attempt to win the Presidency and cross a threshold into a new age of reform and with the withdrawal of the President it was—Indiana, for McCarthy, was a fateful mistake.

Indeed, the decision to enter the primary there was to be the basis for the question which tormented the inner circle of the McCarthy organization when it had begun to scent a possible victory—did the candidate, as opposed to the campaign, really want to win? If he did, why did he not bypass Indiana for the fertile soil of Nebraska, which he believed would yield to him the farm vote, and for cool Oregon, skeptical of Kennedy? Why should he declare for Indiana first, literally forcing Kennedy to follow him? McCarthy was already or about to be involved in ten other primaries—a prodigious effort by any standards. Why didn't he concentrate on them?

McCarthy announced his entry into Indiana on the same day that Robert Kennedy declared for President, and, to a large extent, McCarthy was reacting angrily to Kennedy. He would not give Kennedy any presents, or, above all, show fear of any kind; he would make Kennedy fight for everything.

It was not yet clear whether the President or a stand-in for him, like Governor Roger Branigin, would be on the Indiana ballot. If

Kennedy went in, and McCarthy didn't, he would be giving Kennedy the protest vote. He might permit Kennedy to begin building a momentum which would be impossible to stop.

In part, his own candidacy had been meant to be inspirational, to prove to the young that politicians are not necessarily gutless, ready to deal and take the easy way out—and now he did not want to seem to back off. Besides, his supporters in Indiana were pressing him and presenting what was later known to be exaggerated claims about the strength of the state McCarthy organization.

Finally, there was McCarthy's view of the primaries and his own position in them. He did not take the conventional view that 1968 was 1960 when a candidate could be knocked out in one or two bruising fights. The primaries were a steady growth in a general contest. He, as the total underdog even after New Hampshire, had little to lose and much to gain in a primary of almost any kind, and as the underdog he was forced to take risks.

The candidate sounded confident as the test approached. "Bobby's campaign is like a grass fire—it will just burn off the surface. Mine is like a fire in a peat bog. It will hold on for six months," and, after the President's exit: "Until Lyndon got out it was like three-cushion billiards. Bobby could hit me only when he banked a shot off Lyndon. It was a case of who could hate Lyndon the most, and he seemed to be winning. Now he will have to attack me directly." Beneath the surface, he was less certain. His campaign was being forced to start again against new opposition. And that opposition, after all, was a Kennedy, rich, tough, organized, famous, imbued by the mass media with a mystique a Roman emperor would have envied. Kennedy was ahead in the national polls. Indiana, for him, would be a re-creation of West Virginia in 1960 and, as Humphrey had fallen then, McCarthy would fall now.

Indiana was supposed to be the "crossroads of America" but whose crossroads and which America? In the north were the industrial towns like Gary, Hammond, and East Chicago, jammed with Negroes, heavy with smoke; in the south the big black barns with the signs: CHEW MAIL POUCH TOBACCO. The fields had an odd mottled color—"because of the glaciological history of the region," McCarthy told a reporter. Pronunciation was provincial—Dooboys County, Vinsens, Terry Hoat, Indanapolis, the capital (with an abundance of fallout shelters and War Memorial Plaza—"War Monger Plaza," some called it); the local papers seemed almost to wish for a higher Indiana casualty rate in Vietnam to prove the state was doing her patriotic share. It was Klan country, Bible Belt country, labor-union country, Negro country, ethnic-group country, and a Southern state masquerading as middle Border. It was tough country—one local McCarthy leader, a former bookie in Lake County, made a practice of drawing his pistol out of the pocket of his shiny silk suit and laying it on the desk before sitting down to talk with the national McCarthy representative. People were suspicious and the information level seemed low ("Does McCarthy know the enemy is training *gorillas* to attack our boys?" a lady anxiously asked). The usual answer to appeals to vote for McCarthy was, "Senator Who?"

"The people here don't cut down lilac bushes as they have in other states, and they leave big trees standing in the plowed fields. They like music, too. Those are good signs," said the candidate, always appreciative of regional differences. He tried, wanly, to joke. On the origin of the word "Hoosier": "A long time ago, some pretty violent people lived out here, and they used to bite each other's ears off. There were all those ears lying around, and when anyone picked one up he'd ask, 'Whose ear?' " But the bad signs predominated. As he wrote in a poem about Indiana:

> The first Bad Sign is this:
> "Green River Ordinance Enforced Here.
> Peddlers Not Allowed."

> This is a clean, safe town
> No one can just come round
> With ribbons and bright thread
> Or new books to be read.
> This is an established place.
> We have accepted patterns in lace,
> And ban itinerant vendors of new forms and whirls,
> All things that turn the heads of girls.
> We are not narrow, but we live with care.
> Gypsies, hawkers and minstrels are right for a fair.
> But transient peddlers, nuisances, we say,
> From Green River must be kept away.
> Traveling preachers, actors with a play,
> Can pass through, but may not stay.
> Phoenicians, Jews, men of Venice—
> Know that this is the home of Kiwanis.
> All you who have been round the world to find
> Beauty in small things: read our sign
> And move on. . . .

The candidate and his campaigners were the actors, the preachers, the transient peddlers of ideas. Doors were slammed in their faces; townspeople refused to rent empty space for McCarthy storefronts. In Green River and many other places they obviously were not wanted. It had been inconceivable at first that McCarthy, even if he could not top Kennedy, could lose to Governor Branigin, but as he began campaigning McCarthy conceded that he might be lucky to get ten per cent of the vote.

In politics nothing is harder to change than direction. Without question, the campaign had a major weapon in the performance of the candidate on television. Calm, cool, quick, direct, splendid in what television folk call "tight shots" or close-ups, he was the best television performer among the Presidential candidates.

But the money was not spent showing the candidate in TV ads; it went into local organization.

McCarthy could not hope to take over the existing Democratic

Party structure, which was locked into the campaign of the governor, who in turn represented Hubert Humphrey. This was the old, old politics—state employees had to pay a two-per-cent party tax, with contributions elicited as well from people with patronage. The McCarthy forces had to create their own state-wide organization. The sentiment building for McCarthy was such that Gans was able to get some seven hundred full-time field workers in Indiana. The expectation was that they would organize the students who would pour into the state; with students carrying the McCarthy message, the candidate would repeat his feats in New Hampshire and Wisconsin.

But two things went wrong. Even as the excitement about the McCarthy kiddies' crusade was at its apogee, the collegians were starting to cop out. The Kennedy entrance had confused them, and then, with college students like everyone else, styles change. They were coming but not in the flocks that had reached Wisconsin, and they needed to be cajoled into the busses. But suddenly, in April, there were no busses either. The McCarthy campaign, it seemed, had run out of money.

"The McCarthy campaign was the most factionalized campaign I've seen in my life," remarked, with bewilderment, Patrick Lucey, former Lieutenant Governor of Wisconsin, after working with the McCarthyites at the Chicago convention. Good people ought to be able to work together for a common objective, in theory. This warmhearted notion, however, overlooks pride, ego, territoriality, immaturity, self-interest. It ignored the tested dictums of the old politics: "The campaign manager must be able to say 'no' or 'yes' and stick with it. . . . He must sometimes say 'no' to the candidate. . . . Commitments must be kept. . . . Divisions will ultimately produce disaster. . . . A campaign must have unity and move from its starting position steadily to victory."

Behind the smiling posters of the candidate in Indiana, the campaign was breaking up into warring groups. There was the Senator's Washington staff against the newcomers. There was the war of the tube. The latter, which like all the rest was to continue in one form or another till the very end, consisted in Indiana of a clash between Carl Ally, a high-powered New York advertising man who had volunteered his services, and Bill and Kay Nee. Nee, on leave from his Minnesota ad firm, consistently fought for a "cool" approach, emphasizing issues and the low-keyed personality of the candidate. Others thought the Nees' work too homey and called the couple "Ma and Pa Kettle." The Nees won a clear victory over Ally in Indiana, and Ally left the campaign. From then on, the campaign had no agency with responsibility for the national effort. In the remaining primary states Nee utilized local agencies and, while the advertising seemed well attuned locally, it seemed to lack a national thrust.

There was the struggle between the national staff headed by Gans and the Hoosier McCarthy organization. The Hoosiers, laboring under the well-publicized delusion that students were running the campaign, filled the top campaign positions with college kids. The national staff, experienced now and a few years older, brushed them aside like leaves.

And there was the war of the bankbooks. This was to be a three-sided contest, with Gans on one corner, the financiers on the second, and Stephen Quigley, Abigail McCarthy's brother, on the third. Quigley, fiftyish, dark, a Ph.D. chemist, had been asked by McCarthy to head the Washington finance office. Abigail had at last become concerned that her husband would be strapped with an enormous campaign debt. Indeed, as the bills arrived from New Hampshire and Wisconsin it became apparent that the campaign was already deeply indebted—perhaps $150,000, even without Indiana. Quigley shared the growing apprehension about the efficacy of the national staff. Even if it was good it was expensive, for the volunteers had to be housed and fed. He was appalled by the money spent on such things as printing (without competitive bids); the telephone (the national staffers were addicted to long-distance phone calls, including those to parents at home—the Indiana McCarthy phone bill came to $78,000); rented cars; air travel (over a dozen "Q" air-travel cards, which could be used by anyone, were in general circulation); and the like. "Just anybody could obligate the campaign," Quigley explained, and indeed there seemed almost no way to say no. A request for a $10,000 order for buttons and literature was vetoed in Washington but bought anyway. One girl from the East sent a group of kids to Indiana on a plane she managed to charter and charge to the campaign without anyone's knowledge, much less authorization. Quigley began asking questions before he paid bills.

To the national staff, working under extreme pressure, the delays caused by Quigley were treasonous. The word was that Quigley was antiyouth—though a mild, middle-sized fellow, he was portrayed as an ogre who began eating babies at the toes. As cautious Quigley tried to foil the grandiose plans of the national staff he developed swift opposition from still another quarter, tho big money men.

The financiers were not partisans of the national staff; quite the contrary, they felt that most of the prodigious sum of $800,000 which was to be spent by McCarthy in Indiana was being wasted, largely through inefficiency. As one of them, Arnold Hiatt, put it, "We financial guys had an instinct to do something. You couldn't just stand by in all that chaos." Corporate officials and businessmen, mostly, they wished to exert some political control over the campaign and to do so they had to have the treasury. (A little ungraciously, it seemed to some, McCarthy was to remark later: "Our problem was too much help and too much financial support . . . it was like three times as much as we expected. People moved in, you know, who wanted to raise money. It's pretty hard to say no. They'll do it on their own, anyway. Run kind of separate efforts.")

The principal money men were Hiatt; Stein; Robert Pirie, thirty-five, a major shareholder in Carson, Pirie, Scott Department Store in Chicago; Werner H. Kramarsky, on leave as Assistant Mayor of

New York City (John V. Lindsay, the Mayor of New York, had not discouraged several of his top aides from working in the campaign, but he was increasingly irritated by McCarthy's refusal to talk about specific issues); and Martin Peretz, a bearded assistant professor of social studies at Harvard. Like the volunteers, this group had mostly been brought into national politics by the Mc-Carthy campaign. They were among the chief raisers and/or givers of large donations which, in two instances, exceeded a quarter of a million dollars. (Then, and later, most of the big donors came from New York City, like Martin Fife and General Motors heir Stewart Mott. Unlike many large political givers, McCarthy's did not seem to want special favors, even if their candidate was elected.)

Even with the efforts of these men, the financial condition of the campaign was desperate. Since money came only in spasms, there was no way to plan to keep costs down—it was typical, for example, to have literature printed on weekends, with overtime, because the money hadn't arrived until Friday. The only reason the campaign ran at all was that there is a practice called kiting. In simple terms, kiting means to overdraw your account. The campaign's version was rather like the operation of a semishady business about to go on the rocks. As a check was coming due, a deposit would be made from another bank, and to that bank from still another, probably from out of state, so that a check might take a week or more to clear. If possible, the campaigners would find banks which were not yet computerized, to slow up the process. During the interval, frantic calls and telegrams would be sent to the donors in hopes that their contributions would cover the checks. A really quick banking system would have killed the McCarthy campaign.

The big money men in the campaign did not want to put the resources in grass-roots operations but rather in television, radio, newspaper ads, direct mail—more traditional ways of reaching voters. But now, having raised the money and deposited it in the Washington accounts, they found that Quigley would not readily give it back. For him the central problems were still the debt and the eternal question of who, if anyone, was entitled to authorize an expenditure. Quigley dragged his feet while the money men urged spending now and paying later.

Having lost all patience with Quigley, just as Quigley had with him, Hiatt proceeded to march on Washington and what ensued was the McCarthy campaign's private battle of the books. Officially, Hiatt was treasurer of the campaign, but Quigley's credentials were just as good—no, nothing could be settled by titles. Hiatt formed a new team of wealthy volunteer businessmen to help him and, determined to wrest control from Quigley, tried to take over the books and the lists of Washington contributors. Quigley resisted. He changed the locks on the finance office doors and would not furnish Hiatt with information. Hiatt responded by firing Quigley's staff but Quigley fired Hiatt's. Back and forth they wrestled.

A resourceful and tested business executive, Hiatt pondered. He was getting nowhere with Quigley and decided to copy Stein, who himself, quietly, had adopted a practice already flourishing in the campaign, although on a much smaller scale, known as bootlegging. Frowned on by Quigley, who yearned for a centralized system of finance, bootlegging consisted of having independent sources of income, outside the mainstream of McCarthy money. If you were a bootlegger, you contacted a rich contributor and urged him to donate money directly to your branch of the campaign, not to the Washington office, and every branch, and usually twigs on the branches, had secret bank accounts and secret sources of money. Campaign manager Clark's bootleg account, for example, was called Clergymen for McCarthy and was located at the Freedom National Bank in Harlem. Stein himself had amassed a bootlegged fortune which, he announced magisterially, would be used *only* for McCarthy television. Hiatt, observing that Stein was successful, embarked on the most massive bootleg scheme of all. He determined to have the Washington mail sorted before Quigley got to it and the large checks sent to him. In this way he would starve Quigley into submission. Quigley, down to a few paltry thousands of campaign dollars, seemed beaten, when Stein, by accident, slipped Quigley $50,000 and he was back in business.

Not all of these events had occurred by the end of the Indiana primary, but they are a fair sample of how everybody was "doing his thing" for Gene McCarthy, much of which the candidate, still yearning for a small and simple campaign, would have preferred be not done at all.

For the candidate these were not happy days.

The essential strategy was to hit the smaller cities and towns, partly because McCarthy had done so well in such places in New Hampshire and Wisconsin, and partly because these were supposed to be the centers of the Branigin vote which McCarthy must break down if he was to win. He was endlessly on courthouse squares and steps, hand thrust forward, introducing himself to tiny knots of voters, and sometimes he would appear in the same little town more than once. There were good moments—at one courthouse he was met by a string quartet which played Vivaldi and Bach— but for the most part it was the kind of campaigning least suited to inspiring a candidate to peak performance.

And whatever was done for him, it often seemed, was done wrong. Who would read a brochure issued by his headquarters entitled "The Policy Record, Principles and Visions of Hope of Senator Eugene McCarthy"? His cavalcade rolled down the road: a motorcycle cop, a bulldozer, the candidate's car, a garbage truck, a pickup truck, the press bus. The press, on whom so much depended, would somehow arrive at a different airport from the candidate and miss his speech. His advance staff, such as it was, could never be depended on. McCarthy would arrive at plant gates early or late. Mary McCarthy recalls arriving at a "coffee" at which two guests appeared; the hostess was delighted, having expected one. At an airport, as McCarthy was speaking, the tire of his airplane suddenly exploded with a *whoosh!* and that sound, for the Indiana effort, was the epiphany.

"EUGENE'S HITTING THE VOTERS WHERE THEY AIN'T" or "MC-CARTHY LEAVES BACKERS WAITING" the headlines said, and it often appeared that the candidate was only going through the motions of a campaign. "Where am I? What am I doing here?" he would ask frequently. His personal staff was given the right to make or break appointments at will—and not always with perfect political judgment. The scheduling became so erratic that McCarthy turned the whole thing over to Eller, who wouldn't answer telephone calls from staffers who wanted advice on the Senator's schedule or from advance men who needed to know his itinerary. The schedule was never approved until it was too late to raise crowds for the candidate; it was changed, scribbled over, en route to destinations. Because the planning was so bad, the candidate began skipping scheduled appearances until he dropped at least one a day. (Once he halted the cavalcade for a picnic and baseball game, completely missing a crowd that was waiting for him.) He was overscheduled, underscheduled, lost, driven impossibly long distances, and later estimated that he wasted eighty per cent of his time. He would return at night with his pockets stuffed with poems people had handed him during the day, but the poetry vote, it seemed, was all he was getting.

He was doing even poorer in the ghettos than in the white areas. "I will not make racial appeals," he had said, "to either black or white. I will speak the same to all—and there is no reason not to, for all are men and all are Americans." Yet he would wear a Martin Luther King button and defy Roy Wilkins' command that he avoid Atlantic City while a National Association for the Advancement of Colored People convention was under way there; McCarthy did not take kindly to ultimatums. So he campaigned in the ghettos in Indiana but not happily. The sparse crowds made him look silly;

to repeat and repeat his record on civil rights was repugnant to him. One problem was that whenever he walked into a crowd where there were more than three or four Negroes, his aide-de-camp, Charlie Callanan, "would think it was a mob riot and take him out of there, quick," complained a staff member. Without such connections with the black community as Kennedy had, it was impossible to know the black power structure—*whom* was the candidate talking to? What did he represent? McCarthy would go to the ghettos, but he did not put himself out. The Indiana ghettos were for Kennedy and would give him eighty to ninety per cent of the vote.

If McCarthy did not stir the hearts in black Indiana communities, he did not seem to try to undo the negative impression the blacks had of him. On the day after Martin Luther King was shot, McCarthy was campaigning in California. He walked through Watts—to the trepidation of his staff—but he mentioned Martin Luther King only once, when he spoke of "reconciliation of the races." He went to the funeral in Atlanta but stayed conspicuously out of the television cameras. He seemed constantly afraid of trading principles for votes.

Abigail McCarthy had known Coretta King when both had served on the board of United Church Women. She was in the Atlanta airport about to catch a plane to another destination when she met the distraught Mrs. King there. Coretta King asked Abigail McCarthy to come to her house, which Mrs. McCarthy did, leaving as the dignitaries began to stream in. The few McCarthy campaigners who knew about this incident realized at once the significance stories showing a King-McCarthy connection would have. Abigail McCarthy refused to discuss it and asked a New York newspaper reporter, informed of the event, not to write about it, a wish the reporter respected, and the candidate continued to be regarded by the ghettos as distant and uninvolved.

If the candidate was discouraged, so were the workers at headquarters in Indianapolis, two floors of the Hotel Claypool—

known as the Cesspool, the upper six floors having been burned out. They lived in another hotel famous for the size and rapacity of its cockroaches. Their food allowances had ceased to arrive, and they lived on sandwiches provided by the good ladies of the city. During a heat wave the sandwiches went bad and there was a daily sick call for food poisoning conducted by Rosanne Stavis, the generous housemother for the whole campaign. Doctors warned about vitamin deficiencies and donated great vials of vitamins.

Into Indiana the McCarthy campaign poured its battalion of stars, who acquitted themselves with valor. Paul Newman, who made fifteen campaign swings for McCarthy, opening eleven storefronts in one day, amused himself by driving a policeman's motorcycle around the block. Myrna Loy, campaigning in Indiana, learned about the generation gap. Appearing at a college radio station for a broadcast, she was asked politely by the young announcer, "Myrna Who?" As recruited by a capable group of women headed by Bobbie Handman, Sandy Johnson, and Sandy Silverman, the stars included Rod Serling and Garry Moore. Dustin Hoffman was introducing Simon and Garfunkel when a stink bomb exploded, injuring someone in the audience.

For all its style, energy, and charm, the McCarthy campaign was not coming off. Overshadowed by Kennedy, it lacked cohesion and a focus. The candidate, in the lull in Vietnam discussion following the President's announcement of a bombing halt, seemed to have no real issue. Although it came too late to be effective in Indiana, the issue was finally found—Kennedy and the question of power.

Kennedy's announcement of candidacy immediately after the New Hampshire results had raised the hackles of the McCarthy forces, but there was a feeling of inevitability about Kennedy, and the bulk of the McCarthyites would at this time have supported Kennedy if their own candidate had been defeated. Indeed, in Indiana there was a certain sympathetic bond because both candidates—Kennedy even more than McCarthy—were being unfairly treated by the state's largest paper, the *Indianapolis Star,* and the afternoon paper, the *Indianapolis News* (both owned by Eugene C. Pulliam), whose coverage and even cartoons were obviously against both camps.

The Kennedy headquarters was located down the street on several stories of a movie house which was playing *Gone With the Wind.* The relations between the two camps, at first cordial, became hostile. The incidents seemed small at the start. The Kennedyites had approached some of the McCarthy kids with cash offers to change sides. That was probably acceptable behavior, though few McCarthy campaigners went over. Less so, thought the McCarthy forces, was the attempt by a prominent Kennedy person to rent the Claypool headquarters out from under them. Cash in hand, he offered double the price the McCarthy campaign had paid, but the landlord stuck by the original bargain. The talk of Kennedy's attempting to buy the election in Indiana even reached the editorial page of the *New York Times,* and the McCarthy people could observe glumly that the Kennedy campaigners were generally paid while the McCarthyites were volunteers, starving at that. Kennedy literature changed its contents in the southern part of the state, where the space given in the north to advocacy of civil rights was devoted to law and order. The McCarthyites moralized a little on that, but the regional adjustment of appeals seemed to be part of politics, too. The McCarthy campaign did not always parade its dovishness, either.

Then, inexplicably to the McCarthyites who thought McCarthy support would be essential if Robert Kennedy was to win at the convention, Kennedy people launched an attack on Eugene McCarthy's record in Congress.

The charges had originally come from Citizens for Kennedy in New York, though Kennedy's press secretary, Pierre Salinger, said that there was "not anything being organized by the national headquarters of the Kennedy campaign." The charges also appeared as ads in college newspapers as far away as the West Coast. Mc-

Carthy could not take them without remonstration. He reflected upon this period later, in an interview with the *Boston Globe*: "You see, once he [Kennedy] came in it was old politics, pretty much. It wasn't really the challenge to the Johnson position, it got into the question of what's your record on civil rights, and why is your attendance record bad? And all these other side issues that Bobby introduced. The question of my being for a guaranteed annual wage, stuff like that, that changed the whole context of it."

At five p.m. on May 3, in the McCarthy suite at the Marott Hotel in Indianapolis, there was a council of war, with McCarthy; Gans; Jeremy Larner, novelist and free-lance journalist who was a McCarthy speech writer; John Cogley, who had joined the campaign as a special adviser for a few weeks; and Philip Murphy, former financial editor of the *Boston Herald Traveler,* who had become the press secretary. The decision was clear: Go after Bobby.

McCarthy began that night in a speech at Butler College in Indianapolis. Until then he had been kidding around with remarks like, "He plays touch football, I play football. He plays softball, I play baseball. He skates at Rockefeller Center, I play hockey," which were recorded with gravity by serious-minded reporters. Even his challenge for a debate had been uttered with a touch of whimsy—he would meet Kennedy, alone, high-noon style, in the old shooting town of Scottsbluff, Nebraska. But on this night the campaign changed. McCarthy defended his record, revealed his net worth, thirty thousand dollars (probably too high), challenging Bobby to reveal his, and he said, "The time has come to begin to judge the opposition." Did Robert Kennedy, he asked essentially, measure up on the overreaching issue of the uses and abuses of Presidential power?

There was a rustle of hope the last weekend in Indiana. Money had come, and there was television advertising and busses for the kids. They, some seven thousand of them, had turned out in response to the desperate appeals from Indiana. The "Long March" crowd came—mostly on half-fare student air tickets, from the East; the "Dirty Nuttin' " busload all the way from Texas—Johnson, it seems, had referred to some demonstrators as "Dirty Nuttin's,"—and they arrived wearing Dirty Nuttin' buttons, one of which was worn by the candidate. Another story cannot be substantiated but serious people swear it is true. Sammy Davis, recruiting for Kennedy in Chicago, offered free tickets to his show for students who went to Indiana and canvassed for Kennedy. Several busloads arrived at Kennedy headquarters in Indianapolis. The students alighted, said "Thanks," and marched en masse to McCarthy headquarters.

It was not enough. McCarthy was outcampaigned, outorganized, outspent. An NBC pre-election poll gave Kennedy 43 per cent, Branigin 26, and McCarthy 19, with the rest undecided, and the only comfort the McCarthy people could take as the returns came in was that the final tally read: Kennedy 42, Branigin 31, McCarthy 27. The candidate had done better than predicted and Kennedy, who needed 50 per cent, had been slowed, though in the manner of a tank going around a slight bend in the road. Generous journalists like Tom Wicker would say that McCarthy "proved that he was a serious contender for President of the United States," and Gene McCarthy would get wild cheers at the Claypool on election night when he said, "I didn't come here to dismiss the troops." The candidate had a moment at least to share the television screen, if not the debate platform, with Robert Kennedy when CBS, as Kennedy and McCarthy were interviewed in separate studios, managed to link them up to Kennedy's surprise and great irritation. There had been some good moments in Indiana, but it was a bruised, battered, and dispirited group of McCarthyites that pushed on.

Nebraska was Indiana only worse. Indiana had been a vampire, sucking the blood from the McCarthy organization—every cent, every volunteer, every moment of the candidate's time, and for Nebraska there was nothing left.

And this was a state which the McCarthy people had originally expected to win. Not because they had a strong local organization —no McCarthy group had ever taken root, and not one single Nebraskan of local importance supported the Minnesota Senator; and not because there was any keen interest in liberal politics there. The McCarthy people hoped for a victory because of a reigning myth. *Farmers* would vote for him because of his agricultural record and because he was from farm country himself.

Though $150,000 was spent by the McCarthyites in Nebraska, almost all of it in the final week, the campaign was a chronicle of errors. Yet the results were probably foreordained. NBC, as if McCarthy no longer mattered, gave the Kennedy campaign five minutes on election eve to one minute for the McCarthy effort. Kennedy, not McCarthy, got 60 per cent of the farm vote. He also secured 85 per cent of the Negro vote and nearly 60 per cent of the blue-collar vote, with a total of 51 per cent, to 31 per cent for McCarthy and a few per cent for Hubert Humphrey. Pierre Salinger was only echoing general sentiment when he said, "Senator McCarthy is no longer a credible candidate." Theodore Sorensen said the Nebraska result would knock McCarthy out of the race. Kennedy said, "I would hope, based on what has happened so far, that we could join together, work together, in Oregon and California."

McCarthy might say gamely, "So now we come to the difficult part. On the old Oregon Trail it was always easy enough to get the wagons to the Missouri River, but it was those that made it right through to the West Coast that really proved they had it in them," but the political truth was that few candidates had taken two primary drubbings, as McCarthy had in Indiana and Nebraska, and gotten up again. The McCarthy campaign was on the mat and the referee was counting.

7 | The Oregon Trail

The out-of-state campaign manager who arrived in Portland mid-April to take up his duties was not precisely what the Oregonians for McCarthy had been looking for. A prickly bunch, they had already expelled two previous envoys as disruptive and indigestible. A New York Jew, or half-Jew, who was a writer without previous political experience except in the McCarthy campaign, was not their idea of an answer to Lawrence F. O'Brien. Nonetheless, they gave me a try.

Oregon was to be McCarthy's Marne, and it was petrifying that I, who had never set foot in the state, should now be virtually in full command of the make-or-break McCarthy effort. At least for the first few weeks, I would work almost without aid or consultation from anyone in the national campaign. There had been one assist on my first evening in Portland. Jerry Eller, the Senator's lovable, roguish administrative assistant, had arrived for a meeting with a group of Oregonians for McCarthy. Neither Eller nor myself realized that this assemblage had been meant to lay the base for a McCarthy fund-raising drive, and Eller proceeded to deliver one of his pseudoserious political monologues. A "true believer," he said, shouldn't spend all his time inquiring whether Senator McCarthy had a good voting record. Women became involved in a political movement such as this as a sex substitute like bowling, Eller said. Scholars, he insisted, hand over old theses and articles instead of trying to develop new ideas for position papers. The scholars screamed. The Republicans in the room cried out that freedom of inquiry was being stifled in the heart of a people's democratic crusade, and the women stared quietly at their laps. The meeting broke up in disarray, and it took the campaign manager days to get the Oregonians back on the trail. Henceforth, I decided, I would try to coordinate alone.

Spreading out my assets and liabilities, I was depressed, but only up to a point. I knew about the prospects for defeat in Indiana and Nebraska. I had brought the spectacular sum of two hundred dollars from the campaign treasury, and, since Oregonians for McCarthy was almost broke, this was all we had. Against our meager forces would be ranged the foremost campaign intelligence in America: O'Brien, Steve Smith, Fred Dutton, Theodore Sorensen, Ted Kennedy, a pantheon of stars!

But there were a few good omens glittering in the heavens for the McCarthyites, too. Except in Indiana and Nebraska, the candidate was doing unexpectedly well. From nowhere, he had moved up in the polls and the *U.S. News & World Report* rated him first. *Time*'s "Choice '68" poll among college students placed him ahead of Kennedy, and he towered over Humphrey. His shoestring operation received 44 per cent of the vote in a Connecticut primary which would not have been held at all if McCarthy supporters hadn't carefully inspected the law. In Pennsylvania he had beaten Robert Kennedy 7 to 1 and Humphrey 10 to 4, though the latter votes were write-ins. Write-ins, too, were the 28 and 19 per cent of the vote received respectively by Kennedy and Humphrey in Massachusetts, to McCarthy's 50 per cent. Maddening to the manager in Oregon, desperate to boost morale, was the reporters' refusal to make the connection: Rockefeller beat Nixon on write-ins in Massachusetts, while Kennedy, on write-ins, lost decisively in his home state.

And in Oregon one could see what McCarthy had ignited in America. Not merely enthusiastic, desiring significant changes,

Oregonians for McCarthy was prepared to work and existed in organized fashion all over the state. Here was a strategy that might be successful against Kennedy—even without money or political professionals: outorganize him.

Kennedy might also help defeat himself. The television showed him tugged and buffeted by screaming mobs of California high-schoolers. Kennedy doubtlessly was trying to create an impression of irresistible popularity, squeezing the crowds into cul-de-sacs or narrow streets to heighten the impact of congestion, a favorite Kennedy crowd-building technique. Kennedy had to start his bandwagon rolling at high speed to shatter the flimsy McCarthy barricades and the Humphrey gates. Though Kennedy would subsequently, and perhaps imitatively of McCarthy, tone down his style, his approach was questionable for a state with one of the highest education levels in the nation. I had heard of a remark of a prominent Kennedyite's wife: "The McCarthy people have no *right* to be in this election. Imagine, amateurs running a campaign!" Gazing at Kennedy headquarters—which shared an entrance with, but seemed a part of, a boutique, with cute dresses and gewgaws—I felt that the Kennedy campaign was slightly precious. Yes, there were signs, faint but unmistakable, that the Kennedys were overconfident. They were neglecting the front lines.

As the McCarthy forces moved from state to state they found themselves confronted with a hodgepodge of election laws. In New Hampshire, there was a classification known as Independents, who remained such only if they did not vote in a primary election; if they did, they lost their virginity and were henceforth identified with one of the parties. In Wisconsin, Republicans and Democrats could cross over at the polls, while in Indiana crossovers were not permitted—unless you got away with it. The regular Democrats were publicly encouraging Republicans to cross over and vote for Branigin. In Oregon and California, Republicans could vote Democratic in the primary if they reregistered. The reregistrations might not seem important in terms of round numbers, but in close elections they could be critical. A reregistration drive conducted by the McCarthy people in California got about three per cent of the Republican vote, and that would have been enough for Senator Thomas Kuchel to defeat Dr. Max Rafferty in the Republican primary.

Eager to get the campaign off the ground, I conferred with the Oregon leadership: Dr. Joe Allman, a professor at Oregon University at Eugene, the state chairman; Blaine Whipple, a real-estate man, vice-chairman; Howard Morgan, a construction-materials man and former Federal Power Commissioner, and Jean F. Delord, finance cochairmen; Dr. James Watson; John Callahan, a professor at Portland State; Gene Hogan; John Painter, a local reporter who acted as press secretary; and several others. They wanted to begin a Republican reregistration drive and looked to the penniless manager for funds for a television show. The manager, by accident, got word of a thousand-dollar check which had been sent by Republicans for McCarthy in New York and was being held by one of the Oregonians against what eventuality no one knew. Extracting the check almost by force, I purchased a half hour of television time. Intelligent Republicans on the show would explain why they intended to reregister and vote for McCarthy, but to convince the audience a sample of the candidate was also needed.

This was one of these times when one discovered the meaning of amateurism. After months of campaigning, the McCarthy movement had almost nothing usable as television footage—no commercials, no documentaries about the candidate's life—nothing but a few half hours of the candidate on platforms in other states. One of these was edited, with space left for the live Republicans, and the show went on the air. It was as important internally as without: the Oregonians for McCarthy knew at last that they had a campaign.

Next, a headquarters. The Oregonians had rented a few rooms in an office building, probably in the secret hope that the national staff would overlook them altogether in its rush to California. The national staff would be coming, though, panting for battle, in numbers I dared not mention to Oregonians concerned with deficits.

Already in the first week after my arrival a dozen workers had come and new ones popped in every day. From the manager's associations in previous McCarthy campaigns came Maryanna Henkart, a Harvard biologist. Born in Portland, where her revivalist father had her singing hymns to drunkards at age two, she, gentle in manner, would handle relations with Portland groups. The then assistant librarian at Yale, David MacLaren, would work with the offices around the state, while Dan Singal organized students; Michael Mills, a student at Reed College in Portland, who had been working in McCarthy's Senate office, would assist the campaign manager. To help came Steve Thomas, a Boston writer; Diana Green, a communications expert from Wisconsin who would tape the Senator's speeches and feed them, by special phone hookup, to local radio stations; Patricia O'Connell, a former reporter from the *New York Herald Tribune*; Claire Svourc, a journalism major from the Midwest; Andy Teuber, an Eastern actor; and my wife, Lael Scott, till then a reporter on the *New York Post*. Susan Thomases from New Jersey, in one day, became an expert in campaign office management—she knew how many telephone lines nestled in a cable and how to get credit from the phone company. Eleanor Goldman, wife of a poet-professor from Columbia University, would organize the committees of physicians, professors, lawyers, artists, and so on with which the manager planned to blanket the papers in the final week of the campaign. The first job of Starry Krueger from New York was to organize a committee of nine college presidents in the state to call for a McCarthy-Kennedy debate. Wired to Nebraska, it was refused by Kennedy.

Such a crew needed space—lots of it. I also wanted to give the impression of solidity and scope. The McCarthy campaign gloried in spectacular headquarters and in Oregon it outdid itself. There was just enough money to rent for a month what had been the Portland Elks Club and then a sports club. On three floors of this vast unused building the McCarthy organization settled in.

"Nothing works here but the people," I told the reporters. One of the beauties of a volunteer effort like this was that there were always skilled hands. An artist devised a canopy—a huge outdoor cloth banner that said McCARTHY—and lighting, and psychedelic drops for the lobby. One of the best calligraphers in the country came from a local college and devised a big sign to put around the building, McCARTHY. THE MAN THE PEOPLE FOUND, and the slogan was echoed, as soon as the money came in, on distinctive blue-and-white billboards around the state. I insisted on a kiddies' room on street level, where passersby could easily see it. Suddenly there it was, a big CHILDREN FOR McCARTHY sign on a clean plate-glass window, and a brightly painted room with hobby horses, toys, and a full-time volunteer so that women could leave their children and work upstairs.

The headquarters was interesting enough to fetch the reporters and the stories brought in more volunteers. Toward the end of the campaign there were hundreds of people working there at almost any time, day or night. From the lobby a flight of marble stairs led to a chandeliered room for advance—laying the ground for the candidate's visits—and scheduling, another for Women for Mc-Carthy. (Women for McCarthy, with its own officers and budget, was now active in seventeen states with something like 170 offices. Abigail McCarthy was one of its chief attractions, and there were also the flying nuns. Encountering a nun working at the headquarters, I asked what she was doing there. "Oh," she said brightly, "I just flew out from Minnesota for the weekend to campaign!") There was the press section huddled in a dark corner of a ballroom and the basic organization took place in a large wood-paneled "State Room," the manager lurking in a small room off it. Up one more flight of stairs was a huge ballroom with a stage where dozens of long tables were set up. The McCarthy campaign did poorly in the large cities partly because they were not as easy to canvass as smaller places. McCarthy had to carry Multnomah County, which encompassed most of metropolitan and suburban Portland, to win in Oregon, and the county was to be organized down to the last doorstep.

Portland organization, good as it was, was nothing compared to the miracles performed in the Fourth Congressional District, around Eugene, by Harriet Civin; in Lynn County by Nan Culver, who had mastered all the McCarthy campaign techniques; in Washington County by Harry Shaick; in Columbia County by Dolores Hurtado. And there were offices opening all over the state, forty-five in all, ten around Portland alone, including a McCarthy office at a salmon fishery from which the good woman who created it had to walk a half mile to the phone. The one Negro community in Oregon of any size was the Albina district in Portland, and there a Kennedy Community Center had opened. This, since there was no such Kennedy center anywhere else in Oregon, struck the McCarthyites as condescending. They proceeded to establish a McCarthy campaign *headquarters* in Albina. The campaign paid the rent for the whole summer, donating it for community use when the election was over. (McCarthy did much better with the black vote in Oregon than in previous states.)

As the Nebraska campaign ended, Gans, because of the money shortage and the increasing resistance to the national staff from local people, had begun to disband his troupe. The majority were asked to go home and perform for McCarthy there; most of them packed, said good-by, and hitchhiked to California to work in the campaign. Sixty selected national staffers were flown into Oregon, where, at the airport, they found twenty cars had been begged, borrowed, or stolen for them. Arriving at headquarters, they looked like a Hertz ad. The manager gave them a lecture; they were desperately needed, but they were to help the local people, not command them. They were to be friendly and mannerly and to avoid smoking pot in the storefronts. It was pronounced Oregun, not Oregawn.

Following the Nebraska debacle, McCarthy was low and exhausted and turned down appearances on the "Today" show and "Meet the Press." His campaign had been inept, as he was well aware, and if he should not have entered Indiana, he had clearly spent too much time and money there. The campaign was headed toward insolvency. Once a campaign has begun to flounder, the trend is hard to reverse—as on Wall Street, a bearish psychology sets in. The money vanishes, and the candidate sinks.

Just after Nebraska, McCarthy finally yielded to the promptings of those who had been urging him for months to reorganize his campaign. Now entered two new figures, Thomas Finney and Thomas McCoy.

Thomas Finney—forty-four, slight, horn-rimmed glasses, from Idabel, Oklahoma, soft Oklahoma voice—was a CIA man for several years in the 1950s. He headed Stevenson's convention fight in 1960, was an advance man for Jack Kennedy, and a former administrative assistant for Senator Mike Monroney of Oklahoma, managing his successful campaign in 1962. He was an unofficial White House aide in 1964, a law partner of Clark Clifford's until he became Secretary of Defense, and he was considered to be one of the best campaign managers in the business.

Thomas McCoy, fifty, was the son of a local politician in Connecticut. Tall, gray-haired, humorous. He had just retired from the CIA, where he had worked in the clandestine section, responsible for all of Asia.

Finney and McCoy, close friends, had both strongly opposed the Johnson Vietnam policy since 1963 and made their feelings known by personal contact and memorandums circulated in the government. Each had been in contact with McCarthy for some time— Finney had talked of the candidacy with McCarthy in August—but neither had joined the campaign: McCoy because he was still with the CIA; Finney because his partnership with Clifford, then advising Johnson, made his participation in the McCarthy campaign inappropriate. The President's withdrawal solved Finney's conflict of interest over Clifford and he thought McCarthy's cause no longer hopeless. Finney offered to help, but it took him a month to get through the blockade of McCarthy's Washington staff. Finally, after close friends of McCarthy's had made strenuous efforts to bring the two of them together, Finney was on a plane to Minneapolis, where McCarthy was staying the night. It was the day after the Nebraska primary. McCoy, John Safer, Maurice Rosenblatt, and a former McCarthy aide were with him. The group had a fair idea of what should be done, and on the way out Finney scribbled notes. They had hoped to see McCarthy that evening but, on arrival, were told by the ever-present Charlie Callanan that the Senator had gone to bed. It was, it seemed, Callanan's eternal refrain.

McCarthy was due in Florida—a primary he had entered on Eller's advice—the next day, and the five men traveled with him. On the flight Finney argued that McCarthy could beat Kennedy in Oregon and California, go to the convention as a compromise candidate, and win the nomination. But he had to campaign differently. He had to stop making nostalgic speeches about the snows of New Hampshire and being the first man into the race. He must take a fighting stance and use his time more efficiently. He could not afford such an elaborate campaign—other campaigns were cheaper because they relied on local people not a large national staff—and he should spend most of his money on television. The Kennedy campaign was polarizing the country. McCarthy should offer to unite it.

Finney left for Washington at the first Florida stop. Blair Clark went to Florida that day and McCarthy told him that Finney would become over-all coordinator for Oregon and California, with McCoy staying on the plane as liason with McCarthy and the press. Additional television advisers would be mustered, and the fighting financial group brought under control with strict budgeting. Every cent would be poured into Oregon, which had to be won if McCarthy was to stay in serious contention.

A larger meeting was set for Saturday in Washington. Gans, alerted to the administrative changes, flew in from California. He marched into McCarthy's office before the meeting began. It was a difficult moment for him. Through heroic effort he had put together the organization of field workers, the core of the McCarthy movement, as he saw it, and now, as though the full blame for Indiana was being placed on him, he was, it seemed, being demoted. It looked to him as though the original McCarthy ideas about "participatory democracy" and the "new politics"—in a campaign which was giving political education to large and growing numbers —was about to be scuttled in favor of old, conventional politics. Perhaps his pride was offended as well. He told the candidate that he was leaving the campaign. McCarthy told Gans that he was undoubtedly overtired and overworked and should stay for the meeting. "Good luck, Senator," Gans said, and departed.

For the candidate it was a difficult moment, too. He had always been loyal to those who had joined him early, when he had nothing. He was exhausted, having just finished two hard primary battles and being already engaged in Florida, where, against a Humphrey slate, he was not doing well. (He was to get 25 per cent of the vote.) That evening he was to address the annual convention of the Americans for Democratic Action, which would endorse him, and the following night an enormous rally at Madison Square Garden (which raised $500,000) and then to Oregon—the scheduled appearances seemed to stretch forever. He had neither time nor inclination for staff problems. He convened the meeting, comparing it to a skull session of a football team before the last two big games of the season. After that came the bowl game.

Around the table in McCarthy's Senate office were Finney; Eller; Clark; Stein; Hiatt; Hemenway; Quigley; Safer; McCoy; Peretz; Levine; David Garth, a television expert Finney had brought in from New York; Maurice Rosenblatt; Edward N. Costikyan, a prominent Democrat from New York; and Martin Stone, the President of Monogram Industries and a McCarthy leader in California. There was no agenda. McCarthy said that he had been hurt by the ineptness of his campaign. His organization had to be better in the last primaries. He repeated the arrangements made the previous day, when the group had traveled to Florida, and said he would leave the details to them. He was about to depart to prepare his evening speech when he was asked two questions. The first from bearded Martin Peretz: How would the press react to news that Finney had joined the campaign? Wouldn't his former connection with Clark Clifford make him seem an Administration plant and represent a tacit joining of McCarthy and Humphrey to stop Kennedy? McCarthy replied that it was not a problem—Finney was an old friend from Stevenson days. He was a McCarthy, not a Humphrey, man. The suggestion that Finney was a Humphrey man did appear in the papers, but its greatest impact came later, within the McCarthy ranks.

Martin Stone raised the second point. The departure of Gans, he said, would be a disaster. The national staff was loyal to him and there might be large defections. Under his breath, McCarthy said that he thought the loyalty was to him, the candidate, not to others. He thought that Gans would change his mind. "Work it out," he said to Finney and Clark, and left the room.

The meeting continued. Finney planned to fly to California the following day to set up a communications center to ensure instant contact between the candidate and his staff and a fast reaction time. The Senator, he said, should be scheduled to be in bed by ten p.m. —Finney thought McCarthy's speeches were showing fatigue. Garth would direct television which would be harder-hitting. Stein, though an amateur, had taken an active part in television programing—he would now concentrate on fund-raising. The group wondered what was happening in the satrapy of Oregon, which seemed to be pursuing an independent course. Nobody was optimistic, but then nobody talked about McCarthy's chances.

Boarding the plane for California the next day were Finney, Mc-Coy, and Norval Reece, a former ADA official from Pennsylvania who had helped manage the McCarthy effort there and who would handle scheduling. Reece had taken the position on two conditions, that he and he alone be in charge of McCarthy's schedule and that any commitment, once made, be kept. The group was determined to put the campaign in fighting trim. Traveling first class, they discovered Curtis Gans (apparently flying to California to conclude his campaign affairs) in the tourist section, and Finney went back to talk with him.

Finney had contradictory evidence. Gans, though a good political intelligence, was said to be an inexperienced administrator who had difficulty delegating authority. Some thought he was more interested in preserving the integrity of the movement than trying to elect the candidate. Others believed in Gans' leadership and contribution to the campaign, and in this group were Clark and Abigail McCarthy, who had urged Finney to pull Gans back in. Though he would later discover that the candidate did not always agree with his wife, Finney thought she spoke for him now. Most important, Finney was affected by the news stories claiming the McCarthy campaign was being taken over by Humphrey forces, which Gans' departure could only strengthen. After talking with Finney on the plane, Gans rejoined the campaign, and Finney and Gans held a press conference in San Francisco to say so. Gans would be in charge of "political operations," although, in California, he was to remain in the south because the northern California McCarthyites were intensely hostile to the national staff. In Oregon, the manager would be left alone unless he made a major blunder.

The manager there was satisfied with the progress. Relations between the local people and out-of-staters had been almost ideal. The local scheduling and advance work had been put under the direction of Blaine Whipple—in Oregon, at least, McCarthy would be scheduled by someone who knew the state. Whipple was helped by an imaginative though excitable law student from Yale, Steve Cohen, while Bob Terry, a national staffer, ran the advance group. It consisted of over a dozen young men, and when they had lost their rough edges (one rented McCarthy's suite at a downstate hotel two weeks before the candidate was scheduled to arrive and lived there with his girl friend), they were as good as anything Kennedy could put in the field.

The campaign was like a science-fiction monster, growing uncontrollably. I would discover a new group had materialized from nowhere, set up shop in the headquarters, and had a sign out like: LABOR FOR MCCARTHY, or MCCARTHY FARM BUREAU; or a black group, headed by Bob Slaughter and Skip Bracken, which had organized despite the candidate's strictures on the subject. One day I happened to open a door to a tiny room. I was facing two young men sitting at a table which consisted of two sawhorses and a board, on which two candles burned. There was no other illumination. Incense smoldered.

"Who the hell, please, are you?"

"We are the transportation bureau," they chimed.

Horrified, I looked at the wall. There was a large chart, topped by a skull and crossbones. It was a very bloody chart, with space designated for deaths, hospitalizations, minor injuries, damaged vehicles, and lost vehicles. I was appalled to see there had already been, without my knowledge, several accidents, one hospitalization, and several "missing" rented cars, a few of which were never found. "Nothing to worry about," the transportation bureau assured me. I left, issuing strict instructions: the press was not to be admitted to this room.

When it came to charts, I was usually an advocate. Great charts, lots of them, mounted on walls and drawn on blackboards, with the names of Congressional Districts, cities or wards, with numbers and symbols, gave the impression that the campaign was molded, sculptured, presided over by intelligence, invincible in its sweep. I believed in openness—what was there to hide, except the absence of money?—and anybody could penetrate the inner sanctums. One day I saw a familiar face spying on the charts.

He was a top Kennedy dog, William vanden Heuvel, the Kennedy campaign manager in Oregon and, like myself, also from New York. With him was another Kennedy luminary, Herb Shmerz. Scandalizing my staff, not for the last time, I invited the two into my office. We bantered. "Why won't Kennedy debate our man?" "I'll debate you instead." "I'll debate *you* if Kennedy will debate McCarthy." "Not unless the Humphrey campaign manager is on the platform, too." Vanden Heuvel became serious. "Don't you think we should get together? Wouldn't it be a crime if we only succeeded in electing Humphrey?" "Who gets together with whom? Will you come over if McCarthy wins in Oregon?" "Surely," he said, with an expression that said not a chance for poor old McCarthy. He went on: election night in Indiana not a single McCarthyite came to Kennedy headquarters to offer congratulations. It wasn't gentlemanly. I assured vanden Heuvel that I would come to offer congratulations in the event of a defeat. I was satisfied to let it go at that. I liked vanden Heuvel but did not want to tell him about my feeling, growing slowly but inexorably, that McCarthy would win in Oregon.

Some days gloom filled the headquarters, thick as smoke, making it hard to remember the fun had ever been there. What occasioned the deepest gloom in Oregon were the Kennedy attacks on McCarthy's voting record, the "smear sheets," as the McCarthyites called them. They were reprints of ads in California student newspapers, sponsored by one or another *ad hoc* committee, and the Kennedy forces in Oregon and all over the country denied official responsibility for them. Steve Smith, Kennedy's brother-in-law and campaign manager, later told me that the Kennedy leadership was not responsible for the attacks.

Unlike 1964, when we did attack Keating's voting record, it was our judgment that an attack on McCarthy's record should be kept out of the campaign, and the attacks that did occur were not supported by anyone on top of the campaign. But in a volunteer effort you can't control everyone. Had it been our attack we would have done a better job.

Still, it was possible to get a copy of the smear sheets by asking for one at Kennedy headquarters. The pattern of distribution of the charges which appeared in New York, Nebraska, Indiana, Washington, California, and Oregon strongly suggested an organized effort, which in turn suggested that while some Kennedy leaders were undoubtedly not involved a few may have been.

Kennedy himself did not deny the validity of the charges; in Oregon, for instance, he told a group of rabbis that they should study the record and judge for themselves. McCarthy was convinced that the Kennedys were trying to create "expanding doubt" about him, as he put it, and he was deeply upset because no prominent Democrat stood up for him. "If they can do this to me, they can do it to any member of Congress," he remarked. The smears showed, he said, that Bobby "was unfit to be President."

For a time McCarthy's campaign was collecting evidence—Kennedy had been accused of such tactics before, in his Senate campaign against Keating—for a court case against the Kennedy campaign, but the plan was dropped. It was hard to prove falsehood in the gray area the charges covered, and unless the McCarthy forces could win, and speedily, there seemed no point in giving the accusations still more publicity.

The charges were, in fact, partially true. McCarthy *had* missed a key vote to invoke cloture and permit the Civil Rights Act of 1968 to pass. If the Senate voted down cloture by a narrow margin, McCarthy would have had a heavy responsibility. He *was* guilty of voting against a reduction in the oil-depletion allowance, *did* have a poor attendance record in recent years, to cite just a few of the "facts" listed. The first target of the charges was college students. The attacks were supposed to prove that McCarthy was a tarnished idol. They succeeded, too, for many questions were asked and it became increasingly difficult to mount the student canvass drives. I was particularly depressed because the charges seemed to neutralize the students who had been so long in turning on.

Of course, the Oregon staff issued detailed rebuttals. McCarthy's attendance record had dropped in 1967 and 1968 because he was campaigning. He had usually voted in favor of reductions in the oil-depletion allowance but he favored review of depletion allowances for the whole mineral industry—to single out oil, he felt, was a purely political gesture, a genuflection to liberals who love to hate Texas oil millionaires. He had broken a heavy campaign schedule to get to Washington in time to vote for imposing cloture, but the vote lost and Majority Leader Mansfield was unable to file for another vote until after the weekend. McCarthy returned to the New Hampshire campaign trail. On Monday he flew back to Washington. A Senator tried to call McCarthy to warn him of the vote but the lines were busy and his staff procrastinated. The vote was close. This time it won—and the minute the vote was in Vice-President Humphrey banged down the gavel. McCarthy had finally gotten word but he walked in three minutes too late. "I've sat in the gallery and watched I suppose a hundred votes," said Washington civil-rights lawyer Joseph Rauh, "but I've never seen a time when the vote wasn't held for a Senator known to be in the building. If necessary the Senators stall for each other. This time none did. I think the Humphrey crowd was deliberately getting Gene."

The denials were boring to read and difficult to digest. They sounded defensive. They made McCarthy appear fallible, a sin in American politics. In the heat of the campaign, the truth was too difficult to communicate—McCarthy, doubtless, was not a "perfect" Senator. A Senator makes several hundred legislative decisions a year and not all of them will suit everybody. In the complicated judgments and compromises that went into the votes, he had probably made mistakes, even by his standards, as all Senators had. It would not help to say this or to point out that the leading figures in the National Committee for an Effective Congress and the Americans for Democratic Action, the principal liberal groups watching Congress, supported McCarthy, not Kennedy. The bark of the underdog would have been heard in an announcement that McCarthy had voted the same way Kennedy had in twenty-two out of twenty-nine key issues since 1965.

So, while the respected Howard Morgan went before Oregon television cameras to denounce Kennedy tactics, I was sure that simple denials would not be enough. I had had the experience of appearing, since there was no one else, as McCarthy's representative before leading members of the Portland Jewish community. (It says something about the balance of power that the other side sent Ted Kennedy to talk to the same men.) Would McCarthy send Phantom Jets to Israel? the Jews wanted to know. I assured them, not wishing to commit the candidate, that a President McCarthy would certainly not stand by idle if . . . True peace could be obtained in the Middle East, the Senator had said, only if there was a broader agreement with the Soviet Union. The gentlemen pressed on. What about the voting record? I learned I had to do more than say that the charges were untrue.

If I were to say later to vanden Heuvel that it had been a clean fight, and vanden Heuvel were to agree, I was sincere. Politics was simply tough. The manager knew that anti-Kennedy feeling in Oregon was strong. The Gallup poll said that many, fairly or not, considered Kennedy opportunistic, immature, ambitious, trading on his brother's reputation, a schemer, and so on, and in Oregon anti-Kennedy feeling was especially strong. Kennedy had aroused animosity by what was said to be his highhanded treatment of Oregon labor leaders and of the mayor of Portland some years before. There was no difficulty collecting a group of people prepared to vent their feelings on the air. The Oregonians recorded commercials, played many times on the radio, in which housewives, a doctor, a lawyer, and a businessman detailed the reasons why they would not vote for Kennedy.

The week following the Nebraska primary the candidate finally arrived in Oregon. The countryside pleased him, the people were more liberal than in the Midwest, and for once he had a solid organization behind him.

He had been humbled in Nebraska and Indiana into accepting a campaign organization, even though he may have still believed he could handle it alone. Norval Reece, arriving in California to discover that the candidate, typically, had two packed schedules, in Oregon and California, for the same day—May 23—ably began cutting through the underbrush that hindered McCarthy's movements. "I inherited a lot of taboos which turned out to be false," Reece said. "Zoo trips, motorcades, even airport rallies. Ghettos. Hoopla. The Joey Bishop show. It was true that on some days he vetoed anything, but, with McCarthy, you waited until he was more receptive. He was a cooperative candidate who did ninety per cent of what I reviewed with him. He wouldn't suggest hoopla and rallies, for instance, but he would do them. He liked the big crowds, though he didn't like the preoccupation of the press with the trappings of a campaign rather than the content. He would do anything if he felt it was valid and important." [1]

[1] There were those who said McCarthy wasn't campaigning hard, and even the candidate said he might be guilty of "acedia"—sloth. This was his May schedule:

May 1. Columbus, Bedford, Madison, Evansville, Indiana and Louisville, Kentucky
  2. Evansville, Vincennes, Gary and Fort Wayne, Indiana
  3. Fort Wayne, Kokomo and Indianapolis, Indiana
  4. Scottsbluff, Nebraska
  5. Crawsfordville, Lafayette and South Bend, Indiana
  6. Richmond, Indiana
  7. Indianapolis, Indiana
  8. Grand Island, Hastings and Lincoln, Nebraska
  9. Omaha, Nebraska
  10. Portland, Pendleton, Oregon, and Sacramento, California
  11. Fresno, Los Angeles and San Diego, California (cont. on p. 162)

Reece and the team in Oregon had independently reached the conclusion that McCarthy should not try to campaign all over the state as Rockefeller had done in 1964, demonstrating energy and concern by visits to boondock and berg—as Kennedy was again attempting. The mood of Oregon in 1968 was not as it was in 1964. People were serious and frowned on ventures that smacked of the circus, though McCarthy, engulfed in a yellow Mae West, would paddle a canoe in the Willamette River and make the cover of *Life*. McCarthy stayed almost entirely in the tricounty area around Portland and in the Willamette River Valley, where the vote was. It would still be a McCarthy-style campaign: "It's downbeat because that's deliberate," the candidate said.

It's not hard to turn them on, to turn the heat up, you know. But I thought it better to play it this way because it makes a contrast with the others. Maybe when we come to fight the Republicans we might open it up a little. I don't necessarily mind the motorcade situation, but speeches and so on have to be tempered to the audience.

---

12. McCook, Kearney and Lincoln, Nebraska
13. Nebraska City, Beatrice, Omaha and Lincoln, Nebraska
14. Lincoln, Nebraska
15. Aberdeen, Brookings and Sioux Falls, South Dakota, and Minneapolis, Minnesota
16. Tallahassee, Jacksonville, Orlando and Tampa, Florida
17. Miami, Florida
18. Washington, D.C.
19. New York City
20. Portland, Oregon, and San Francisco, California
21. Klamath Falls, Coos Bay, Corvallis and Portland, Oregon
22. San Francisco and Riverside, California
23. Ontario and Los Angeles, California
24. San Francisco and Eugene, Oregon
25. Eugene, Salem and Portland, Oregon
26. Portland and Medford, Oregon
27. Portland
28. Chico, Eureka and Sacramento, California, and Portland, Oregon
29. Stockton, Concord and San Francisco, California
30. San Francisco and Los Angeles, California
31. San Diego and Long Beach, California

Still, in Oregon, there was a difference: the self-confidence of the candidate, perhaps. *He liked big crowds.* How else can a politician—and politics is part profession, part trade, part artistry—measure the impact, even the meaning, of his words except by the size and enthusiasm of the audience? Could his own political emotions be roused by a handful of unresponsive listeners? Can we imagine Pericles in Wabash? Brutus in Kearney? Demosthenes in Gary? If McCarthy did not empathize with the crowd he lost enthusiasm. "He's an honest man," said a television reporter in all seriousness. "If he doesn't feel like giving a good speech he doesn't give one." In Oregon the audiences were large—on his first day in the state, in Portland after a good job by the advance staff, he outdrew Kennedy, who had campaigned in the same shopping center, for the first time—the crowd was with him. So he began to open up, and the crowds became steadily more responsive. Only one element was missing—a unifying theme.

He found it, in a fashion that tells much about American politics. It happened on May 21, on the campaign plane from Klamath Falls to Coos Bay when McCarthy gave a combined interview before portable cameras to Jack Cole of Metromedia Television; E. W. Kenworthy of the *New York Times*; and Harry Kelly of the Associated Press. Cole asked the candidate a few standard questions about progress in Oregon, and then the important question: What would McCarthy do if he lost Oregon and California? Would he support Humphrey or Kennedy? "I never expected an answer," Cole said afterward. "Certainly not that he would acknowledge that he might lose." Nevertheless, McCarthy's anger at Kennedy for the attacks on him was clear to Cole, who once again, having rephrased the question, tried to coax McCarthy into saying to whom he might throw his support if he were in effect out. Finally, McCarthy dropped a thin veil of a hint that he might support Humphrey—*if* he changed his position on the war.

The key part of the text was:

COLE: Senator, is what you are saying then, that you anticipate a possible change in position on Vietnam by Humphrey?

McCARTHY: Well, am I supposed to answer that one? I thought I wasn't supposed to. I don't think—it is not impossible —if peace negotiations proceed he might even re-evaluate his position or reassess it as other politicians have been reassessing on other matters. I don't see that reassessment is necessarily out of order.

COLE: Is that a condition precedent [*sic*] for your endorsement of Hubert Humphrey, if you drop out?

McCARTHY: Well, I would think his position with reference to the war would influence very much what my attitude toward him as a candidate may be.

This statement was consistent with his belief and feelings. He had known Humphrey for a long time—E.J.M.–H.H.H. says a silver plate on the telephone in his study, a present from the Vice-President—and, if his choice was to be judged on personalities, McCarthy would have preferred his friend Hubert, but, as he kept saying, only *if* he changed his position on the war. For the candidate was still a man of issues and, as he said later on, he could have swallowed Kennedy if his Vietnam position was acceptable and Humphrey's was not. All things being equal, though, he preferred Humphrey.

It was an honest answer but the full reasoning, evidently, was difficult to communicate in a noisy airplane. The reporters were searching for news and the "ifs" got buried in their zest for headlines—McCarthy was edging to Humphrey—though the three who filed were careful to say that he had "indicated" or "hinted" his support. Within a half hour after the plane landed in Coos Bay the story was on the radio. It brought a volcanic reaction within the campaign. To suggest the likelihood of defeat was discouraging. While feelings were strong about Kennedy, he was still a dove; and if McCarthy was about to embrace Humphrey, then the stories about the Finney connection with the Humphrey camp had new significance. Eugene McCarthy was selling out! There were immediate threats of mass resignations.

While Pierre Salinger was trying, unsuccessfully, to buy the Metromedia film for Bobby's campaign, McCarthy's immediate reaction was to pooh-pooh the importance of the whole thing. This proved impossible, and next his press secretary said that McCarthy's remarks had been off the record, though made in full view of Cole's television cameras. Finally, McCarthy tried to say that what the reporters said he said was not what he said. It was not enough.

McCarthy spoke that night in Corvallis about the processes that had led to the American involvement in Vietnam, especially the military role. "We must be on our guard lest militarism become really institutionalized in this country, and no longer accountable to public judgment and public will." At the very end of the speech McCarthy repeated a remark he had made, without fuss ensuing, earlier in the campaign. He said that better educated people would vote for him, not Kennedy.

The Kennedys quickly replied that McCarthy was an intellectual snob. (As it happened, the Kennedy ads to this effect may have backfired, encouraging people to vote for McCarthy to prove they were highbrow.)

The candidate appeared to have made two first-class errors on the same day, and on the plane back to Portland that night the talk was about the speech McCarthy was to deliver at the Cow Palace in San Francisco the next evening.

McCarthy's two young speech writers, Paul Gorman and Jeremy Larner, did not normally offer gratuitous opinions on the candidate's conduct, but this time, thinking about the Humphrey statement, Gorman said, "You'll blow it, Senator." Gorman, slight and quick-talking, thought that McCarthy must push forcefully to separate himself from Kennedy and Humphrey. Gorman had worked for Kennedy in 1964 and had been the staff man for a group of liberal Congressmen. He had been torn when Kennedy entered, but stayed with McCarthy because the Minnesota Senator had set the events of 1968 in motion. Like many, he was also "fascinated" by the candidate. Since then, Gorman had been increasingly down on Kennedy, who, it seemed, was moving steadily to the right on Vietnam and other issues, while McCarthy was slowly emerging as the left-wing Democratic candidate. McCarthy, Gorman advised, must make clear that he and he alone was free from the institutions of government which had impelled the U.S. into the Vietnam war. He must attack Humphrey and tie Vietnam to the U.S. ghettos. McCarthy, who had had a similar suggestion from Finney and Morgan, agreed.

Gorman stayed up all night with the speech and Larner was still typing revisions in a cab taking him to the campaign plane in the morning. McCarthy's Cow Palace speech attacked Kennedy and Humphrey alike, though McCarthy slurred the remarks on Humphrey, suggesting that he found them distasteful. Vietnam, he said,

> is no accident—no departure from otherwise sound diplomacy. It was the consequence of policies which have long been the principal guidelines for American policy in the world. . . . America will need leadership whose independence from the errors of the past is indisputable . . . [It] must be leadership with no old policies to defend, nor failures for which to apologize.
>
> During the early 1960s Senator Kennedy played a prominent role in formulating policies which resulted in disastrous adventures. Those policies were not merely the product of specific misjudgments. They grew from a systematic misconception of America and its role in the world. . . .
>
> The same assumptions, institutions, and leaders found in the past three years a new champion in Vice-President Humphrey. At the very time when American foreign policy grew more disastrous, Vice-President Humphrey became its most ardent apologist. Not merely did he defend the war; he defended every assumption which produced the war—America's moral mission in the world, the great threat from China, the theory of monolithic Communist conspiracy, the susceptibility of political prob-

lems to militaristic solutions, and the duty to impose American idealism upon foreign cultures.

All these myths—so damaging in their consequences—have had the enthusiastic support of Vice-President Humphrey. And those who sought in the best American tradition to question those policies were subject all too often to his ridicule and scorn.

McCarthy emerged from this speech with a central issue of his campaign fully elaborated. He repeated the theme before a tremendous audience in the Portland Coliseum the Saturday evening before the election, and its enthusiasm was almost frightening; the campaign had begun, indeed, to look like a crusade. McCarthy then did a half-hour television show—the time had been bought by the McCarthyites and an invitation sent to Robert Kennedy to appear with McCarthy; a letter of refusal was brought to me by vanden Heuvel—and then McCarthy went back to his hotel.

The campaign had been unable to afford de luxe accommodations. McCarthy and his entourage were staying at the Congress, a clean, simple hotel, while the Kennedys camped at the luxurious Benson, a half dozen blocks down the street. Returning to the Congress, McCarthy was joined by Robert Lowell, a big man inclined to morose expressions, who had been with the candidate frequently since New Hampshire. Lowell's role, he told a reporter, was to provide a human contact for the candidate. A leading novelist who watched candidate and poet together was convinced that Lowell brought a change in McCarthy. Around Lowell, McCarthy was inclined to show off.

It had been one of the most successful evenings of the campaign and McCarthy wanted to relax. Out loud he read a description of a wolverine which he planned to use as the basis for a poem on politics. While speech writers, press aides, and others waited in the hall, McCarthy and Lowell discussed the poem. The phone rang. It was James Reston of the *New York Times,* who wanted to interview the candidate. "That Presbyterian," McCarthy said. "Well, I guess I have to see him."

He did not put on his jacket or ask anyone to leave the room. Reston sat around awhile, getting nowhere and evidently unhappy, and then he asked for a staff car to take him to the Benson. Those in the room smiled. Staff car? This wasn't the Kennedy campaign. Reston was advised to take a cab. After Reston departed, McCarthy remarked, "Oh, well, he's for Humphrey."

McCarthy was back at work on the poem with Lowell when Peter, Paul, and Mary arrived. They had been campaigning hard and, for them, McCarthy put on his jacket. Peter, Paul, and Mary had written a ballad, "Vote for Gene McCarthy," and now sang it, while McCarthy and Lowell began discussing it favorably, line by line. Then Lowell read some of his own work. McCarthy seemed moved.

About one a.m. most of the guests departed and the staff, eager to talk business, rushed in the door. McCarthy ushered them out in a few minutes and soon he was back working on the poem.

Kennedy, meanwhile, was campaigning furiously by train, stopping at small and large towns alike on a line which had not carried passengers for years. Fully a week before the event, I was told by a Kennedyite that Bobby would do something spectacular "that pertains to water." I waited apprehensively. Then, walking down an ocean beach, surrounded by reporters, Kennedy suddenly stripped to his shorts and plunged into the Pacific. It was daring, heroic, but Oregonians never swim there till late summer because of the cold water and the tides.

The Kennedy emphasis on the spectacular seemed to the McCarthyites the wrong tactic for the state, and the McCarthy stress on local participation and organization was beginning to show. Our campaign was ubiquitous in Oregon. The student canvassers—perhaps two thousand of them, from Montana, Idaho, California, and Washington, as well as Oregon—had not come out in the same profusion as in other states, slowed by final exams and the Kennedy charges. If a crusade it was to be, it had to be an adult one. A doctor in the town of John Day, population 1500, set up a headquarters and bought a billboard; in Baker a woman opened a McCarthy headquarters in a tent. Serious efforts were under way in communities of older people, Oregon having one of the highest concentrations of people over sixty-five in the country. There were Salmon Fishermen for McCarthy, cake sales, art shows, a lightplane canvass, mobile units, and MAKE THE GENE SCENE and MC-CARTHY IS A GROOVY TRIP signs—the broad base is indicated by the contributions. Hundreds of Oregonians poured money into the campaign, in addition to contributions from Washington and money arriving directly from McCarthy groups over the country. The official Oregon campaign expenditure report reveals almost no local Kennedy financial support.

According to the report, McCarthy outspent Kennedy in Oregon, about $350,000 to $290,000. McCarthy local contributions more than made up the difference. Since many bills were paid from Washington after the Oregon campaign, the final McCarthy total was probably $500,000, while the true Kennedy figure was surely higher than the reported one as well. The big McCarthy money was spent on advertising and almost entirely in the closing days of the campaign.

Some weeks before, considerable time had been reserved on television and radio. (It is true that the law demands equal time for candidates, but it does not specify when or whether the media must sell it to candidates at all.) Each day, inspecting the bank accounts, I would cancel the time for the following day, and I continued to do this for weeks, grinding my teeth as Kennedy ads filled the air. With Finney governing the financiers, money at last flowed in quantity to thirsty Oregon. Now the McCarthyites mounted an intensive media barrage. Our television—there were still no packaged half-hour campaign shows except "All the Way to Jerusalem," an excellent film on the students by Eleanor and

Frank Perry who made *David and Lisa*—featured the candidate on issues, while the newspaper ads developed the campaign themes.

Political advertising tries to accomplish several things at once. The McCarthy ads, prepared with the advice of Bill Nee and a Portland advertising agency, Bachman Ferris Associates, tried to strike motifs which would be appealing in Oregon. More and more, the candidate was emerging as a loner, his campaign a triumph of individuality. The ads were headed ONE MAN HAD THE COURAGE; MAN VS. MACHINE; IT DIDN'T JUST HAPPEN—PEOPLE STARTED IT; PARTY PROS DON'T UNDERSTAND HIM—ONLY PEOPLE DO. They spoke of maturity—"The sure and rational voice," or, "Only one man has what it takes to unify America." One asked, the words superimposed on a photo of McCarthy alone in a field of cobblestones, DO YOU HAVE WHAT IT TAKES TO WALK WITH EUGENE MCCARTHY?

The ads tried to contrast Kennedy and McCarthy and often challenged Kennedy to a debate. The debate issue was extremely dangerous for Kennedy and, even among his own staff, controversial. Robert Kennedy, faced with WHY WON'T YOU DEBATE? posters at every stop, was noticeably defensive as he explained again and again that Humphrey had to be on the platform, too. McCarthy tracked him on this issue like an Indian pursuer, even breaking off a day of Oregon campaigning to race to San Francisco, where he hoped Kennedy would appear on the same platform with him before the AFL-CIO. Though Robert Kennedy's name had been printed on the dinner menus, Ted Kennedy came. Finally, McCarthy caught up with Kennedy at the Portland zoo.

It was the Sunday before election day. McCarthy was walking toward the terminus of a miniature railroad which carried passengers from the arboretum to the Portland zoo when he heard that Kennedy was alighting from the train. McCarthy began to walk faster. Kennedy, hearing that McCarthy was approaching—they were now fifteen yards apart—said, "Is he? That's too bad." He jumped into his car and said to the driver, "Let's get going." From the crowd came the cry, "Coward, coward."

The Kennedy forces were far from pessimistic—their own polls showed Kennedy ahead—but their campaign was plainly losing ground, and the day before the election they thought they had found an issue. Kennedy's own strategy had been to ignore McCarthy altogether, not even to mention his name, but his commercials explained that McCarthy was no longer a serious contender —a vote for him was a vote for Humphrey. Annoyed by this, the McCarthyites answered with a postcard mailing and radio spots that appeared the day before the primary. Citing national polls, the ads said that McCarthy could beat Nixon but Kennedy could not. If you wanted a Democrat in the White House you had better vote for Gene McCarthy.

Now Pierre Salinger was charging the McCarthy forces with fraud. One of the commercials used poll results which, unfortunately, had not been thoroughly checked and had been superseded by another poll, favorable to Kennedy. An honest mistake, this commercial was promptly pulled from the air but the other, whose poll information favorable to McCarthy was valid, remained. Salinger then held a press conference to air the Kennedy grievance, but it was too late to matter.

The NBC-Quayle poll predicted Kennedy would win narrowly in Oregon, but the McCarthy manager put more faith in the gambling odds at Las Vegas and the Waterhouse postcard poll—also called the gamblers' poll, since gamblers used it—both of which indicated McCarthy was running stronger than generally predicted. The NBC local outlet predicted a Kennedy victory on election eve and then, at four p.m. on election day, the prediction based on interviews with people leaving the polling places, the station claimed a Kennedy victory. A Polish reporter filed a story saying Kennedy had won. The tension was palpable at McCarthy headquarters that night—a defeat here in a state with a relatively homogeneous population, with no strong minority groups, after a well-organized effort and a superb performance by the candidate, would be insurmountable. "There will be no excuses," I told the press. A few minutes after the polls had closed CBS said that McCarthy had won, hands down. The building shook. The manager kissed his wife, hugged Eve Bachman, his Oregonian assistant, and pounded people over the shoulders. The jubilation from California McCarthy headquarters should have broken the long-distance wire. McCarthy took 45 per cent of the vote, to Kennedy's 39 and Johnson's 12. Gamely and ruefully, Kennedy said, "I'm taking an entirely new look at my organization. I'm going to send Freckles home." But nobody from Kennedy headquarters came to offer congratulations.

8 | California: a Denouement

There was exhilaration after Oregon, almost an alchemical change. The antiroyalist, antiestablishment rebel brigades had beaten Kennedy! It was possible to imagine that our Cromwell would sit in the White House.

Oregon had proved the depth of anti-Kennedy sentiment—the convention could not risk Kennedy, the McCarthyites reasoned. McCarthy would be the natural compromise candidate. Of course, the logic was precarious, for to remain in serious running McCarthy could not lose by much but he could not win by much, either—within the campaign a few people actually hoped that McCarthy would lose California by, say, four percentage points (the actual result) so that Kennedy would not get out. McCarthy would beat him in New York—of that the McCarthyites were confident.

Such were the dreams before the shots in the night, and the question California was supposed to solve was whether America was Indiana or Oregon. Oregon was homogeneous in population, liberal, educated; Indiana was the reverse. The Kennedy forces were claiming that Oregon wasn't representative. There wasn't enough poverty or racial strife. California, then, would have to prove whether there was a powerful national constituency for McCarthy, perhaps a new voting class.

Its outlines could be vaguely discerned though perhaps it was a chimera. It was now clear that McCarthy should not look to the rural or farm vote, for all his knowledge about hog calling. His appeal was to the educated voter, to those millions American universities had been pumping out since World War II. He seemed to have great strength among the Jews, as Stevenson had had, and the academic community was united behind him. At cocktail parties in the suburbs and exurbs, where some of the largest concentrations of people existed, McCarthy could inundate any Democratic and probably Republican opponent. Here, one could almost scent the difference between the McCarthyite and Kennedyite. The Kennedy supporter was practical, hardheaded, striving. The McCarthy person seemed, on the whole, somewhat to the idealistic left of him. McCarthy appeared to be drawing out not just the anti-Vietnam constituency but a progressive vote which was eager for change but leary of means that employed traditional uses of power.

From the political view, the trouble with white liberal Democrats is that they are easily splintered and factionalized. Kennedy thought he could count on the support of at least three groups in California, part of the labor movement, such as the United Auto Workers, the Negroes, and the Mexican-Americans. McCarthy, without blocs, had to build support as he went.

The candidate's position on the California ballot would be determined by the order in which petitions bearing 13,467 signatures were presented on filing day. Lying low to fool the opposition, the McCarthy people, largely organized by the California Democratic Council, held 500 petition-signing cocktail parties throughout the state on filing eve in March. The petitions could not be signed until March 14, and so between midnight and nine a.m. the McCarthyites—there was even a Paul Revere horseback petition campaign in Beverly Hills—collected 30,000 signatures. The result was that primary-election day radio commercials would say (electioneering on election day is permitted in California), "The first name on the Democratic ballot is Eugene McCarthy. The first man to give politics back to the people. Vote for Eugene McCarthy today."

Clever the California McCarthyites evidently were, but unable to suppress their ideological differences. What seemed to some, at any rate, as potential votes for a peace candidate had gone off and organized on their own—as the Peace and Freedom Party, with Eldridge Cleaver as candidate. (There had apparently been some chance to forestall this, but McCarthy's staff had been sensitive about radical support.) The northern McCarthyites battled with the southern ones, and regular Democrats who had come over were at odds with the California Democratic Council because it was thought to be left-wing and diffusing its energies by supporting candidates for other offices, some of whom were backing Kennedy.

Because of its size, the state had been organized as two separate campaigns, north and south. The northerners, headed by Gerald Hill and G. W. (Joe) Holsinger, would permit the out-of-staters to campaign only in a few counties where they were weak in local supporters. Gans brought the bulk of the four hundred national staffers who eventually arrived in California to the south, a place of internal complications and hidden wars. One McCarthy national staffer in San Fernando Valley recalls that he had to clear a decision with fifteen different California factions.

For their part, the Californians were sometimes stunned by the antics of the McCarthy national staff. At the Westwood-Los Angeles headquarters, for instance, a meeting called for nine p.m. was held at three a.m., with the staffers killing the hours playing volleyball in the enormous office—without a net.

Many of the out-of-state campaigners slept on the headquarters floor or worked all night and slept on the warm beach during the day. Naturally, they resented the older staff people for living in the luxury of the Beverly Hilton, where coffee cost sixty cents a cup. Indeed, the campaign was a place of endless contrasts, with staggering hotel bills alongside a treasury so empty that Blair Clark had to make a sizable personal contribution to keep operations going at all. (Clark didn't tell the candidate until after Chicago.)

Idealism, sacrifice, pettiness, inefficiency existed side by side. Only in California would a marijuana pusher contribute half his weekly take to the campaign.

California was a campaign manager's nightmare. The ten thousand students recruited for McCarthy vanished like fish in the huge, unbroken sea of suburbs. It was plain that the usual McCarthy techniques would not win in this ocean of people. Everything had to be organized for publicity and visibility. For a one-hundred-dollar contribution a woman could have herself redone by the beauty editor of *Glamour* magazine, the papers said, or, if you were a really far-out McCarthy girl, you could enter a topless contest with the proceeds going to the candidate. It was a strange world.

The campaigners at Westwood decided to use Ricky-Ticky-Stickies, plastic transfers in the shape of flowers. They would be blue and white with GENE MCCARTHY printed across the center. The campaigners wanted $4000 worth of these. At an emergency midnight meeting, held in one of the financiers' de luxe suites at the Beverly Hilton, which the Westwood crowd called Xanadu, surrounded by canapés, club sandwiches, and real flowers, the McCarthy leaders solemnly discussed the pros and cons of spending four grand on plastic doodads. Gans and company won the fight and were proved right when national television came to shoot four coast-to-coast minutes of McCarthyites sticking Ricky-Ticky-Stickies on sunbathers at the beach.

There were the stars (no novelty here), the folk singers, like Phil Ochs and Tom Paxton, and the notables: Erich Fromm talking about radical humanism to suburbanites; Arthur Miller, Jules Feiffer, and William Styron (arriving together earlier in Oregon, the three had held the ultimate in whimsical non-press-conferences—Feiffer talked about his mother); Robert Lowell; Wilfrid Sheed; Vance Packard; Leonard Lewin (*"Iron Mountain Report"*); and Jason Epstein. Our writers were bigger than theirs, though they may have had the edge in stars. Is Robert Vaughn switching to Kennedy? It was fun, but to do any good it had to get in the papers or on television, which was the job of McCarthy's capable press secretary in California, Wally Bruner, now emcee of "What's My Line?"

To reach those madding millions, a tenth of the United States population, whose antennae sprout from San Diego to Sausalito and Newport Beach to Needles, would require television and a great deal of it. The McCarthyites proved skillful at finding shows on which the candidate could appear—for free—but political commercials were needed too. Finney was in possession of a voter-profile analysis of Californians which showed that while McCarthy was admired he was not considered aggressive and tough enough to be President. The negative "image" had to be counteracted. Werner Kramarsky had estimated that an all-out McCarthy effort in California would cost two and a half million dollars at least. But Kennedy could be expected to spend two dollars for every one McCarthy dollar, and besides, the McCarthy campaign was strapped.

One possible channel for funds opened and quickly closed. Finney argued that it was in everybody's interest not to let McCarthy get crushed in California. Kennedy would need the McCarthy votes at the convention, while Humphrey needed McCarthy to stop Kennedy. Indeed, Humphrey contributors, with permission from the Vice-President's camp, gave $50,000 to the McCarthy campaign, but the flow was stopped by the regular Democrats of California, who didn't like the idea of helping McCarthy.

After Oregon, Finney was determined to put the main McCarthy resources in California into television. The effort was to be marshaled and managed by David Garth, a Stevenson organizer in 1960 who now directed television for John Lindsay. Garth had also been the manager for the unsuccessful campaign for the New York City Civilian Review Board. A round, short, ebullient man in his late thirties who knew his own mind, Garth was a professional television man in noncampaign life. He brought with him other volunteers, like Daniel Melnick, a partner with David Susskind in Talent Associates, and Ruth Jones, a charming and experienced television time buyer. "Unless you've got a fortune to spend you don't want too many commercials," Garth said. "You want just a few good ones—like a woman's basic black."

Inspecting what television commercials the McCarthy forces had managed to assemble, Finney and Garth were certain these would not counter the negative impressions of the candidate. There was one half-hour documentary of McCarthy's life; they agreed that it could not be used—McCarthy was colored bright yellow. The fault was corrected, but when the McCarthy people bought a half hour for it in California the Kennedyites instantly tried to buy an adjacent half hour on the same station for *their* documentary, as if to contrast the wares. The Nees in Oregon had made some worthy short commercials but they featured the candidate answering man-on-the-street questions. Garth wanted something hotter.

He proceeded to shoot a group of spot commercials. A few showed scenes from the campaign, with the candidate in motion, while a voice said, "He has the courage to tell you" or "His courage is the kind we must have in the White House" or "This quiet man toppled the President. . . . It took unusual strength to do what McCarthy did." One featuring the actor Eddie Albert said that McCarthy had "guts." Another bore in on campaign posters of the three candidates fastened on a brick wall:

Shot of Humphrey poster
Election music under
This man wants to be President of the United States.
Qualifications?
Four years as apologist for an escalating war.
Four years as participant in forming the Johnson Administration's policies.
Four years of rising racial disorder and division.

Cut to Kennedy poster
This man also wants to be President.
Although he supported President Johnson for the job until the New Hampshire primary changed his mind.
He has a slight edge: the best financial political machine in the history of American politics.

Cut to McCarthy poster
And this man wants to be President.
His credentials?
He's fed up.
He's fed up with all the political opportunists who didn't speak up when they were needed.
He's fed up with a senseless war.
He's fed up with the rottenness in the cities and the causes of despair in the ghettos.
Are you fed up with these things too?
Vote for Eugene McCarthy.

The commercials were a switch from the usual picture of the issues-minded, professorial candidate. McCarthy suddenly looked tough and formidable, as indeed he was. Now the storm descended. Finney, only a few days before accused of being a Humphrey man, was excoriated for being hard on Humphrey. Some of the "astrologers"—as the campaigners called McCarthy's personal friends who constantly second-guessed the campaigners—felt that the Garth ads, using words like "guts" and "fed up," were not consistent with McCarthy's "image." The Nees, who were in charge of television for the campaign, and believed that the candidate should not be packaged, sent telegrams from Oregon forbidding the use of the commercials. But Garth was also in charge, and he put them on the air. "Amateurs!" he barked at the opposition. "You don't understand that commercials appear between 'Gunsmoke' and soap ads. No one remembers the words—it's the feel."

Garth was sufficiently disgusted by what he considered the un-professionalism of the McCarthyites that he swore never again to work for the campaign. But the controversies were suddenly suspended. Kennedy had agreed to debate!

California poured out for McCarthy its human riches. One day at a shopping center where 2000 had been expected, 15,000 came. McCarthy went in the wrong door and was pushed and jostled until he almost went over a balcony. Leaving, he was perched up on top of the back seat of an open convertible when the driver, seeing the crowd approach, put the car suddenly in gear and McCarthy flew nose first into the seat in front. Pulled and tugged, he was being received like a Kennedy.

He was also making a dramatic recovery in the polls. Once strong in the California polls, he had dropped to a low of fifteen points after Indiana. Now he was only a few points behind Kennedy in some polls, and one, the Mervyn Field poll, showed him to be the only Democrat leading all Republican prospects. He was gaining on Kennedy and he had found the rhythm of eloquence.

"My position," he insisted, "is the essence of conservatism." He was only asking his audience "to clear your vision, and clear your mind" to decide the country's fate. But when he spoke of what should be done, it was increasingly apparent that he was to the left of Kennedy. (Gun control—McCarthy advocated Federal registration but state enforcement—was one exception.)

The principal campaign issue was foreign policy. Both candidates agreed that Vietnam was consuming, tragically, the nation's energies and riches, but McCarthy had moved toward a total critique, toward examining the stance of a whole generation of national leaders who had held the world-wide American commitments, usually supporting the *status quo,* as necessary and inevitable. The assumptions that went into this judgment had escaped sustained and vigorous public scrutiny, he felt. He was concerned with sophisticated questions about government operations and the sort of men who are chosen for the key positions and why. When he spoke of removing the fence from the White House—he would not even *live* there, he joked—he meant that the fence of secrecy ought to be removed, the fence of overcaution should be torn down, the fence of timidity demolished. The nervous, high-powered style of American government was part of a "process" in which those engaged too often were really seeking power for themselves. His kind of Presidency would be "open." Part of this openness would be to give greater powers to the Cabinet, which in turn would engage in dialogue with the Congress and the people. He was a neo-Jeffersonian opposed to the coercive use of power and he was presenting the nation with the first serious political analysis it had heard in many years.

Some felt, perhaps correctly, that he failed in his obligation to articulate specific solutions possibly out of laziness. McCarthy argued that there were enough laws on the books—hadn't he voted for a bill which decreed that wheels must be round?—and while to others the difficulties lay in the area of enabling legislation to enforce laws, for McCarthy the peril was in the area of national spirit and will, in philosophy. He would advocate chopping the budget of the Department of Defense by fifteen billion dollars, using the money for the ghettos (here was a solid demarcation between McCarthy and the Republicans, whose ideas his own superficially resembled), he would urge that the ghetto dwellers depart their inner-city enclosures and move to the suburbs where jobs were, and that training, transportation, and housing be provided. He was a believer in integration, certainly, but he saw the race issue in terms of the common troubles of American life, whose "sameness and lack of variety" concerned him. He was not sure how to deal with racism; he would give the Negro full economic equality and then see what happened. In the end, he said, "You get down to the hard core of what is a man."

One of the most discouraging aspects of the McCarthy campaign was the difficulty of communicating McCarthy's views and record on civil rights and migrant labor to the minority groups, who, perhaps for reasons of their own, often seemed uninterested.

"Gene's stand," remarked the Negro leader and McCarthyite Hebert Reed, over the summer, "is perfectly adequate so long as he is willing to recognize that there is an intermediate stage before total integration in which there must be ghetto self-improvement, self-leadership, and so on. And he does see that. The man is good and great and honest, but he does not move as fast as the black community is accustomed to seeing politicians move. Kennedy has a head start in the ghettos and a better staff for working with the blacks." Kennedy also had more money, and both sides knew that to obtain endorsements of some black newspapers it was necessary to purchase advertising space—just as happens in some white papers.

The McCarthy forces worked hard in the California ghettos. In Watts alone they passed out 60,000 copies of a record of Martin Luther King praising McCarthy after Kennedy had announced. (He had praised Kennedy, too.) McCarthy was to meet with four of five black militants at a radio station in Los Angeles. The leader of the group, Ron Karenga, leaned back in his chair while waiting for McCarthy to show up and someone spotted a hidden microphone underneath it. They immediately suspected McCarthy people of having "bugged" the room but soon decided it was probably the station that had done it. When McCarthy arrived he spoke to them of "colonialism" in America. "He really turned them on," said twenty-five-year-old Massachusetts Institute of Technology graduate Tony Podesta. "He seemed to communicate better with the black radicals than with the liberals." Karenga liked him so much he did a few radio spots for the campaign and then accompanied McCarthy on a tour of Watts. The candidate had shed his reluctance to campaign in the ghettos—he seemed eager to go. On one occasion, returning to Los Angeles from a speech, he got word that Louis Lomax, the Negro writer, was about to endorse him in Watts. The thinking at the Beverly Hilton was that the press bus should be sent to Watts but not the candidate, because maybe the news of the endorsement was false—so much of the news arriving at headquarters was. McCarthy, however, went to Watts headquarters instantly, arriving before the reporters, and gaily answered the telephone. "McCarthy for President," he said. Meantime, no Lomax. Frantic calls went out all over Los Angeles and finally Lomax arrived to endorse McCarthy.

Courting the black vote was an extremely delicate, mysterious business involving complicated judgments of who—the black-power leaders or the moderates—was in charge; how much to believe of what various leaders said; how far to move toward the black position without violating the candidate's determination not to appeal to special interest groups. One evening at the Westwood headquarters the mimeograph team refused flatly to print an appeal which the leadership upstairs had prepared. They felt it was demagogic, and the result was a long midnight discussion between the mimeograph team and the campaign leaders about the literature. The mimeo people won—the candidate was later to say he agreed with them. Whatever it may have lacked, the McCarthy campaign was democratic.

Little by little, McCarthy made progress among the Negroes. The entire black Kennedy slate on the ballot was threatening to bolt to McCarthy. It had begun to look as though McCarthy would carry a sizable portion of the ghetto ballots—the indications, however, were wrong. Kennedy's margin of victory in California was the black and Mexican vote; for the latter McCarthy might have campaigned harder.

The Kennedy people were afraid of serious losses of strength among every segment of the California Democratic electorate. It was their turn to feel gloomy. Now, after Oregon, Robert Kennedy agreed to debate, although it meant revising his strategy which had called for a blackout on McCarthy. Each side was aware of advantages and disadvantages, and each agreed to the debate for its own reasons.

Kennedy had to reverse his decline in California. He had to dispel the belief that he was ambitious and ruthless. A debate would deprive McCarthy of a principal weapon, the taunt that Bobby wouldn't. But the risks for Kennedy were great. McCarthy was handsome on television, bigger, older, smooth, a strong debater. Still, there were some in the Kennedy camp who doubted whether McCarthy had the lust for the jugular.

For the McCarthyites the debate seemed a wonderful opportunity but not without danger. The candidate would have national as well as California exposure, and some believed that if McCarthy did a brilliant job he would win the Democratic nomination. But since McCarthy had asked for the debate, since he was still behind in the Presidential race, he must clearly win. A draw would have the net effect of a loss; a loss would be disaster. And McCarthy could lose. Kennedy, who would doubtlessly be drilled by his experts, with every nuance studied, was no slouch. The McCarthyites were fearful of the Kennedy team—they shared the view that the opposition was ruthless and capable of mischief. So there were deep discussions over such matters as who would sit in the control room and how to safeguard McCarthy's microphone so that it would not be fixed to make his voice sound odd.

The debate was scheduled for the Saturday afternoon before the election on a special edition of ABC's "Issues and Answers." (Kennedy had refused to let the debate be heard on all three networks.) McCarthy was unhappy because it was not to be precisely a debate—instead, three reporters, Frank Reynolds, Robert Clark, and William Lawrence, would ask questions of each candidate, and each would also be given an opportunity to rebut. By Friday evening, the McCarthy briefing team was getting ready. Led by Thomas B. Morgan, a group of a dozen people, working throughout the night, produced a document which purported to predict the questions the reporters would ask the panelists and in what order—as well as the answers. As it turned out, they were right on every question.

One item which greatly concerned the briefing team were the anti-Kennedy newspaper ads which, prepared in New York, had appeared in the California papers. Some of these ads were tough by McCarthy standards—"FOR SALE—THE PRESIDENCY OF THE UNITED STATES"—and one of them contained an embarrassing error. Though Finney was later held accountable for it, the ad had been read to someone else over the long-distance phone and the offending paragraph had slipped through. It said: "Kennedy was part of the original commitment. He participated in the decisions that led us to intervene in the Dominican Republic." Of course, Kennedy had not been in the Cabinet when that decision was made. The line could be costly to McCarthy, putting his veracity in doubt and throwing him on the defensive. Two responses were possible. One was simply to apologize, but the McCarthy semi-pros believed that politicians must never admit culpability. The second course, the one Finney urged, was for McCarthy to approach the line in the context of his campaign arguments. Kennedy had been a participant in the foreign-policy making *process* which had engaged America in the Dominican Republic and Vietnam.

On Saturday, the briefing papers in hand, Finney flew to San Francisco to meet McCarthy at the Hotel Fairmont. He was like a manager with his boxer—he wanted McCarthy to rest, work on the questions and the answers, and spend the afternoon alone, undistracted. He should be "up" for the bout. There had been already some intricate discussions about tactics, probing the mind and psyche of Kennedy. McCarthy was considered the better debater. He should start jabbing Kennedy from the start. At the beginning he might stand to shake hands, forcing Kennedy to do the same and contrasting the difference in height. He should be aggressive, mentioning the smearsheets and the wiretapping—the story that Kennedy as Attorney General had ordered a wiretap of Martin Luther King's phone had just broken. Kennedy would be thrown off balance. He might get riled, utter a harsh word; the important thing was to get him to appear less gentle, for the McCarthyites were certain Kennedy would come on soft.

McCarthy appeared to listen attentively to the briefing. He sat at a table in the middle of the room, carefully folding some of the sheets as he read, as though to be read again, dropping others on the floor. Finney left and later returned. He was disturbed by what he found.

For McCarthy appeared to be having an amiable afternoon. Lowell was there (the campaigners heard that Lowell opposed the debate). Lowell knew and liked Kennedy and had been to see him that morning, saying, "I feel like Rudolph Hess parachuted into Scotland." Kennedy had not been amused, but McCarthy was. So McCarthy was relaxing with friends before the big event, which was understandable, but Finney was instantly depressed. McCarthy, he feared, would lose his fighting edge.

Before McCarthy went to the studio a priest arrived to celebrate mass with the candidate in his suite. There was confusion outside the hotel. Two identical cars were waiting. The campaigners muttered that one had been placed there by Kennedy's jester, Dick Tuck, to rattle McCarthy. Then, driving over, McCarthy and Lowell played at rewriting a seventeenth-century verse in modern idiom. The car detoured briefly so that McCarthy could look at Alcatraz out in the bay. He arrived at KGO-TV, to find it besieged by supporters. There were few Kennedy signs to be seen. He went upstairs and Kay Nee made him up: colored make-up (a necessity on television), not grease (pores aren't right), a little light pancake around the mouth and the eyes. Don't try to transform the candidate—he's got to look the same on the street.

There were rooms adjacent to the studio for the press and guests, since only a press pool would be let into the studio. In the McCarthy guest room the places had been reserved primarily for the large contributors. Tension was such that some guests were tranquilizing themselves liberally with alcohol. For the first minutes of the debate McCarthy was strong, sharp, clear, dominating the ring. He backed Kennedy into a corner almost at once, saying that Kennedy had misrepresented his position on Vietnam, contradicting him with authority. Kennedy seemed to duck and hold. McCarthy broke free and was at him again. His hand went to his pocket—he was about to pull out the Kennedy attacks on his voting record, one thought, but the hand-to-pocket gesture was merely characteristic. Inexplicably to his eager campaigners, McCarthy now backed off, leaving Kennedy leaning on the ropes. Was it embarrassment over Kennedy's mention of the Dominican Republic ad? (McCarthy apologized.) Was he too much of a gentleman to bang away at Kennedy in public? Had the absurdity of perhaps settling the future Presidency of the United States on one program got to him? (But it had been McCarthy who said that debates were important among those whose positions were close, in order to illuminate the differences.) Had he, far more nervous than he seemed, clutched? Or had he (one could whisper it) merely grown bored? For his style became lackluster, almost tired. He hardly bothered to fight back when Robert Kennedy hit him below the belt—in a play for the law-and-order crowd—with a remark that McCarthy advocated moving ten thousand Negroes to white-backlash Orange County. Both men fought for the Jewish vote—Kennedy won that, too, with more pro-Israel mentions, one so obviously thrown in where it didn't fit that the studio audience laughed. For the rest of the hour they sparred, limply, with Kennedy increasingly dominating the camera, though McCarthy finished strong with his explanation of why he should be President. The only real winner seemed to be a popular show on another network.

The McCarthy amateurs were puzzled as they filed out of the suite. Our man had not shown all his stuff but he had been good enough and not made any serious mistakes and perhaps he had won on points. McCarthy himself, shaking hands in the hall, looked grim to the point of ravishment: one sensed that he was not happy with his performance. Finney, the manager, seemed bland. Afterward, however, he lost his aplomb. "He flubbed it! He flubbed it!"

Finney cried, pounding the seat of the cab with his fist. "Blew it! Threw it away! How can you get him elected?"

For Finney had been watching with a different set of eyes and ears. What mattered to him was not the individual debating scores but the over-all impression left by each candidate, which might, in the voter's cranium, take several days to settle. McCarthy had failed to undo the impression that he was not sufficiently strong and aggressive; perhaps he had even confirmed it. Kennedy *had* demonstrably succeeded in his goal, which was to dispel the aura of ruthlessness. McCarthy had failed to show significant differences between himself and Kennedy, and in the absence of a clear Mc-Carthy victory the bout had to be given to Kennedy by a big margin. It had been an important fulcrum, one of six or eight on which the fate of the McCarthy movement would balance.

The next morning McCarthy seemed to feel he had been too easy on Kennedy. He snapped at interviewers on a CBS-TV show who mentioned the voting record again. He appeared eager to move in hard, as he had not on Kennedy. He pressed the re-porters, Jimmy Breslin said, and left them hanging on the studio wall. That day, too, he struck back in a release in which he ac-cused Kennedy of "scare tactics" and "crude distortion" on the Orange County reference; Kennedy's Vietnam program, he said, would end the war no more than Johnson's. It was too late. The Kennedy forces made a phone survey which revealed that eighty to ninety per cent of the viewers believed Kennedy had won. The de-bate seemed to have turned California around.

This impression was borne out in the last two days, for McCarthy crowds appeared to have shrunk and, except for an en-thusiastic rally at Santa Monica, the steam had suddenly left the campaign. Kennedy's last-minute ads were against Humphrey—they warned the voters not to be misled by the Lynch slate, named after State Attorney General Thomas C. Lynch, which appeared uncommitted but was, in reality, composed of Humphrey supporters. They also attacked McCarthy as weak on the law-and-order issue. There was nothing to do but wait for the outcome.

CBS, according to Schoumacher, is still uncertain why its early election-eve prediction, 52 per cent for Kennedy, 39 per cent for McCarthy, was so far off the final count. Despite the gloomy look of things, the McCarthy forces were still optimistic at midnight. McCarthy was ahead in votes. Perhaps CBS was wrong, as the predictions had been all along. The candidate came down to the Beverly Hilton ballroom, said a few words to his followers, and went back upstairs via the hotel kitchen. An hour later, at the Ambassador ballroom, Kennedy took the same route. But now let us listen to Mary McGrory:

> Eugene McCarthy was sitting in his seventh-floor suite at the Beverly Hilton Hotel with his managers, drafting a congratulatory telegram to Sen. Robert Kennedy on his California primary victory when the news came.
>
> "I think," he had just said to Blair Clark and Thomas Finney, "that we could say 'fine' instead of 'splendid,' because I don't think the percentage will go that high."
>
> At that moment, there was a knock on the door. David Schoumacher, a reporter for CBS who had followed McCarthy since New Hampshire, came into the room.
>
> "Sen. Kennedy has been shot," he said.
>
> McCarthy and the others looked at him in total disbelief, and someone said, "You're kidding."
>
> Schoumacher said, "I'm not. I'll go back and get more."
>
> The Senator's wife and his two daughters, Ellen and Mary, came in from an adjoining room where they had been following the returns during an inconclusive evening. The other guests, too nervous to wait for the Los Angeles County returns, had drifted away.
>
> Schoumacher returned in a few minutes to say that Kennedy had been shot in the hip.

McCarthy, sitting in a chair in the corner, put his hands over his eyes, and then looked up.

"Maybe we should do it in a different way," he said. "Maybe we should have the English system of having the cabinet choose the president. There must be some other way."

The color of ash, McCarthy returned to the ballroom and told the campaigners to go home and pray. Upstairs, he said, "Bobby generated so much emotion that this could have happened."

Was he himself in some involuted sense responsible because he had goaded Bobby into the debate? No, the event fell somewhere between an awful accident and God. The next morning his campaigners went to Kennedy headquarters to help them sweep up. It was all they could do.

At seven-thirty on the morning after the shooting McCarthy, unshaven, wearing a bathrobe and with three hours' sleep, asked about Kennedy. "He's not going to make it," one of his campaigners said. McCarthy thought it would be better if he returned to Washington. On the way to the airport he went to the hospital where Kennedy lay. He asked the policemen leading his car not to use their sirens, but because of the traffic the police did anyway, right to the hospital door. "I heard they complained that when I did come to the hospital, I came with the sirens on," he said. "Well, when you get into that kind of response, why, you just figure it is best not to try to prove anything any more." He was embarrassed by the sirens and, after learning that Ted Kennedy and Ethel Kennedy were sleeping, he proceeded on his way.

Part IV | HUMPHREY

9 | McCarthy Summer

The candidate returning to Washington was a shaken man. He had not revered Kennedy in life, but he felt the shock, the outrage to national institutions now threatened by a pattern of political assassinations, the grief of Kennedy's family and friends. McCarthy had not been culpable of moral mistakes but he had permitted his campaign to turn toward conventional politics after Kennedy entered, and their rivalry in the primaries had raised the level of acrimony.

And what of his own political responsibilities and prospects? In the brief afterglow of New Hampshire, he thought he could beat Johnson in most of the primaries if Kennedy stayed out of the contests. If Kennedy hadn't come in until the summer, McCarthy said, "I think he probably would have been nominated." Not everyone agrees with him. But Kennedy had entered, and McCarthy's victory in Oregon had given him a chance of winning the Democratic nomination as a compromise or unity candidate. If neither could win the nomination, Kennedy and McCarthy together could have exerted a powerful force on the Vietnam plank—"I think we would have effected it," McCarthy said. "I think we'd have had Humphrey take a softer line, and created a Democratic victory in November." Both in the platform and the Cabinet the McCarthy views would have been reflected. Such speculations were shattered by the assassin's bullet. McCarthy could not quit—he had attracted too large and faithful a following—but his appraisal of his chances or future influence was somber.

In Washington the candidate attempted to relax, but Secret Service men, just assigned, were a constant reminder of recent events. At the house of a friend he swam in the pool, but pleasure merely served to recall pain. His friends described him as "haunted."

On the way back to Washington with McCarthy, Tom Finney worked on a statement for McCarthy to deliver at his first press conference after the assassination. It should, Finney thought, have the quality of Lincoln's Second Inaugural Address. McCarthy should call for reconciliation and unity. Pointing out that the combined McCarthy-Kennedy vote—averaging over eighty per cent in primaries which they had contested—had been a clear repudiation of the Administration, McCarthy should tell Humphrey to stand down. Other contenders should come forward at the convention, not just McCarthy. If the Democrats listened to the voice of the people by offering change, Kennedy's death would have meaning, and tragedy would be illumined. McCarthy almost appeared to agree: a strong statement was prepared by his speech writers and released to the press, but at the last moment McCarthy drew back. He canceled the statement and changed the press conference from the Senate Caucus Room, because Robert Kennedy had announced there—so, of course, had he—to the far smaller Agricultural Caucus Room, where there was not nearly enough space for the press. His statement was flat and restrained. Ever fearful of pandering to sentiment, of making political capital from another's misfortune, he would not give the rallying cry.

"His face," said the *New York Times,* "was almost as strained as the morning after the shooting of Senator Kennedy." "We've given it a pretty good run," he remarked about this time, but he appeared to have lost all appetite for an active campaign.

There is probably nothing in American politics more quarrelsome than liberal reformers, and nowhere are they more factious than in their bastion of New York City.

After 1952, the Stevensonians had done precisely what McCarthy would urge in 1968—they had gone home and taken over the Democratic organization in many neighborhoods. As reformers they had been successful, too successful, perhaps. There were now more reform than regular Democratic clubs in Manhattan. They had gone through the same life cycle as regular clubs before them. Powerful, they had become the fiefdoms of the few, often more interested in fighting among themselves than working for a common local issue or a national candidacy.

Despite McCarthy's strength among the New York liberals—almost all the reform clubs supported him—the inability of the reformers to cooperate had led to a vacuum of leadership. It was filled by a new organization called the Coalition for a Democratic Alternative, which hoped to solidify McCarthy support and usher the new politics into New York. Organized by Democrats like Paul O'Dwyer, Sarah Kovner and Eleanor French, both reform Democrats, a law student named Harold Ickes, the Negro leader Clarence Jones, Richard Lipsitz, and others, CDA was one of the most effective McCarthy groups in the United States, but its flavor was closer to the peace movement than to reform politics practiced by Democrats of the Stevenson-Lehman-Roosevelt stripe. Often new to politics, the CDAers displayed the relentless energy and wild imagination of amateurs. Easily and even happily, some lost their cool.

Partly because CDA appeared to them too disheveled, contentious, and even radical, the ex-Stevensonians, under Thomas Finletter, John Shea, and Laurence Levine, formed still another McCarthy organization called Citizens for McCarthy. They reasoned that CDA's objectives were cast in broader political and ideological terms than many potential McCarthy supporters could accept, and Citizens would provide a collection point for contributions from donors, especially large donors, who would not give to CDA. (Citizens raised substantial McCarthy money but not as much as its founders hoped; the broader based CDA raised a great deal more. It had poured well over a million dollars into McCarthy efforts in other states.) Rightly or wrongly, the CDAers believed that Citizens was attempting to assume political leadership, and feelings ran high. The CDAers were, for example, sufficiently dissatisfied with Citizens that they tore up a press release announcing Citizens' formation which had been brought to the CDA to be mimeographed. Before the Kennedy assassination brought an end to such plans, the McCarthy campaign leadership intended to stay at a hotel equidistant from CDA and Citizens headquarters to avoid even a hint of favoritism.

CDA remained the operational wing of the McCarthy campaign in New York and it organized storefronts over the state. It viewed with dark suspicion Curt Gans' national staffers and firmly told them to stay out of the state, and it also disagreed with the candidate. In the wake of the assassination, McCarthy was drawing back, discouraging activity in his behalf, and, they felt, letting a golden opportunity slip. They agreed that it would be in poor taste to campaign circus style but, even within the limits imposed by the tragedy, McCarthy could still make appearances and talk on the issues—which was what the campaign was about. Sarah Kovner tried to reach McCarthy to explain their position, but repeated calls went unanswered. Ultimately, the candidate did return the call, but now Mrs. Kovner was furious and refused to speak to him. "Tell him," she told McCarthy's secretary, "that I'm too busy trying to win the election." The New York primary would be held on June 18.

The New Yorkers prepared an ad which expressed their feelings: "WAS PEACE ASSASSINATED TOO?" It evoked a storm from McCarthy headquarters in Washington. Not only did the candidate balk at the ad's propriety, but the best politics in this period was deemed by him to be no politics. The voters would be offended at any rapid resumption of the campaign. A McCarthy representative was dispatched to New York, but only after a meeting which came close to physical blows did the New Yorkers submit. The ad that was then printed was a classic in nonpolitical advertising: "YOU CAN'T VOTE FOR EUGENE MCCARTHY ON PRIMARY DAY."

Although the New Yorkers suspected the candidate would have preferred voters to take this call literally, it wasn't really meant to be a plea to vote for Humphrey. On a ballot at least as clumsy as any in the country, the names of the candidates the delegates supported were not listed. The ad pointed out that if you wanted to vote for McCarthy you had to know who his delegates were in your district. This required effort and a rekindling of popular enthusiasm, which in turn meant—to the New Yorkers—the presence of the candidate.

McCarthy had been clear about the limits within which he would campaign. He would speak very occasionally, with tortured restraint, before special groups like the Fellowship for Reconciliation in New York or would talk quietly to delegates, as he was doing in the West. But he would permit no hoopla, and no rallies, no real activity. On the eve of the New York election he was scheduled to speak at a fund-raising event for the Poor People's Campaign at Lewisohn Stadium. Though the CDA had been generally careful to bill the appearance as a benefit and not a rally, though it was virtually his sole visible public appearance before the New York primary, the candidate canceled it. Calls of despair flew West, including one from a prominent psychoanalyst whom McCarthy respected. The candidate relented and came.

McCarthy's New York victory was one of the most significant showings made by the candidate since New Hampshire. It brought new life to a campaign that seemed to have died with Robert Kennedy. McCarthy delegate slates won about half the vote and 62 out of the 123 delegates elected by popular vote, compared to 30 Kennedy delegates and 10 for Humphrey, with the rest uncommitted.

(The CDA's candidate for the Senate, Paul O'Dwyer, scored a significant victory in the Democratic primary, though he was to lose to Jacob Javits in November.) In beating Humphrey on the order of six to one, McCarthy proved not only that his candidacy was alive but that Kennedy voters were turning to him even if the leadership was not. But the joy felt by McCarthy's campaigners was tempered by the actions of the regular Democrats. McCarthyites asked for half the 65 at-large delegates on the basis of the popular vote. They got 15½, some of whom were not even McCarthy supporters, though some said the McCarthyites lost a few votes by being unwilling to compromise.

In other words, even in a comparatively liberal state, the McCarthyites could not obtain proportional representation. The regular Democrats relied on two arguments—the preprimary votes for district leader, they said, had been won by regular Democrats, and it was a fairer test than the primary because of the light primary turnout, only twenty per cent. The McCarthyites answered that the district-leader elections had really been organization elections; the light turnout should have favored regular Democrats, whose showing, in the New York primary, only underscored their weakness. The McCarthy forces walked out of the bargaining. They were awarded a few more votes and arrived at Chicago with the grand total of 86—somewhat short of half the delegation's 190 votes. (On the same day as the New York primary the Democratic National Committee chose Humphrey supporters for the top convention jobs.)

Not surprisingly, it was plain from the events in New York that those who had power in the Democratic Party would not relinquish it easily. The at-large delegate selections had been made principally by county leaders, on the basis of favors. Profit, prestige, party politics were the determining factors. The Kennedy forces had begun to resemble an independent army with its own generals and commissary. It would not disband. Indeed, Theodore Sorensen, who had once said that if Kennedy lost he would support

McCarthy, was now made a delegate-at-large, although New York political practice decreed that a beaten candidate is not then appointed; Sorensen had lost the election to the McCarthyites two to one. New York showed that McCarthy had great popular support, but also that victory in Chicago would require an energetic candidate, adept organization, and a large measure of luck.

After the New York victory, the candidate seemed easier and happier, readier to recommence. There were various things that he might do. Groans met one idea—a trip to Europe. (In the Robert Kennedy camp, Pat Lucey had planned to recommend a European trip to his candidate after California.) So McCarthy stayed and campaigned, but in his own way. He would return to the issue-oriented politics of New Hampshire. He did not think he would win many delegates by strong pleas to vote for him. His only opportunity—if there was one—would be panic at the convention: the delegates might know from the polls by then that Humphrey could not beat Nixon. They would pick McCarthy because he was the man who could win in November. This scenario was what McCarthy had in mind when he said, in July, that his chances were "fifty-fifty."

He would not campaign too hard, reserving several hours a day for writing poetry. He took out nearly a week for a retreat to his alma mater, St. John's in Minnesota. The Benedictine monks were given *deo grazi,* or the permission to speak. They talked with McCarthy about the decline of monasticism—the Secret Service men, the candidate maintained in high good humor, were the only real monks left; they kept the vigil. McCarthy read his poetry to the monks and nuns at a campus coffeehouse in the evenings. He hiked, played tennis, and talked about his days in the Great Soo League. He pitched for the nuns against the Secret Service—the nuns won 17-0—and stayed up late into the night reminiscing with the priests over highballs. At mass he wryly read an epistle from Saint Paul's letter to the Philippians: "I know how to be poor and I know how to be rich too. I have been through my initiation and now I am ready for anything anywhere: full stomach or empty stomach; poverty or plenty. There is nothing I cannot master with the help of One who gives me strength."

To many of his campaigners, the candidate seemed changed. In New Hampshire, where the possibilities of political humiliation had been real, he sometimes accepted advice, though rarely sought it. Now, he retreated, and seemed aloof from the battles which were beginning to burn over how to win the nomination if it could be won.

The weeks following the New York primary election were critical ones for the McCarthy effort and would answer a central question: Can a man who, with every philosophical justification, does not like the exercise of power obtain power in our society?

Within the campaign, the estimates of McCarthy's chances ranged from nil to moderately good. The bleakest view, naturally, favored cutting costs drastically, for if nothing could be done why waste money? But even for those who thought McCarthy had some chance, there were sharp divisions on what, exactly, to do. One group, interested in continuing the movement that had sprung up in McCarthy's name as well as winning the nomination, wanted a strategy called People Power. The group believed that a massive grass-roots effort would sway the delegates and lay the ground for total reform in the party. A second group determined on an approach we shall call "confrontation politics"—less grass roots and aimed at the convention. It hoped that a series of tough challenges at Chicago would shift the convention to McCarthy. The third group saw McCarthy's central difficulty as the delegates' fear of his party irregularity. Confrontation, for this group, was the best way to insure that McCarthy would not get the nomination. It favored neither organized grass-roots activity nor brutal convention challenges, but a small, fairly traditional operation, putting heavy leverage on the party power centers.

With the candidate appearing indecisive, all three groups fought for supremacy, with the first and second groups forming a loose alliance against the third. The McCarthy campaign, as it raced to Chicago, had fatal contradictions and flaws.

The strategy of confrontation was led by Stephen A. Mitchell, Chairman of the Democratic National Committee from 1952 to 1955. A gray-headed lawyer in his mid-sixties, Mitchell was normally a gentle man, but causes aroused a combative streak in him and he had a temper. Mitchell brought in Martin Gleason, a friendly thirty-seven-year-old Illinois businessman long interested in state politics. "I've got a reputation," Gleason remarked, "as a political alley fighter." Not everyone grouped about the McCarthy banner was principally interested in stopping the war in Vietnam. Gleason was not opposed to American policy there, and Mitchell's doubts about it were recent and not a governing reason for his joining the McCarthy campaign. Both were believers in Democratic Party reform. (Which group one fell in with anti-Vietnam war campaigners or party reformers—was a distinction of some importance. For instance, the party reformers, having achieved many of *their* objectives at Chicago, found it much easier to join the Humphrey campaign. Mitchell did, almost at once. Those strongly opposed to the Vietnam policy found the transition much harder, if not impossible.) A decade before, Mitchell had described the forces within the Democratic Party that worked against irregulars like the McCarthyites.

. . . One of the clear trends of 1959, in both parties, is the movement from what may be called the "old-style" to the "new-style" political organization. . . . The essential difference between the old and the new is the same everywhere: the old is characterized by exclusiveness, a minimum of party activity, and an absence of democratic procedures; the new is characterized by expansionism and independence which may approach the evangelical, greater activity, and a devotion to democratic procedures. . . .

Since the county chairman is elected, through direct or indirect processes, by the party members in his county, he inevitably realizes that his best chance to maintain his chairmanship lies in manipulating a low level of political activity, especially in the primaries. Too often he tries hard to exclude dissenters and potential leaders from the organization. . . .

Those who guide this process can recognize the symptoms of aging and guard against them. If they fail, the cycle enters the next stage. The enthusiasm of the revolution wears off, and activities decrease. Once the old leaders are rendered incapable of a return to power, the new leaders may begin quarreling among themselves, permitting cliques to form. Party officers who have overstayed their welcome begin to think of extra-democratic ways of retaining office.[1]

While Robert Kennedy was still alive, Mitchell and Gleason, over three long evenings in Chicago, mapped out a complicated strategy by which, they thought, McCarthy could win the nomination. It had been presented to the candidate at seven-thirty a.m. in San Francisco, the morning after the Kennedy debate. By eight-fifteen the meeting was over. McCarthy not only approved the scheme but had some ideas for strengthening the attack. "Stevenson would have agonized for five weeks over what Gene approved in forty-five minutes," Mitchell remarked.

"Nobody knows much about this business—I'd never run a big convention operation before and no one else in the campaign really had either," Mitchell said later. One could only make assumptions and hope they were right. For Mitchell and Gleason, McCarthy's only slender hope to win the nomination was to make the dynamics of the convention work against the prospects of Hubert Humphrey. "We'll fight in every place we can stand and shoot," Mitchell said. They would overlook no opportunity for a scrap. The Humphrey host, they reasoned, was composed of three unnatural allies—

[1] Stephen A. Mitchell, *Elm St. Politics,* New York, Oceana Publications, Inc., 1959, pp. 26-29.

Northern Democratic leaders with a heavy debt to organized labor, the South, and President Johnson. The interests of these three parties were not identical. If the proper wedges could be driven between Humphrey's forces his army might collapse in disarray.

The weak point in the Humphrey lines, Mitchell and Gleason discerned, was Texas. It was not a popular place—one reason so many people disliked Lyndon Johnson was his state of origin. As Democratic National Chairman in 1952, Mitchell had been forced to endure the defection of Governor Alan Shivers to Eisenhower. He had a strong dislike for politics as practiced there. Now, he thought, the anomalies of Texas could be made to work for McCarthy. Texas Democrats employed the unit rule from the precinct level up, so that dissidents could be systematically excluded. Credential challenges took care of insurgents who managed to get to the district- or state-convention level. Negroes and Mexican-Americans had small voice in party matters—only a handful of them were on the 1968 delegation, though they constituted twenty-seven per cent of the state's population and a higher proportion of the Democrats. Senator Ralph Yarborough, a liberal insurgent who supported McCarthy, could win by sizable majorities, but the Texas delegation was almost entirely party regulars.

Mitchell did not want to turn his big guns squarely on the racial or national-origin composition of the delegation. To do so would have been to put the battle in the Credentials Committee, and credentials fights tended to be complicated and legalistic, so that a delegate could explain away a bad vote when he got home. Mitchell's thrust would be at the unit rule, in the Rules Committee. He would demand an abolition of the undemocratic unit rule, which was then used to exclude political as well as racial minorities, not simply for future conventions but for this one too.

The issue Mitchell would fasten on, hammer home, was bossism, as practiced in Texas, and elsewhere. Bossism was fairly acceptable in the South, but in the North it was a fighting word. Northern bosses don't like to be identified as bosses. Northern labor-liberals, the "lib-labs," could not vote in favor of bossism. They would vote against the unit rule and the Texas delegation.

This would put Humphrey in an untenable position. Which way would he go? To vote with the South would put the Northerners in arms. To vote with the North was even more dangerous. Mitchell believed that neither Johnson nor Texas Governor John Connally would permit the immediate abolition of the unit rule. Their power in the state depended upon it. Johnson might pull away from Humphrey. The Southerners might stay with favorite sons or even field a candidate of their own. Humphrey would somehow have to hold onto his Southern support, which was exactly what Mitchell wanted. He would identify the Vice-President with the unpopular President in every way he could, and he would push the notion that Johnson's real choice for Vice-President in 1968 was John Connally, unpalatable to the North.

The intention, then, was to break delegates away from Humphrey on issues other than the candidacy of Eugene McCarthy, to split the Humphrey camp into quarreling factions. Mitchell and Gleason would raise many other challenges in an attempt to do just that.

When there had been Kennedy to contend with, the plan was to make the unit rule and other fights McCarthy-led battles. The Kennedy forces to some extent could have been depicted as machine politicians themselves. Humphrey would lose strength and at the same time Kennedy would not have the votes to win. The President would have done everything in his power, the theoreticians believed, to stop Kennedy. The Southerners would have found McCarthy more acceptable than Kennedy. If they did not like McCarthy's Vietnam position, they might agree that he was a realist in the end. They would appreciate his nonemotional approach to the ghettos and find solace in his limited view of Presidential power. With Humphrey collapsing, Johnson and the South would put McCarthy over.

Before Kennedy died, McCarthy had spoiled the scheme a little by announcing on radio in California that he intended to make a fight on the unit rule. Mitchell and Gleason had hoped for surprise. Now, with Kennedy gone, it would be harder to mount the necessary leverage on Humphrey—the scheme depended on Humphrey's not being too far beyond the nomination point in delegates—and a further blow was given by Humphrey in July when he said he supported the abolition of the unit rule. But it was not clear how consistent he was about abolishing it, and Mitchell, perceiving Humphrey's support to be shaky, decided to go ahead with all cannons blazing. In some minds, his battle plan was to come tantalizingly close to success.

The second general approach, People Power, was that of Clark and Gans and meant mobilizing the vast pro-McCarthy sentiment in the country and focusing it on the delegates and influencing the polls. Huge rallies; nation-wide canvassing; silent, street-corner vigils by millions; McCarthy headquarters everywhere (staffed by housewives whose untended homes carried signs reading WE'RE DIRTY FOR GENE); letters, calls, and visits to delegates, who would also be subject to pro-McCarthy talk from their mates, their children, their dentists, doctors, lawyers, Indian chiefs, and almost everyone with whom they came in personal contact—by such manifestations would the delegates learn the nation's choice. This strategy was to be unfurled by Curtis Gans at a meeting in Chicago starting June 19, with about two hundred of the faithful flown in from all over the country on the campaign's "Q" air-travel credit cards.

Gans thought he had the candidate's permission, but McCarthy had begun to question the cost and wisdom of the enterprise, which required an elaborate national staff operation. Now Quigley, more than ever said to hate youth, suddenly canceled the meeting. To Gans it was too late to stop and he proceeded to buy a large bloc of tickets, taking the precaution of purchasing them at TWA on the American Airlines credit card so that only the total bill, not the individual ticket stubs with names on them, would be returned to

Quigley. At Chicago Gans was faced with more trouble. A delegation of national staffers had trapped the candidate in a New York hotel bedroom—they wanted *some* leadership, Gans' or not was immaterial—and at the Chicago meeting the revolt broke into the open. If this was people's democracy then a leader's right to lead could be questioned, and the national staffers did so. By now it was generally known that McCarthy was displeased with Gans and many staffers feared that Gans' uncertain position was coming between the candidate and the kids' projected summer program of delegate-storming. If this was truly the case, the kids wanted Gans to resign. Gans said it was not.

Some even believed that Gans, like Macbeth, was afraid to sleep because he might wake to find he had lost control. Should he be toppled from his seat of authority? But, after all, as one of the first supporters, he was pre-eminently entitled to wear the proud button FMBNH (For McCarthy Before New Hampshire). He had contributed mightily to the victory there and in Wisconsin and the troops were loyal. He could stay, on sufferance. But the only results that Gans could announce to the group was that there would be no funds for the summer program. The campaigners should go home and stay there. The conclave—including some $90-a-day accommodations, the only ones available in convention-filled Chicago—cost between $25,000 and $50,000, depending on the version one listened to.

If nobody actually left the campaign after this meeting it was because nobody wanted to go and there was nobody to make decisions stick. The candidate, when the chips were down, did not want to be tough on his troops. Nor was he interested in details. As Maurice Rosenblatt remarked, "He could do all the impossible things but not the easy ones. He was not operations-minded. Lincoln would spend two hours talking about armor plate with the Bureau of Ordnance. Gene is too abstract to be interested in what kind of an envelope brings back campaign money. His was the way of the prophet."

The candidate, too, was tired from the primaries—he had given a tremendous amount of himself. Some believed the campaign took a few years off his life. His staff, knowing his distaste for operational matters, tried to protect him. McCarthy would arrive at a staff meeting with a small agenda. Is anybody talking to the Southern delegates? Yes. (Nobody was.) Is the money all right? Yes. Well, work it out as you go along.

The money was far from all right. California alone had cost more than a million and a half dollars, and early in the summer McCarthy learned that his campaign was more than a million dollars in debt. If he could not be held legally liable, he would clearly feel a moral responsibility for the debt. It was not a pleasant prospect, and McCarthy was alarmed. He needed help. He could not be expected to enunciate policy and run an organization too. "What do I have to do to convince people I can't be concerned with *everybody?*" he asked plaintively. He was unable to get his troops to "hang up their sweatshirts," as he requested. He wanted a strong man, and in desperation he turned again to Finney.

After the New York primary McCarthy had invited Ickes and Mrs. Kovner to breakfast, congratulated them on their effort, and joked that perhaps he did better in states where he did not campaign so much. The CDAers were still upset by the quality of the campaign's leadership in Washington, and said so. McCarthy answered, "You'll like Finney. I think he'll take charge now." He turned to his aide, Callanan. "Where is Finney?" he asked. "He's left." McCarthy said, "Why did he go? He hadn't seen me." "You'd gone to bed," Callanan said. "Why didn't you get me up?" McCarthy said. He looked annoyed.

Finney had agreed to stay on only till the end of the California campaign, but it was generally thought he would remain with McCarthy after that if asked. Before the situation could be discussed, though, Finney learned the day after he returned from California that his father was mortally ill. His father subsequently died and it

was two weeks before Finney returned to the campaign from Oklahoma.

Finney was not a "pro"—he did not work in politics full time—
but he had largely managed the Stevenson effort in 1960 and was
the floor manager for Stevenson's convention fight.

Theodore H. White (in *The Making of the President 1960*)
had called him "extraordinarily able and articulate." Finney was
probably less concerned with Democratic Party reform than some
others in the McCarthy effort—for him the locus of change was
likely to be in the Federal Government in Washington, where he
knew his way in both the executive and legislative branches. He had
ties to Johnson and Humphrey and he had argued the dove position
with his former law partner, Clark Clifford, the Secretary of Defense. For Finney the central issue was Vietnam.

Finney had strong friends in the campaign—the ex-Stevensonians in New York, the CDA, the finance people like Hiatt and
Pirie, some campaign advisers like Maurice Rosenblatt, Russell
Hemenway, and John Safer. They had urged McCarthy to get
Finney back in action. Finney had been home from Oklahoma
barely an hour when the phone rang. It was Tom McCoy, urging
him to go to New York to see McCarthy that Wednesday night,
the day after the New York primary. Finney and McCoy climbed
on a plane for New York, and Finney, after a harrowing day, did
not arrive at McCarthy's hotel until ten-thirty. He was met by
Callanan, who said, "The Senator has gone to bed."

Finney had a business appointment in Washington the next
morning and at seven a.m. wearily caught a plane back. He did not
meet McCarthy until Sunday, when the candidate asked him to un-
dertake the leadership of the campaign. Finney, a volunteer, said
he could not: his professional responsibilities, his exhaustion from
the California campaign and his father's death, and a very real apprehension about being caught in the coils of the McCarthy organization determined for him that he should take a lesser role. He

would lead the hunt for delegates and attempt to restructure part of the campaign for that purpose.

Finney agreed that McCarthy had been hurt politically by Kennedy's assassination, but not so badly, he judged, as McCarthy thought. Alone, McCarthy had too few delegates to command the necessary leverage. But Humphrey was beginning to sag in the polls. It was conceivable that the Vice-President's strength would crumble seriously before the convention—as it was indeed to do, far more precipitously than anyone in the McCarthy campaign could yet imagine. Finney, as McCarthy's chief delegate headhunter, had to prove to the politicians that McCarthy, able to beat Nixon while Humphrey could not, was their principal hope to stay in power.

To Finney the delegates were chosen in antiquated ways, but they were more responsible than the McCarthy organization usually allowed. They had to believe the man they chose would make a good President. McCarthy's Presidential credibility was under attack because of his supposed weakness as an executive. The delegates were concerned, as well, by the insurgent tone that rose from the McCarthy ranks. Would the Senator bolt the party if he were not nominated? What would he do with the party if he were? Would it be better to pick a loser than to have McCarthy's young mavericks throw the party regulars out of their jobs? These fears Finney sought to dispel, and the last thing he wanted was for the McCarthy campaign to arrive in Chicago disruptive and making unnecessary trouble. When McCarthy was elected there would be time to disrupt the Democratic Party.

To Finney, then, the candidate should appear frequently on television and the delegates should be talked to quietly and persuasively. Finney set up his own experienced delegate-gathering operation: G. W. Holsinger, vice-chairman of the Democratic Party in California, to be floor manager; Mayne Miller, from the Stevenson campaign, to work the South; Edward N. Costikyan for the East and Illinois; Gerald Hill for the Western states; and others. Finney could not move quickly; he needed private-poll results to show to the leaders and he had to prepare charts and graphs —Finney was almost compulsively careful and logical. He could be heard smoothly on the phone: "I've got a California poll that is just fantastic. I've got an Iowa poll that is three to one. I feel we'll start doing better in the South and Negro areas. They are keeping the thing reasonably close. The Humphrey thing is starting to crumble. The real thing that's bugging the country is the fixing of priorities. Given the decision to remove urban blight, the organization of the machinery is not the critical element. It's the commitment. I think Gene's got that."

Finney's strategy included a bold design which, if known, would have been regarded by many other campaigners as fantasy, treason, or both. "I believed," he was to say later, "that there was a real possibility that the McCarthy candidacy could have been supported by elements of the party that most people in the McCarthy campaign were ready to assume would be antagonistic." He talked to John Connally, whom he found "open-minded." The Southern governors and Connally were not wildly enthusiastic about McCarthy, but Finney did not unearth deep dislike, either—Connally, after all, supported McCarthy in 1964. Finally, there was the most powerful Democrat of all, the President.

"I don't think," Finney noted, "that the President did anything to capture votes for Hubert Humphrey." Through his former partnership with Clark Clifford and his own work for Johnson—he had conducted several personal missions for the President and had served unofficially on the White House staff—Finney thought he knew something of the President's mind. In his view, Johnson rated McCarthy high, despite the challenge of New Hampshire, and thought him well qualified for the Presidency. It had been the Kennedy threat, more than McCarthy's, which had driven the President to withdraw. The gap between Johnson and McCarthy on Vietnam was not a chasm. McCarthy's position was that the bombing halt was of secondary importance to a commitment to a political settlement and military de-escalation. There were grounds here for an accommodation between the two.

There was no hope, of course, that Johnson would endorse McCarthy before or perhaps even during the convention. What Finney looked for was a slow building of political circumstances. *If* Humphrey began to fade in the polls and looked as if he would take the party under, *if* McCarthy seemed a much stronger candidate for November, *if* Johnson was as down on Humphrey as Finney suspected, *if* the delegates were satisfied about McCarthy's party regularity, *if* the Democratic leaders, fearful of defeat of state parties, were gradually and delicately brought into the fold—or at least persuaded to stay neutral—*if* all these events could be made to occur, then Johnson, quietly, might switch horses or at least let it be known that he would not stand in the way of McCarthy as the convention's choice. Independently, Eliot Janeway had reached a similar conclusion. "A deal could have been made with Johnson," he said later. "Johnson would have had to be given concessions on the war, but it would have cost McCarthy his reputation in show business."

Finney's return to the ranks was noted, by columnists like Rowland Evans and Robert Novak, as the first sign that McCarthy, however unwillingly, was prepared to make the steps necessary for nomination; but within the campaign resistance grew with each step.

Although Finney was to head the delegate hunt, he soon learned that he could not touch one part of the campaign organism without getting a reflex action from the next. Finney wanted a smaller, more easily directed delegate hunt. That seemed to fit with the candidate's designs to save money, and McCarthy directed Finney to cut back on the staff. Two days later, without warning Finney, he suddenly authorized a $160,000 budget for the national staff, apparently under the misapprehension that this money would not otherwise have flowed into the campaign. Finney, unaware, started to prune, and was instantly identified as the enemy of the grass roots and the new politics.

Finney was not against the national staff but he thought it had to be controlled. That the McCarthy kids, enthusiastic but inexperienced, should be directly contacting delegates—as they were being instructed to do by Gans—was, for Finney, a sure way to make McCarthy's nomination an impossibility. A compromise was reached: Curtis Gans had divided the country into eight regions, each region with a deskman in Washington and staff people in the field, modeled after the Kennedy campaign of 1960. (The financial problem of the McCarthy campaign was nowhere clearer than in its inability to mount a delegate operation in the nonprimary states, where most of the delegates were, until the primaries were over. A little group headed by Genie Gans, Curt's wife, Don Green, and Dave Mixner had done their best, stealing buttons and literature from the primary campaign. As the candidate ruefully noted, they even managed to bring down in a local contest McCarthy's old friend and former campaign manager, Herman Schauinger, because in their eyes he hadn't worked hard enough for Gene.) Gans' deskmen would gather intelligence for Finney, whose own group would make the contacts. Finney would work out of his law office and not in the turbulent campaign headquarters. Not wishing to become involved in the campaign imbroglios, he became difficult to reach by phone and the kids said that he was doing nothing for McCarthy.

Finney's metabolism was a strike against him—he did not stay up all night or operate in a continual rush. But, at least by his lights, he was proceeding. The mailings were not going out, so he hired a professional mailer, as well as a communications expert for the convention. He began to think about television commercials. Slowly, because he didn't believe he had a real weapon until the poll results were in his hand, he began to contact key Democratic leaders. One of the first was Jesse Unruh of California, and now

Finney found there was more trouble. Richard Goodwin had already been there. Complicated schemes were afoot.

Goodwin, following the Kennedy assassination, had rejoined the McCarthy campaign. His energy, his view on Vietnam, and his love of the political struggle made it impossible for him to stay out of the campaign long. He was now paid a thousand a week, with liberal expenses, and to the treasurers' despair he had a habit of renting cars and forgetting them as they sat in a garage. Goodwin was impatient—some found him abrasive—with the in-fighting at the headquarters. He believed you had to make *some* decision and do *something,* right or wrong. "In a campaign," he said, "you take one step after the next. If you look too far ahead you're likely to stumble." Finney's seeming lack of action was bound to strike Goodwin as the way to lose.

"The cards are really all dealt," McCarthy, displaying fatalism, had told Goodwin, who thought the chances were small but worth a try. Goodwin was more of a free-lance campaigner than an organizer; he was forgetful of details though rapid in thought. One of his assignments was to try to bring in the Kennedy supporters, many of whom were bitter toward McCarthy for his attacks on Kennedy during the Oregon and California primaries. They appeared to have forgotten the attacks on McCarthy's voting record which had provoked him to retaliate. Goodwin believed that the campaign would not have seemed so bitter to the Kennedyites in retrospect had Kennedy lived. Now the Kennedy people appeared to want to withdraw from active politics, though most of them shortly reappeared. Since they did not join McCarthy, some observers felt that they were not sincere in their desire to change the Vietnam policy and that Kennedy's had been a compaign of new-politics issues run by old-politics managers. Their solid support would have been the last source of momentum for McCarthy after the New York primary. But their concept of politics essentially opposed the McCarthy idea of a popular movement whose power lay in the people; and they disliked McCarthy more than most McCarthyites imagined. As one Kennedy chieftain told me, "We regarded Gene as a dangerous man. We didn't like his concept of the Presidency and we thought as an individual he raised enthusiasms without following through. We much preferred Humphrey. Maybe even Nixon."

Meetings were arranged between the Kennedy staff leaders and McCarthy, but the talks were not satisfactory to the Kennedyites. They could not get over their resentment at McCarthy, and the candidate, reluctant, as always, to ask for help, did not make it easier for them. But if active support could not be had from former Kennedy staffers like Kenneth O'Donnell (four top McCarthy workers spent a full day in travel to reach O'Donnell at Cape Cod, only to be rebuffed), Theodore Sorensen, or Pierre Salinger, more of an inroad, it seemed, could be made along Kennedy-identified *politicians* like Governor Harold Hughes of Iowa or Jesse Unruh, Speaker of the California Assembly. These were men with political constituencies whose own careers might well depend on the backing of McCarthy supporters. (The Kennedy *voters,* the polls showed, backed McCarthy more often than Humphrey.)

Unruh, especially, would have been a prize. Along with Stanley Steingut, the Bronx district leader; Richard Daley, who before the convention was by no means considered a villain despite his use of police force against demonstrators that spring (McCarthyites then thought him one of the best bosses); and a few others, Unruh was an authentic power broker. He had ambitions to be governor in a state where Humphrey clearly could not win though McCarthy probably could. Unruh had expressed himself about the President to Murray Kempton: "A man said to me the other day that 'if this cowboy is elected President next November, we won't have a Democratic President in this country for the next twenty-five years.' You can write that down; I didn't say it." It looked as though Unruh might support McCarthy, and Mitchell decided to bait the hook.

He suggested that Goodwin make the contact. Goodwin met with Unruh in July at a memorial dinner for Kennedy in South Dakota.

There, Goodwin had a chance to do some politicking. Patrick Lucey apparently wanted to support McCarthy but had sincere doubts about his capabilities as President; if McCarthy lacked administrative ability—no one really knew—Goodwin assured him it was not critical. Leadership, vision, imagination were, and McCarthy had those. Lucey did not commit himself. At dinner, Goodwin sat next to Unruh and explained what Mitchell had in mind. Would Unruh like to run for Permanent Chairman of the Democratic National Convention against Representative Carl Albert of Oklahoma, the House Majority Leader, who had already been designated for the post by the Democratic National Committee? Unruh said he might be interested in the idea. Back in Washington, Goodwin began collecting information on the civil-rights record of Carl Albert as potential ammunition.

The Unruh candidacy offered several advantages. If Unruh, with the backing of the McCarthyites, the Kennedyites, and, later, the McGovernites, could actually win the Permanent Chairmanship that would be a significant triumph for the peace forces. It would also offer a screen for Unruh, who had difficulty supporting McCarthy openly because of the splits among the California Democrats. But for Unruh to run for Permanent Chairman meant that he had to avoid public identification with McCarthy; that was a minus and the McCarthyites could not have it both ways.

Finney—hearing about the plan from Unruh's office—offered more objections: by tradition, the House Majority Leader was Permanent Chairman; there would be no basis for the fight—Albert would be fair; finally, if McCarthy won the nomination he would face a hostile Majority Leader. Again, Finney's position next to the others was cautious and traditional; the split in the campaign was deepening.

Finney's main antagonist was Mitchell, and the trouble lay in words which no one had clarified: "Convention arrangements." McCarthy had put Mitchell in charge of them, but Finney's assumption was that "arrangements" meant mechanical functions, not strategy and organization. Mitchell thought of the "arrangements" in terms of his own strategy, also authorized by McCarthy, and the two experts were on a collision course.

The original Mitchell-Gleason convention budget had called for almost a million dollars, including fifty chauffeured limousines, whereas Finney's 1960 Stevenson convention fight had cost sixty thousand. Finney started to prune. He called John Criswell, National Treasurer of the Democratic National Committee, to say that the McCarthy campaign would not need as many hotel rooms as had been planned. Personal dislike and strategic differences made communication between Finney in Washington and the McCarthy Chicago group almost impossible. Now Gleason called on Criswell to demand more space for the McCarthy forces and Criswell reported that Finney had already said the opposite. Mitchell shook them up; Finney placated. The same happened when Finney strongly opposed a McCarthy foot canvass in Illinois. Finney thought the canvass would irritate Mayor Daley of Chicago and ruin any possibility of getting at least some Illinois delegates for McCarthy. Finney was less than keen about many of the challenges Mitchell planned to mount. Each side thought that the strategy of the other was inadequate.

The McCarthy campaign abhorred a vacuum. Impatient with the endless wrangles, futile meetings, and frantic phone calls, the New Yorkers began to move. With the Empire State as a lever, they would try to stage the most impressive grass-roots show of support ever seen previous to a nominating convention. It was to be called McCarthy Summer, the summer of hope, of gathering peace, of reconciliation, and of a redress of power in the United States. A few McCarthy releases recapture the heady mood of those days:

LEADING WRITERS ORGANIZE IN SUPPORT OF MCCARTHY

The McCarthy for President Campaign today announced the formation of the "Writer's Project for Eugene McCarthy," a group of leading writers whose names read like a "Who's Who" of American letters.

The group which includes such writers as Norman Mailer, Terry Southern, Edward Albee, Bruce Jay Friedman and William Styron will mobilize support for Senator McCarthy in the literary community and among the public at large. They will engage in varied activities from writing letters to newspaper editors and to delegates, to participating as delegates at the Chicago Democratic National Convention. A number of the writers were supporters of the late Senator Kennedy.

Mr. William Styron, author of the current best-seller *Confessions of Nat Turner,* said today, "Almost never in the history of American politics have so many serious literary figures felt a kind of desperation about the world. This has provoked not just a remote interest, but an active participation in the events of this campaign year. There is a passion and profound alarm on the part of writers, largely due to the war in Vietnam which has caused us to turn to Senator McCarthy."

DOING YOUR OWN THING IN THE MCCARTHY CAMPAIGN

Thousands of people who have never before actively engaged in politics have flocked to the McCarthy campaign and have organized campaign cabarets, art galleries and boutiques. They have designed dresses, produced records, and other items to raise funds and in California they are turning their homes into mini-sized headquarters.

[Eugene's II] cabaret opened July 1 in Boston's Kenmore Square. . . . For $1 admission, Eugene's features a mixed bag of entertainment—political skits, rock bands, folk music, dancing and political "speakouts." . . . Nightly, a dozen pretty young volunteers turn waitress and service guests ranging from college students to such prominent Bostonians as Dr. Paul Dudley White, the noted heart specialist, Mr. and Mrs. John Saltonstall, Jr., Dr. Jerome Wiesner, the M.I.T. physicist and a member of the Massachusetts delegation to the convention.

[In New Haven] Henry Strauss, a local McCarthy coordinator,

has designed three brightly colored pushcarts called "McCarthy Mobiles." Teen-aged volunteers equipped with vendors' licenses hit the streets daily selling campaign buttons, sweatshirts, earrings, tie clips, posters, stickers and other items.

In New York, "Women for McCarthy," a national group, has opened a "McCarthy Mart" on West 56th Street in mid-Manhattan. Run by Hedda Hendricks, a dynamic woman prominent in civic affairs, the tiny blue and white boutique has taken in more than $20,000 in sales and contributions since it opened last May 26.

In St. Louis the non-pros are also doing their thing. They have converted the front half of their headquarters into a successful art gallery with paintings donated by local artists.

[On the West Coast] the new "McCarthy neighborhood centers" . . . are recognizable by the giant McCarthy flower stickers on each door.

At Oak Ridge, Tennessee, McCarthy supporters have organized a "Eugene's."

Some of the best cooks in Windom County, Vermont, turned out their best dishes and held "Cuisine for Eugene."

But even where there is no formal McCarthy operation, volunteers have struck out on their own. McCarthy supporters abroad are running their own informal campaign in American communities in Paris, the Virgin Islands, Rio de Janeiro, and even Tokyo.

The New York group announced People for McCarthy, who would go door-to-door, coast-to-coast, with People-for-McCarthy kits—stationery, pens, stamped addressed envelopes, to write letters to delegates. Advertisements in each area would explain who the delegates were. The New Yorkers believed that some Democratic leaders got as many as a hundred thousand letters. Frank Rosetti, the Manhattan leader, remarked that he was impressed with the volume of mail. The trouble was that he couldn't find his union pay check in the avalanche. There was also the "telephone revolution" billed as a "massive telephone operation which may revolutionize American politics." In New York, where the pilot project was, operators took calls on fifty phones on an advertised number from seven-thirty a.m. to midnight, and as the phone revolution began they were logging as many as 10,000 calls a day from New York McCarthy supporters. McCarthy Summer would culminate in M-Day, August 15, with rallies held all over the country and the candidate appearing on regular or closed-circuit television. (Led by Hannah Weinstein, M-Day was a highly successful venture, clearing half a million dollars for the campaign. McCarthy workers in Chicago, however, complained bitterly that M-Day drained away all manpower resources during the precious preconvention days.) More than a thousand McCarthy-for-President clubs had sprung up around the country. Preconvention hearings, held by the McCarthyites, heard imaginative ideas for change—Dwight Macdonald's ideas for reforming the Constitution, Michael Harrington's on Presidential commissions on the future, Betty Friedan's on a new day for women. This popular uprising seemed limitless; American politics had seen nothing like it.

The candidate in whose honor such volunteer activity was outpouring sometimes mystified people close to him. Would he be a good President? "Adequate," he said, a charming and obviously honest answer, intellectually satisfying to those who saw the McCarthy campaign as a break from stereotypes, American braggadocio and unrealistic self-appraisals. It was a worrisome response to those campaigners concerned with winning over the delegates. Well, *did* he want to be the President? He was "willing," again the right answer from the intellectual's point of view, but the wrong one from the conventional politician's, who held that a zest for the Presidency was the best guarantee of victory, party regularity, and even of stability in office.[2] Ambiguity appeared to be a quality

[2] "The Presidency is an exacting, even lethal job, and no one can be expected to perform well in it who does not want it with enough zest to pursue it, no matter what misgivings he may occasionally have in the darkness of the night. Were the office really to seek the man, who knows but what he might

which, however human, Americans did not like to contemplate in a President.

The question of the degree of McCarthy's willingness to become President haunted even his campaign chieftains. For one: "I think he was schizophrenic about whether he really wanted it." For another: "His moods seemed to vary by a factor of four. On days when things looked good—and there were such days, no matter what he may say later—he was both exhilarated and depressed. On days when things looked black he was also both exhilarated and depressed, for the opposite reasons." He was sometimes the teacher, acting as though instruction, especially of the young, in democratic politics was his essential mission; he was sometimes the exemplar of good and honest values in politics; and occasionally he seemed like a politician who wanted to win.

His performance before the state delegations, for instance, was uneven. (Some politicians called them love-ins.) Before the Ohio delegation, and later in California—where he brought a smile to Unruh's face by promising him a bright future in Democratic politics if McCarthy was elected—he was a superb campaigner, although he annoyed the California Kennedyites by not mentioning the name of Robert Kennedy. He disappointed his followers in Missouri when he told delegates: "Don't vote for me if it causes you trouble," and infuriated them in Oklahoma when he said he would settle for two convention votes. The McCarthyites there had been fighting for eight votes; after the candidate's visit they got two and one-half. The Washington, D. C., delegation, with a strong component of Negro and white intellectuals, was apparently prepared to go for him. McCarthy was tired and badly briefed, and

---

treat it merely as an honor and only go through the motions of governing? Or worse, elected in such circumstances, he might, for all his modesty, acquire the idea that he was doing the nation a gracious favor by governing it—and that way lie dangerous delusions of grandeur." Robert Bendiner, *White House Fever*. New York, Harcourt, Brace and Co., 1960, pp. 35-36.

he lost votes when, asked about civil rights, he referred a Negro questioner rather tartly to one of his previous speeches.

". . . Not even McCarthy's most fervent advocates can deny that McCarthy hasn't lifted a finger to make it easy for any member of the professional political clubs to even meet him halfway," wrote Eliot Janeway. He would neither change his style nor make concessions. "I'm not going to 'corral' or 'round up' delegates," he observed. "That's Texas language." He was reluctant to conduct the rite of telephone calls to politicians. He seemed above the business of political deals. He did not visit a Senator, said to be sympathetic, whose office was just down the hall, and, though he was in Maine for a brief visit, he did not call on Governor Kenneth Curtis, said to be a potential supporter. Senator Vance Hartke made overtures to work in the campaign but McCarthy declined. Hartke had not helped him in the early days, when he wanted it, and then Hartke had joined Kennedy, calling McCarthy a loser. (Hartke later supported McCarthy.) Governor Philip Hoff of Vermont, a potentially keen supporter, was disappointed by McCarthy's diffidence, though he became an active McCarthy campaigner. McCarthy felt he should not have to beg support from those who agreed with him ideologically, and he was often bitterly unhappy with the failure of the liberal politicians to get behind his campaign on their own. Where *were* all those liberals who had repeatedly urged this or that course of action?

"Why don't you call Hart?" he was asked, and McCarthy would answer, "If Phil's family can't convince him, I can't." Senator Philip Hart of Michigan, one of the ablest of the liberal Senators, typified the position of many liberal politicians whose wives and children supported McCarthy while they did not. Hart's wife and daughter Ann had been active McCarthyites since New Hampshire, and they lectured him regularly. Just before the convention Hart announced for McCarthy and campaigned for him in the Michigan delegation. "The guys who were going to be against Gene would have found some reason for it," Hart has said. "The delegates would say of Gene, 'He'll do those crazy things if we nominate him and he'll blow it.' I said, 'Those are the very things that make him attractive.' "

McCarthy's difficulty—trying to be himself in a political system which demanded stylized performances, like a method actor in the Comédie-Française—was nowhere more obvious than in his meetings with Negroes. He has stated and restated his excellent civil-rights position but, like the white delegates on issues like Vietnam, the Negroes demanded still another restatement of where he stood. Perhaps McCarthy's expressions lacked that nuance which would make the delegates feel his utterances were expressly for *them,* as individuals who mattered, but especially with the Negroes he sometimes seemed ill at ease, anticipating that that same question was about to be asked.

The McCarthy Negro meetings and rallies were complicated by a strange, new, and poignant element in American campaigns, the Secret Service. The campaigners joked that the Secret Service saw to it at last that hotel rooms were reserved and baggage arrived on time, but their impact was no joking matter when it came to the ghettos. The job of the Secret Service was to protect the candidate, while his job was to reach the people, and if those people were black the Secret Service sometimes had objections. The Secret Service could not cancel an event, but it could raise the specter of assassination. Its information often came from the local police—likely distrusted by the Negroes—and Norval Reece, McCarthy's astute scheduler, began examining police intelligence closely. Told, for instance, that McCarthy would be exposed to criminals, Reece was able to determine that the "criminals" were really black nationalists. The Secret Service did not object to a McCarthy appearance in Pittsburgh in a white neighborhood where he spoke to 15,000 people from a raised platform in clear view of surrounding high-rise apartment buildings, but they did suggest canceling a short walk in the Pittsburgh black ghetto. McCarthy went anyway, as usual, but sometimes the Secret Service won. Providing immediacy to the Secret Service warnings was that there had been some trouble. In California a white man had managed to get both McCarthy's hands occupied and swung at him. During the summer in New York a meeting with Negroes was stopped by a bomb threat. The threat was actually called in by a McCarthy campaigner. He had heard that a bomb would be planted, said nothing fearing that McCarthy would not go to Harlem, became frightened, and finally phoned. There was no bomb. McCarthy may have had difficulties reaching the black-desired levels of emotion, but he was not as ineffectual in the ghettos as was sometimes said. There was evidence that McCarthy, as the nominee, would have been supported by the minority groups. Writers like Louis Lomax, Alex Haley, and the Puerto Rican Piri Thomas gave him splendid endorsements. (James Baldwin insisted that he meet McCarthy to make a judgment; laboriously, time was provided in McCarthy's schedule; Baldwin did not show up.) Polls taken before the convention showed (in each instance against Nixon) in Delaware Humphrey with 67 per cent of the Negro vote to McCarthy's 65, in Illinois 88 to 88, in Michigan 86 to 64, in Missouri 89 to 87, in New Jersey 85 to 84, in Pennsylvania 79 to 79.

By the end of the summer he had visited the ghettos in almost every major Northern city. I was with the McCarthy party when, late in the campaign, the candidate came to announce his support of Operation Breadbasket—the Southern Christian Leadership Conference's attempt to impose boycotts on food chains and other businesses which did not work to alleviate ghetto problems—at the Tabernacle Baptist Church in Chicago. They were singing "Let It Shine" as McCarthy entered. It was enormously hot. "We are making an adjustment in our program for Senator McCarthy," said the minister coolly. Noise in the audience. "You white folks keep quiet." Huge cheer. The silver-tongued Reverend Jesse Jackson rose. He said, "Peace is good for black people. . . . Anyone

who will stand up against the racist government we have and declare peace in time of war, against the people who loot the looters
—who could stand up on these principles—they deserve your
ears. Listen to his content. If he has some respect in it. If he has
none let him know. We are first-class citizens."

"Soul power!" they chanted.

But now McCarthy had to wait a full half hour while the collection was taken and, during this long, hot interval, to listen to Reverend Calvin S. Morris, a flute-throated young man. Jackson and
Morris are accomplished—no, brilliant—orators with the capacity
to raise one high or drop him low with no more than a changed in-
flection. I should not have liked to have to follow them on a platform. Julian Bond, no mean orator himself, was there to introduce
McCarthy. The candidate rose, flat and stodgy by comparison.
Was he talking about New Hampshire snow once more? Hard to
tell, because the microphone was not working. Repeating when
the mike was back, he talked faster and suddenly had the beat.
Yes, he had it. "What about us?" he repeated like a leitmotiv.
"Civil rights begins when you resist the politicians. What about
us? I have no obligations and no Maddoxes. What about us? I don't
ask for any easy judgments. What about us—the *people?*"

Then everybody—Jackson, Bond, McCarthy, the campaigners,
even the press corps—linked arms and sang "We Shall Overcome."
At that moment he had every vote in the house.

By mid-July the McCarthy campaign appeared to be breaking
out of stasis and the candidate's feeling that his strength lay in
popular distaste for conventional politics seemed to be proved
right. The Humphrey campaign had stalled, its initial big money
having evaporated after McCarthy's New York showing. Astonishingly for a man whose mercury could once barely be measured
on the national polls, McCarthy was now beating Nixon by a much
greater margin than Humphrey was, according to the Harris poll.
He was also ahead of Rockefeller. (Harris showed a massive shift

toward McCarthy, involving millions of voters, in a single week.)
He led Nixon by 23 percentage points in California, and a Cross-
ley poll showed him ahead of Humphrey by 22 points in Massachusetts. He was getting nearly 20 per cent of the Republican vote,
the poll indicated, carrying the independents, the suburbanites,
people under 35, the college-educated, people with incomes over
$10,000 against Nixon, and defeating Humphrey in all these cate-
gories, running behind the Vice-President only among older
voters, Southerners, and Negroes. Humphrey on the campaign
trail was getting booed. Something of a spectacular change appeared to be happening among the American electorate, which
was showing a strong desire for change, whether leftward or right-
ward no one could be sure.

McCarthy was also attracting enormous audiences at rallies
staged two or three days apart in late July—Richmond, Detroit,
Boston. The one at Boston's Fenway Park was the McCarthy campaign's high-water mark, at least until then. The McCarthy forces,
fearful of not filling the huge baseball stadium, gave away some
tickets and the result was that some people with $100 tickets
couldn't get in. Notwithstanding, it was the largest paid political
rally in 1968, with 38,000 inside the park and 10,000 or 12,000
outside. "I have seen nirvana," cried a youthful campaigner as the
candidate entered the stadium to a resounding roar.

The following morning, flying back to Washington, the candidate had a chat with Washington lawyer Joe Rauh. Long a civil-
rights activist, Rauh thought he had discovered a way to trap
Hubert Humphrey in Georgia. McCarthy approved the plan, and
then he confided, "Well I've got troubles."

Finney had given authorization for a $25,000 set of polls to be
taken (characteristically for the campaign, Goodwin, the same
day, also authorized another $25,000 set) and his contact men
were organized and ready to move. "I was hoping our polls would
show a four or five point difference between McCarthy and Hum-

phrey in the key states, and I thought it might be enough," explained Edward Costikyan, Finney's delegate hunter for New York and other states. "A convention is a limited environment and seemingly small things can make a difference. In the meantime the last thing you wanted to be was offensive, as we were in ads like 'HUMPHREY, ANYONE?' You don't really deal with delegates but with leaders, and you don't quite ask for their vote. You certainly don't browbeat them. You didn't want to say that you hated Humphrey, only that Humphrey, demonstrably, wasn't going any place. Politicians don't look at individual polls, they look for trends, and if they *feel* a trend they are responsive to it. You help them along. You don't bring up the question of whether McCarthy is the better man —the function of the delegates is to find the candidate who is the best risk and who can represent as many approaches as possible. The biggest question for the delegates is not the Negro vote or anything else specific except 'Can he win?' You were trying to change revolutionaries into conventional politicians, but, I'm afraid, the McCarthy movement was basically antagonistic to national politics. I guess I didn't belong in the campaign—I've an orderly mind."

New York was a perfect and dreadful example of a campaign with split leadership. At one point in New York some half dozen different McCarthy delegate operations were at work—Finney and Costikyan, Gans' group, the CDA (mostly through their delegate letter-writing campaign), Jerome Eller from McCarthy's Washington office, assisted by Howard Stein, whose normal beat was Wall Street, and various McCarthy irregulars.

Stanley Steingut was the particular object of McCarthy affection, and, while perhaps amused by some of the not-so-hidden persuasion, he was not at all happy about a Murray Kempton column reporting conversations with the McCarthyites. It revealed that Steingut's principal interest in life was not who became President but whether Steingut could become Speaker of the New

York State Assembly, which, the following January, he did. The revelation of Steingut's private ambition gave the impression that the McCarthyites could not be trusted with confidences.

One of Finney's concerns was simply to keep the few professionals he had, like Costikyan, from leaving the campaign in disgust. Further, Mitchell's bellicose-sounding pronouncements from Chicago were undercutting his strategy—the Humphreyites, it might be noted, were also surprised that the McCarthyites were apparently doing everything possible to alienate the delegates. Finney went back to McCarthy, who told him to take full command of his campaign. Finney replied that he could not assume responsibility without clearly defined authority, and the two agreed that Finney would write a press release announcing Finney's generalship. Finney drew up an organization chart, with McCoy as administrative director and clear lines of responsibility. He brought the release to McCarthy on a Saturday, the day after McCarthy's triumphant rally at Fenway Park, and McCarthy said, "I can't do it, Tom." Finney felt humiliated, not only for himself but because he had involved many others who would now be out of the campaign. "You've got to put somebody in charge," he said, "and I can't take the responsibility without the authorization." McCarthy said, "It'll have to be Mitchell."

Those who knew the candidate well believed that Finney had made an error in attempting to persuade McCarthy to give him full responsibility—the candidate clearly preferred keeping his campaign chiefs equal, even if one had to "work around" some of them. But there was more to it than that. The McCarthy campaign had arrived at an impasse.

The dilemma, for such it was, lay in the candidate and the nature of his campaign. Finney's plan, in a sense, was optimistic because it declared that McCarthy had a chance to win inside the Democratic Party organization. But the Finney approach did not have the thrill of Mitchell's confrontation and it led to a seeming contradiction—to win for the new politics by means of the old. And if McCarthy used the old politics and lost, what would his campaigners have to show for it?

"What we *wouldn't* have had to show for it," Finney said later, "was Dick Nixon. I think the thing at Grant Park wouldn't have occurred, and I think the cause of liberalism would have been advanced. The McCarthy campaign would have fought some credentials fights, certainly, but the right ones with a chance of winning and we might have been able to marshall greater strength on the peace plank, at least. I thought the choice between McCarthy and Humphrey difficult and painful. The real thing was the war, and at that time I was indulging in the hope that if Gene could not win, at least Humphrey's position might be made more pliable by the McCarthy campaign even if it failed. And, probably more than most people in the campaign, I thought Gene McCarthy could win the nomination and become President if he could emerge as the candidate who could bring peace and unify the searing division within the party between North and South."

For those set on reforming the party Finney's notions vitiated the campaign of its revolutionary animus. As Gans said later, "The Finney thing had a great deal of meaning. The question was how you saw the candidacy—if you saw it as an alternative candidacy, to revive citizen participation and build better foundations for American democracy, or if you saw it in terms of an individual around whom to pick up delegates and national support. All the fights were based on the difference between what we saw and what Finney saw. In his view, if McCarthy could get the nomination, O.K., but if not there must still be unity in the Democratic Party. We saw him as an agent for the *status quo*. For us, a strategy of amelioration would not work. We thought to show that Humphrey would divide the party and lose. McCarthy could unite it and win."

Whatever chance there might have been to reconcile these divergent views, at least for the balance of the campaign, was drowned in the rumors that flooded the McCarthy camp. "When we first got the staff together in Washington, I told them we start out with double agents just for openers. They work for me but they're really working for themselves. Then we move to triple and quadruple agents, working for some cause. That's the trouble with all those NSA people, they're too conspiratorial. I'm the cause now, and everyone should be working for me," the candidate had warned, and gone unheeded.

Based entirely on circumstantial evidence, the rumors were revived that Finney was a double agent, doing his best to give the nomination to Humphrey. He was part of the "Oklahoma Octopus"—Albert, Criswell, Senator Fred Harris, and others—which was strangling the McCarthyites. The talk of his association with Clifford was again held against him. Finney's role in the Mississippi compromise at the 1964 convention, when he had been counsel to the Credentials Committee, was cited as evidence that he was a believer in the old politics. (Finney believed that the Mississippi Freedom Party in 1964 did not have legal status or enough votes; the compromise resulted in a call to the 1968 convention to unseat delegations which practiced discrimination.) The "astrologers" thought of him as a public-relations minded "flak," and what were differences in tone and strategy were taken as differences of loyalty.

McCarthy in fact tried to put Finney in charge, but too many of his campaigners were now certain that Finney was a Humphrey man. Perhaps, too, McCarthy was moving ever farther from the Democratic Party and it was too late to draw back. Faced with a choice, he chose against Finney, who faded from the campaign until later events brought him back in a new role. With Finney went all the semiprofessionals like Costikyan.

A week later the *New York Times*, which had the facts, called for Finney's side of it, and in the published result politicians all over the country found their worst fears about the ineptitude of the McCarthy organization confirmed.

While the McCarthy campaign was absorbed by internecine warfare, important developments were occurring on the Democratic front. Humphrey continued to gain delegates, but what was turning into a Humphrey collapse at the polls—"Humphrey couldn't be elected Mayor of Cairo against Arthur Goldberg," a McCarthyite quipped—served notice on politicians that, although the Democrats still vastly outnumbered the Republicans, the voters would reject a Democrat identified with the Administration. McCarthy was failing to move into the vacuum and now his campaign was confronted with yet more opposition, the candidacy of Senator George McGovern of South Dakota.

The McGovern campaign could hardly have been regarded by the McCarthyites as anything but inimical. McGovern had been urged to back McCarthy and was even offered fifteen minutes of television time by the McCarthy campaign. McGovern seemed willing to accept the time but did not want to mention McCarthy's name. McGovern first announced his candidacy in early August at Chicago's O'Hare Field to a group of important Kennedyites —Unruh, Hoff, Hughes, O'Brien, Sorensen, O'Donnell, Lucey, and others—who had assembled to organize support for the Commission on the Democratic Selection of Presidential Nominees, with Harold Hughes as chairman. McGovern's announcement was not greeted with enthusiasm by the group. Some felt that his candidacy would hurt McCarthy, others that it offered no help to beleaguered liberals like Unruh and Hughes. Partly to assuage McGovern, the group now offered him the chairmanship of a new rump group, the Committee for a Democratic Convention, and Lucey announced for the first time that he would support McCarthy. (He had gone to Minneapolis himself to double-check the candidate's qualifications with McCarthy's old friends.) Unruh,

Hughes, and Hoff said that they would support McCarthy, too, although the endorsements would be spaced out rather than given at the same time. From New York, Steve Smith flatly suggested that McGovern not run. The McGovern campaign was thought to have been stopped.

Less than a week later, when McGovern announced, Lucey and the others were surprised. "He just got the bug," one said later. "Besides, he thought he could help his own Senate candidacy." In addition it seemed likely that McGovern, reasoning that McCarthy could not get the nomination, hoped to offer at least a halfway spot between McCarthy and Humphrey, the same role McCarthy originally envisioned for himself. The McCarthyites could argue that McGovern would get no votes that McCarthy would not receive in the end, but McGovern, who only weeks before had fulsome praise for Humphrey, not only ran but began to attack McCarthy in full campaign style. McCarthy lacked, McGovern said, "active compassion." (McCarthy showed how he felt after the convention. The McCarthyites had a $60,000 slush fund raised to aid liberal candidates. How much for McGovern? "Give him," McCarthy said, "$145.50—a dollar for each vote he got at the convention.")

Nothing seemed to go right for the McCarthyites as the summer campaign drew to a close. Gans' deskmen were willing, dedicated, and bright, but this was not their year. No one forgot the day when the phone number of John Gilligan, who had beaten Senator Frank Lausche for the Democratic Senatorial nomination in Ohio, was asked for, provided, and called; the number was a mortuary's. "Oh, well," said one of the McCarthy staffers, "who's John Gilligan? We never call him."

The kids did not have the political pull to call leading politicians, so the job often fell to Blair Clark. But Clark had no particular standing in Democratic politics either though he "logged," as he put it, hundreds of calls a day. (To the point where he was found crying, "What's wrong with the phone?" It was shown to him that he was holding the receiver upside down.)

If it sometimes looked as though the McCarthy campaign could use a psychiatrist, it had, in fact, not one but two who held a few group and private sessions. They heard plenty. The campaign fatigue had developed into something resembling low-grade paranoia. Almost everybody was suspected of something. A treasurer was said to be embezzling campaign funds; Goodwin was for Ted Kennedy; Lowenstein was CIA; Gans was for the "movement." When Gans sent out wires scheduling a meeting, another campaigner, thinking a different group should be invited, called Western Union, canceled Gans' telegrams, and exchanged them for his own. What other campaign—in a country where "law and order" was a principal issue—would nurture a group called BAM, Black Americans for McCarthy (despite the candidate's distaste for special interest groups)? A relative of a prominent Negro leader was allowed to run up a $1000 bill in a week at a Washington hotel, while at the same time there were attempts to cut back the national staff existing on their pitifully small per diems. These attempts were always frustrated by such ploys as what was laughingly called Project-Adopt-A-Worker—if a staffer was given the ax he would merely double up on somebody else's per diem. Once in the McCarthy campaign, nobody ever wanted to leave it. "The more we fire, the more there are," one of the treasurers lamented. "It's just a New Left political bull session on the payroll. Why, they're already setting up for 1970."

The loyalty to candidate and cause was fierce, often past compromise. A McCarthy half-hour television program was being prepared and a dispute broke out. On one side the Nees and Arthur Michelson, a public-relations man on leave from his job in Minnesota, wanted the candidate to ad lib before the camera, as he usually did. The natural, almost homey flavor of his personality, they felt, was muted if he tried to read from a script. Richard Goodwin, though, wanted McCarthy to read a prepared text from TelePrompTer cards (which Goodwin had to write himself in longhand because the other side "forgot" to order them). Goodwin's goal was crispness and clarity in a strong statement on civil rights. An agreement was reached. McCarthy would tape both segments and the better one would be used.

Once the tapes were made, each side still insisted its version was best. After heated arguments, the matter went to Clark to adjudicate and Clark chose the Goodwin version. Michelson was angry enough to take a swing at Clark.

The "Goodwin" half-hour tape was at an NBC studio in New York for final preparation, to be shown nation-wide that next night. At four-thirty in the morning Goodwin was waiting for an elevator at the St. Regis. He wanted to see the completed film before leaving for Washington. Coming out of the elevator was Michelson, who had, Goodwin thought, an odd expression. Goodwin went straight to the studio and from there he called Stein. "There has been a theft," he announced. "We'd better call the police."

"There has been a theft. There is talk of searching the hotel," Stein called the Nees to say at six a.m. For Michelson had simply taken the film, and during the day the plotters, Michelson and Bill and Kay Nee, sat in a coffeeshop playfully winding the film strip around Coke bottles. They reasoned that with the Goodwin section kidnaped their own would have to be used, but they had miscalculated. Michelson had taken only a copy—the master reel remained at the studio. Learning of this, Michelson dispatched a campaigner from Washington with an entirely different half-hour show which had been used earlier in the campaign. Because of air traffic she arrived late, which was the only reason there was a McCarthy television half hour that night. Goodwin had put a guard on the film, but faced with conflicting instructions, NBC doubtlessly would have canceled the show.

"You're crazy—nothing like this could have happened," an NBC executive remarked in bewilderment about the incident.

The best remaining hope of the campaign was McCarthy's continuing popularity. On a scale measuring sincerity, strength, straightforwardness, coolheadedness, decisiveness, confidence, independence, up-to-dateness, excitement, and good looks he outdid Humphrey in every category. He remained ahead of Humphrey in most polls right to the end, but strength was greatly obscured by the disparity between the Gallup and Harris Nixon-Rockefeller polls before the Republican Convention. Poll results were suddenly in doubt, and the Democratic delegates had one more reason to ignore the McCarthy claims.

In fact, and somewhat mysteriously to his campaigners, McCarthy was not making the same gains in the polls in August as he had in July. Partly, the results appeared to reflect the slow pace of McCarthy's campaign and, partly, according to an analysis prepared by the McCarthy campaign, the poll sample techniques. Why, the campaigners asked, was McCarthy's real strength always underestimated by preprimary polls? For he had run between 4 and 20 per cent ahead of the poll predictions and consistently captured between 62 and 73 per cent of the undecided vote. The answer, the analysis maintained, was that the poll samples were too heavily weighted toward people over 50, with too little emphasis on those between 21 and 29. Older people *registered* with greater frequency, but the *turnout* among younger voters who registered was higher, offsetting the difference. Therefore, it was said, poll samples should be weighted in terms of the eligible-to-vote population, giving greater emphasis to the young where McCarthy was the heavy favorite over Humphrey.

The McCarthy forces could also point out that the polls were really national samples which included the South, where McCarthy was weak. But the South would not go Democratic in 1968, their argument went, and McCarthy showed his serious strength in states which the Democrats would have to carry to win. A Kraft survey, commissioned by the McCarthy campaign, of ten states which had conducted primaries showed McCarthy running stronger than Humphrey in every one—15 per cent in California, 20 per cent in Oregon, 17 in Nebraska, 17 in Illinois, and so on. More important, the poll indicated that McCarthy would or might be able to carry the key states which Humphrey could not—California, Illinois, South Dakota, Oregon, Indiana, Wisconsin. In the national election Humphrey was to lose every one of them. (New York and Massachusetts were shown to be safe for either Democrat and Humphrey won both.)

"Talking to Eugene McCarthy after an interval of a couple of years, one is first of all impressed with the absence of any effect the momentous events of this year have had upon his personality and behavior," wrote the political scientist Hans Morgenthau in the *New York Review of Books* in August. "Most public men—and for that matter, most private men as well—play roles which either they or others or events have assigned to them."

His own man to the end, McCarthy's trouble was that the perceptions of intellectuals like Morgenthau and those of the delegates increasingly failed to square. After a survey of fifty states, Bruce Biossat noted in an August *National Observer*: "Many doubt Senator McCarthy can be elected. Some cite his temperament and personality and conclude that they are unsuitable for the Presidency. Others doubt his seriousness of purpose. Nearly all consider him a maverick, a man who is irregular, unconventional, unpredictable."

He would not—or could not—undo this impression; indeed, in the waning days of his campaign he reinforced it. As Chicago loomed closer, the candidate seemed guilty of political mistakes.

One was the announcement of his future Cabinet. There was a certain detectable frivolity about the assortment—it had been assembled at high speed and names added or taken off on the plane from Washington to New York, where the list was released. Even some of the middle names were wrong—a McCarthy Cabinet would have had not Thomas B. Watson, the IBM executive, but a manufacturer of plumbing equipment. Watson and other businessmen, Coretta King, Republicans, maverick Democrats—the group was not only mostly unnew politics but it was almost a taunt at the regular Democrats beginning to assemble at Chicago.

Another was McCarthy's statement on the Soviet invasion of Czechoslovakia the week before the convention. The news could not have come at a worse time for the McCarthyites, just then releasing their own peace plank on Vietnam. McCarthy recognized the impact the situation would have on his campaign and on his efforts toward peace. Jeremy Larner had prepared a statement for him, but McCarthy brushed it aside in favor of his own and refused entreaties to change it. The President, he said, had acted "out of proportion" in convening the National Security Council to consider what was not "a major world crisis." Instead of calling the emergency meeting on Tuesday night, "I would listen to the news on the radio, check it out with a few people to see if it was accurate, and tell them let's keep informed and we will meet in the morning."

McCarthy meant that Czechoslovakia was not a major world crisis in the way that a potential thermonuclear exchange would be, not that it was no crisis at all. He said in the campaign that hyper-reactions and superfast reflexes caused damage and he was restating that position. Besides, he always avoided the conventional utterances of those like Senator Everett Dirksen or Representative Gerald Ford who were already appealing to patriotic sentiments, which McCarthy, almost above all else, did not wish to trade on. Calling the National Security Council late at night, when it could do nothing, was to him a grandstand play.

Nonetheless, his statement was wrongly pitched, aimed as it was at the American political process and Johnson, not the international situation. He was almost too perfectionistic in not making the simple political gesture, which was probably the President's intention in convening the Council, of indicating concern for the Czech people. McCarthy soon realized he'd made a mistake, and asked his assistant, Eller, to work on a clarifying statement. He said, "Of course I condemn this cruel and violent action. It should not really be necessary for me to say this, but to make clear my attitude, I do." But the damage was done.

Such developments in the campaign shocked many McCarthy supporters and convinced them that McCarthy was "blowing it," as Allard Lowenstein said. Mitchell, working out of Chicago, was upset and said so later: "I always knew Gene was a hell of a campaigner, but something happened to him on the home stretch. He always ran hard at the end and peaked at the right moment. This time he faltered."

He had given up. A week before the August 26 Democratic Convention he told an alert British reporter, Jeremy Hornsby of the London *Express*, that he could not make it at Chicago—a statement picked up, oddly, by only one American newspaper. By then he had called Finney and asked him to step back in the campaign. "What's your reading?" he said. "What's yours?" Finney answered; and McCarthy said, "I think it's gone."

In the last days of the McCarthy campaign the candidate wished to accomplish four things. He wanted to maximize his vote at Chicago, partly to please the troops who had worked so hard for him; to keep his name out of contention for the Vice-Presidency, at least for the time being; to get gracefully out of a scheduled television debate with Humphrey; and to push Humphrey toward accepting some version of the McCarthy peace plank. Finney, who became his chief agent in these negotiations, called Humphrey's campaign manager, Lawrence O'Brien. If the Humphreyites had secured the nomination as they claimed, he said, then they should permit scattered McCarthy strength, locked up in Humphrey delegations by the unit rule or political commitments, to vote for its candidate. McCarthy, Finney said, would campaign for Humphrey only in states where McCarthy got delegate votes. It was a matter of some fifty potential McCarthy votes and

O'Brien appeared to agree, but because of confusion, antagonism to the McCarthyites, and last-minute uncertainty among the Humphrey forces the votes were never delivered. (McCarthy also explored, to no avail, ways in which he might assist Maine's Muskie get the Democratic Presidential nomination.)

McCarthy made clear to Humphrey, at a meeting at the latter's house the week before the convention, that he did not want to be in contention for the Vice-Presidency, even if it were offered. The mere whiff of a deal would cause apprehension among the McCarthy supporters and the uncommitted delegates; just as important, a McCarthy move toward the Vice-Presidency would be interpreted as self-advancement and old politics and would not only hurt his own political future but render suspect the backing he might tender Humphrey. If Humphrey could support a dove plank on Vietnam, McCarthy might be able to come over to him— and there was every reason to hope that Humphrey was changing his stand on the war.

None of these objectives would have been aided by a McCarthy-Humphrey confrontation on television one day before the convention began. It was past the time when a debate could help and it could hurt the McCarthy forces in the platform fights. McCarthy didn't want to box in Humphrey on Vietnam. Finney talked to the Humphrey camp: McCarthy would not be the one to cancel the debate, but if Humphrey, who had no stomach for the debate either, wanted to make a tacit agreement to cancel the debate the McCarthyites would not exploit the situation. Inviting the other Democratic Presidential candidates—McGovern and Lester Maddox of Georgia, who had now announced—to join would have killed the debate, prompting the television networks to cancel the affair themselves. But there seemed to be a real possibility that the Federal Communications Commission would rule in favor of a McCarthy-Humphrey debate, without the other candidates, and an agreement was reached on a statement that, after discussion with McCarthy's staff, the Vice-President was canceling the "Meet the Press" program on the grounds that he did not have time.

This decision was apparently not communicated to Chicago, where most of McCarthy's staff people now were, and they immediately issued statements taunting the Vice-President for being afraid to debate. A bewildered Humphrey, in person, called a McCarthy aide to say, "What the hell is going on?" In the end, it was McCarthy who had to cancel the debate, saying it was too late to have an impact.

The candidate, when he flew to Chicago on the Sunday before the Monday opening, had been on the campaign trail a full year— if one includes his early testings of the potential race. He had campaigned in thirty-two states and visited cities and towns beyond recall. He had traveled well over a hundred thousand miles and the airplanes he had used were talismans of his progress—from commercial airliner to two-engined private planes to a chartered American Airlines Electra and then a Boeing 727,[2] in which he usually sat on the front seat left with his legs on a cushion. Coatless, in suspenders, wearing heavy-frame glasses, smoothing his hair with a flat-palmed gesture, his shoulders high and surprisingly bony, he looked perhaps older than his years. In front of him was a partition on which, before each journey that summer, his campaigners mounted a poster with a photo of Humphrey and Johnson that read: WHY CHANGE THE DUMMY FOR THE VENTRILOQUIST? Patiently he would ask to have it taken down and on this trip he did so for the last time. From small and brave beginnings he had set enormous forces in motion—forces which were not played out and whose impact was yet to be tested at Chicago and beyond.

[2] The 727, on which McCarthy traveled 40,000 miles, cost $11,000 a month plus $200 an hour in flight. The cost was offset, though, by the fact that the press corps on board paid first-class fares to the campaign.

10 | Confrontation at Chicago

A national party convention is a sea of particles, and though the Democratic tides appeared to be running strongly toward Hubert Humphrey no one could be certain that the Humphrey high-water mark might not be something short of nomination. If Humphrey failed on the first try, he might well fail for good. His strength would rapidly recede and the particles begin to flow toward Eugene McCarthy. Much depended then on mood—a candidate who believed he was strong, his optimism and actions reflecting it, might well be a better challenger.

McCarthy's Chicago contingent had been preparing for the convention for weeks and they were far from being as pessimistic as their candidate. On Sunday, August 25, when McCarthy arrived at Midway Airport, they glimpsed a few strong rays of hope. But Abigail McCarthy had called Pat Lucey to say, "Gene's very discouraged. Go cheer him up." Lucey was the first man up the ramp after the plane taxied to a stop near a mass of McCarthy supporters waving signs. "We want a respectable vote," McCarthy said at once, but Lucey answered, laughing, "Don't give me that stuff. I came to get you nominated."

McCarthy stood on a wooden platform on the edge of the field and looked down at a crowd of 10,000 to 15,000.[1] That particular

[1] Norman Mailer's count was 5000, but he may have been distracted by noses. Observing McCarthy's arrival he reported that the McCarthyites had a "com-

morning the lines on roads to the airport were being repainted, ob-
structing traffic—that, of all days: believers in conspiracies were
having a field day in Chicago—but the crowd had come anyway, a
forest of signs: HYDE PARK WANTS GENE; LOVE NOT HATE; LEADERS
OF THE PEOPLE SHOULD BE PEOPLE; RENAISSANCE, NOT REDUN-
DANCE; GIVE THE PRESIDENCY BACK TO THE PEOPLE; DELIVER US
FROM HHH; SEND HUBEY BACK TO THE PHARM; HHH—HOHOHO.

The candidate smiled into the microphone and tried to speak.
The mike was dead. Sabotage? he laughed. He tried the other
microphones. Dead! The crowd groaned, half in pleasure at the
simple-minded perfidy of Chicago police. Let's sing! said the candidate, but they were not in the spirit. They were ready for a fight.
Was their candidate?

In the car, after a short speech, McCarthy listened to Lucey,
who brought him up to date. Sunday and Monday were the critical days. It was not yet over. The night before, Richard Goodwin
had had a long meeting with Texas Governor Connally. Lucey did
not tell McCarthy that, but he did ask, approximately, "What if
you're confronted with the choice of continuing in the Senate or
being President with Connally as Veep?" McCarthy thought the
idea was preposterous.

Among those watching the car leave the airport was *Esquire*'s
"reportage team"—Terry Southern, the novelist, bearded, with
sinister dark glasses; Jean Genêt, the French playwright, in an
open-necked shirt and corduroys, short and bald, resembling a
benign and demure Khrushchev; William Burroughs, the novelist,
tall and thin, all in brown from his shoes to his thrown-back 1930s
newspaperman's-style hat—a lithograph by Daumier. They stared
at the departing caravan and their faces said, "What does this
Democratic National Convention *mean*? Can anybody make
sense of it?"

---

mon denominator—thin nostrils." I was not able, apparently, to observe as
many nostrils close up as Mailer, but the crowd seemed normal nasally,
though perhaps the throng was trying to scent victory.

In Chicago, a group of forty young lawyers headed by Wayne Whelan and John Schmidt had been organizing the McCarthy convention challenges since early July. The lawyers were upset over the treatment of the McCarthy forces in some states like New York and, especially, Pennsylvania, where McCarthy received eighty per cent of the popular vote but a much smaller percentage of the delegates. The pro-McCarthy and/or anti-regular-Democrat sentiment in the Chicago legal community appeared immense —the lawyers were generally from the wealthy law firms, which, though normally Republican, were nevertheless willing to give them time off for the fight. Aided by Jessica Tuchman, the lawyers divided the country into regions and began a full-scale review of the laws governing delegate selection.

The results were not encouraging for the McCarthyites or for democratic choice. In 1967, Richard J. Hughes, Governor of New Jersey and chairman of the Special Equal Rights Committee of the Democratic National Committee, had written to all state party chairmen reminding them of the Call to the 1968 Convention, which stipulated that voters, regardless of color, creed, or national origin, should have a chance to participate fully in party affairs. The party, Hughes said, must make certain that all delegates "are broadly representative of Democrats in the state" and seemed to promise that the Credentials Committee in 1968 would unseat those delegations which did not fill the bill. Quite apart from the question of whether "broadly representative" included Democrats favorable to McCarthy, the Credentials Committee, if it stuck faithfully to this stricture, would have an insuperable task, the McCarthy lawyers thought. In no less than thirty-five or forty states were there illegalities or irregularities. A truly democratic convention would have required throwing this convention out and starting over. The party was resisting fresh blood just when, for the first time in many years, an army of new donors had arrived.

One of the troubles for the newcomers was the question of time.

About six hundred delegates—almost a quarter of the total votes —had been selected by party officials, themselves chosen at least a year before the convention. In Maryland, for instance, the national delegates were picked at a state convention, the delegates to which were members of the state central committee chosen in 1964. In cases like this, changes in the national outlook, shown by the successes of McCarthy and Kennedy against Administration slates, were not reflected in the composition of the delegations. The 1968 Democratic Convention is a dramatic example of institutions unable to prepare for the rapidity of change in modern times. The six hundred, plus the one hundred votes of the national committeemen and committeewomen from each state, were committed to party regularity—which meant the Administration, which meant Humphrey—and this was the springboard from which the Vice President could hurtle to nomination.

In addition to the problem of *when* delegates were selected, there was also the matter of *how* they were chosen. As one experienced observer put it, "through machine politics and confused long ballots [bosses] have perfected barriers which keep opposing party members from finding a way to their positions of command." The reformers concluded that there were only two sufficiently democratic methods in use in the states: direct primaries where all the delegates-at-large went to the winner, as in Wisconsin and Oregon, or the choosing of delegates in district primaries, as in Florida. Most states, though, used one or another variety of party machinery to pick some or all of the delegates, and the result, as the McCarthy forces saw it, was an unfair representation of voter preferences, with minority (or even majority) preferences not given adequate weight. This skewing of strength toward the party regulars was compounded by the unit rule, requiring that the entire vote be cast according to the preference of the majority, used by nine states and territories coming to the 1968 convention, with optional use in eight other states and the District of Columbia.

There was, finally, the issue of race. The Call to the 1968 Convention demanded that state parties represent all citizens equally, and while the percentage of Negroes at the Democratic Convention had been rising—1.5 per cent in 1952, 2.2 in 1964, 5.7 in 1968—it was clear that Negroes were underrepresented in terms of their part of the total population, 10.5 per cent in 1960 and undoubtedly more now. In twelve states and the District of Columbia, the percentage of blacks in the delegations exceeded the percentage of the blacks in the state population, but in many others Negroes were grossly underrepresented. The challenges based on race were similar to those based on delegate selection in that both resulted in systematic exclusion of minorities, one minority racial, the other political.

The Chicago legal group sent lawyers to Texas, Georgia, and Tennessee—they had wanted the challenges to originate locally, but outside help was sometimes needed—and they narrowed the challenges to those which seemed important and likely to succeed. Nineteen McCarthy credentials challenges were eventually filed, three weeks before the convention.

Mitchell had brought in Joe Rauh and Herbert Reed, civil-rights activists, as senior policy advisers, and with them the McCarthy strategy now underwent a subtle shift. Mitchell's central thrust had been on the unit rule and the exclusion of political minorities —this would be the McCarthy "boss" issue and would be fought out in the Committee on Rules and Order of Business. The Rules Committee met only a few days before the convention; the Credentials Committee met first. By precedent the Credentials Committee was the place for challenges based on race. The result was to change the challengers' emphasis from the political minorities to the racial or national-origin minorities. It was symbolic of this change in emphasis that the Texas challenge, largely a matter of the exclusion of political minorities, once the cornerstone of Mitchell's strategy, dropped to second place behind that of Georgia, which was based on civil rights.

Today, civil rights is *the* Northern liberal domestic issue. It was clearly not one the McCarthy forces could lay special claim to pursuing. The original McCarthy plan—to show a consistent violation of the "one-man one-vote" principle throughout the country by hitting at improprieties in states like Washington, Indiana, Michigan, and Texas and, despite the small number of delegates usually involved, to dramatize the condition of the party—was subordinated to more conventional demands for civil rights. Once the McCarthyites were launched on this course, they would concentrate on the Southern challenges and find it easier to compromise on the political ones in the North.

As soon as the Credentials Committee opened its sessions in Chicago, the Monday before the convention was to begin, it became apparent that the underrepresentation the McCarthyites were complaining about was nowhere more obvious than in the committee itself. The reformers (McCarthyites, Kennedyites, McGovernites) could probably claim a third of the convention vote, or more, but they only had 10 or 15 members of the 112-man committee. One of the first rulings of the chairman was to bar a motion that would have prohibited challenged delegations from voting on their own fate, both in the committee and on the floor if it came to a fight. To permit such procedure seemed a clear violation of democratic principles. Indeed, the pattern of events and demeanor of the regular Democrats suggested to the McCarthyites that the Humphrey forces had determined more or less in advance how far the McCarthy rebellion would be permitted to go, and that once that line had been reached the rebels would be crushed by whatever means necessary. The chairman, Governor Richard J. Hughes, in his opening remarks to the committee, complained that some people—evidently the McCarthyites—were more interested in disrupting the convention than electing a President and this theme was repeated endlessly.

The McCarthy bark turned out to be worse than its bite. Only eight of the challenges were actually brought to the Credentials Committee by the McCarthyites and, of these, they thought only a few were serious. All the while calling for party unity, the regulars, on the other hand, acted with the martial spirit the police would soon demonstrate. "You'd have thought we were Trotskyites," a McCarthy Credentials Committee member said bitterly. The regular Democrats, significantly, seemed to have misread the mood of 1968; they were certain that the McCarthyites would rejoin the fold once the nomination was in—as reformist dissidents had done before.

From the outset of the hearings, the McCarthy people were annoyed by the secrecy of the chairman. Executive, closed sessions were scheduled through Saturday; the notion, it seems, was to hold the hearings during the week and reach decisions on Saturday—a means, the suspicious McCarthyites decided, of deferring the seating of the challenged Mississippi delegation until just before the convention opened. It would then be interpreted as a progressive victory, blurring the defeat of challenges from other states. Everyone on the committee knew that the Mississippi challenge would win—the delegation had not met the 1964 directive to convene with a fair representation of Negroes—and the McCarthyites argued that the committee vote should be taken at once. They won their case; the Mississippi vote was held on Tuesday. The McCarthyites scored, they believed, an important victory: Mississippi would prepare the way for successful fights in Georgia, Alabama, and Texas.

The committee turned to the other cases. "There was more under the rocks than we had supposed," said Howard Morgan, a McCarthy delegate from Oregon. "It was an outrage. Terrible. Just terrible. State after state showed massive irregularities." In North Carolina some voter-registration lists exceeded the total population, in one county by over two hundred per cent. The lists had not eliminated the dead and gone and included fictitious names —which evidently could be voted by white people. In three Congressional Districts of Indiana the McCarthy forces had been unable to get the floor at delegate-selection meetings, which had lasted less than five minutes. In Washington State, the McCarthyites claimed, the regular Democrats had used a variety of means to deprive them of votes, including a rigged caucus after which the ballots had been destroyed. The dirty deed was recorded in a poem circulated at Chicago called "The Ballad of Pierce County":

> From the shores of Puget Sound
> The story's going round
> How they burned the evidence
> To hide their crime from view
> One-thirty-seven cast their votes
> Hubert won but it was close
> But the ballot tally was one-forty-two
> (Very strange)
>
> So they burned all the ballots
> Burned up the ballots
> So no one could ever see
> They burned all the ballots
> Burned all the ballots
> In Washington's Pierce County. . . .
>
> Can you picture now the sight in Chicago one fine night
> Someone calls for a recount
> But they're burning the ballots
> It's the politics of joy
> For our pyrotechnic boys
> And the only way to stop them is to vote
> (For Gene) . . .

Some of the challenges were dropped and some pursued without ardor—in any case, the committee voted most of them down overwheimingiy. There would be floor fights on some. This left, for the McCarthyites in the Credentials Committee, two key states, Texas and Georgia. Georgia offered some interesting tactical possibilities before Governor Lester G. Maddox muddied the waters by entering the race. Some weeks previous, Joe Rauh had noted the approach of a rump convention called the Georgia Democratic

Forum. Humphrey was supporting both the Forum and the regular Democrats headed by Governor Maddox, and Rauh saw a chance to pin the Vice-President to the wall. If Humphrey could be forced to choose Maddox, with whom a famous photo showed him linking arms, over the civil-rights-minded insurgents then the Vice-President's conservative base of support would be identified. To do this a grass-roots organization—Rauh, Gans, Sam Brown, David Mixner, Charles Negaro, and others—went to Georgia and worked the Forum, controlled by Humphrey labor-liberals. By the time the Forum opened, the McCarthyites had seventy per cent of the vote, though they offered spots on the challenge delegation to the Humphrey supporters. Humphrey now faced the prospect of backing Maddox or a heavily pro-McCarthy delegation headed by Julian Bond.

The Bondsmen arrived in Chicago expecting to be seated, and the fact that they emerged with only half the Georgia delegation was one of the shocks of the 1968 convention. The Georgia challenge case rested on the premise, as its brief said, that "the Georgia Democratic Party has wholly failed to assume its burden to assure full Negro participation in party affairs." Georgia delegates, under state law, were chosen by the Chairman of the State Executive Committee with the advice of the Democratic governor. The chairman, James Grey, had supported Barry Goldwater in 1964. Grey and Maddox had absolute power to choose the delegates —as Governor, Maddox also picked the State Chairman, Grey— and it seemed abundantly clear that they would not observe the convention's call for full and equal participation by everyone. But now, at Chicago, the regular Democrats urged compromise. Both delegations would be seated in full, with each group getting half of the vote.

Bond did not want to compromise but was under enormous pressure to do so—at one point he called the Vice-President to complain about the treatment of his group and to ask Humphrey's support. Humphrey, too, was for the original compromise plan. It

had begun to look as though the Bondsmen would have to accept
a compromise and, if so, they wanted a good one. The compromise
that Bond would have accepted under duress was that only half of
the regular Georgians be seated, corresponding with half their
vote, but on Saturday, with Bond absent, Hughes announced that
Bond had accepted the original compromise, which he had not, and
his compromise resolution carried. "I have never been so used and
humiliated," Bond said, "though I have dealt with Southern seg-
regationists."

The McCarthy minority was now up in arms and determined to
fight out the Georgia question on the convention floor. The minority resolution was presented to the committee staff late Saturday
afternoon but the bearer forgot the instructions to ask for a receipt
(matters had reached *that* stage), and at six-thirty in the evening
the minority group was told that no report had been filed and it
was now too late, the deadline being past. The McCarthyites went
to the convention leadership for a ruling. Why was there a Saturday deadline for the minority report when the majority report
would not be filed until Monday? If the minority could not file
with the convention, it would do it on national television. The
minority report was then permitted to be filed, but the McCarthy
forces were approaching total alienation. "Hughes," one McCarthy
delegate said acidly, "is so crooked he has to screw his hat on."

The Texas credentials challenge was argued on Thursday. The
dissidents said that the delegation should be reconstituted. It excluded Mexican-Americans and Negroes and liberal Democrats
loyal to the party in favor of conservatives who sometimes even
voted Republican, and it buried the opposition in the unit rule.
(The challengers cited incidents like a reformist Mexican-Ameri-
can sheriff's being dragged through the streets in Bexar County by
Texas Rangers.) They asked for 50 of Texas's 104 delegate votes
and were roundly beaten in the committee. If he lost one delegate, Connally threatened, he would walk out of the convention.

The fight now shifted to the Rules Committee. On Wednesday,

the McCarthyites had met to discuss strategy, and they decided to try to get the unit rule abolished, not just in the permanent rules, which would apply to future conventions, but in the temporary rules, which would apply to this one. The trouble was that the temporary-rules decision would be among the first on the convention floor on Monday, and voting against it would be the states bound by the unit rule and the regular Democratic delegations which might be unseated in the credentials fights that came afterward. It was something like getting beheaded by the man you intended to behead the following day.

By Thursday, when the Rules Committee opened, the battle lines were drawn and it was the McCarthyites vs. Texas, the self-appointed defenders of the *status quo*. The Texans argued that the unit rule was not only constitutional but, as Governor Connally put it, "the very essence of pure democracy." (Connally was plainly annoyed. Was the Mitchell strategy beginning to work after all?) Mitchell hotly argued the case against the unit rule before the committee on Thursday. It was, he said, "infamous," and he was grilled mercilessly by the unit-rulers. The McCarthyites were not gentle either, and the Texans threatened to put President Johnson's name in nomination. One Texas delegate went so far as to say, "If we knew the unit rule would be broken we wouldn't have put the minorities on the Texas delegation!"

The unit-rule question now went to a drafting committee, and the McCarthyites were still convinced that the regulars did not clearly comprehend the distinction between temporary and permanent rules. For their amendment to abolish the unit rule as a temporary rule, for the voting in this convention, was accepted, and this became the majority report of the Rules Committee, with an enraged Texas filing a minority report. But though the regulars were willing to abolish the unit rule at the convention level for this and subsequent conventions, they would not accept the McCarthyite proposal to ban the unit rule down to the precinct level and to insist that delegates be chosen in the calendar year the convention

was held. That, the regulars said, violated States' rights. The Mc-
Carthyites then filed a minority report too.

That was where matters stood on Monday, when something
curious occurred. Hy Raskin, the convention's parliamentarian,
called the McCarthyites to say that the temporary-rules amendment was out of order procedurally, citing chapter and verse. The
McCarthyites said it was not and, besides, to reverse the decision
of Samuel Shapiro, Governor of Illinois and chairman of the
Rules Committee who had permitted the amendment (though perhaps not understanding it), would make Shapiro look like a fool.
Raskin let the amendment stand.

Meanwhile, another great fight was brewing over the plank
on Vietnam, first in Washington where the Committee on Resolutions and Platforms had opened its hearing and then in Chicago
when the committee moved there. About three hundred witnesses,
including Cabinet members and United States Senators, were to
speak, but, despite the impressive testimony, the foreign-policy
planks—and probably the others—had already been prepared for
the committee staff and cleared through the Federal bureaucracy
in a memorandum[2] which made clear the Vietnam bias of the
committee staff. It accepted uncritically the Administration's stand
on the bombing halt: "We support a complete bombing halt in the
North as soon as Hanoi shows a positive sign of reciprocal restraint," and omitted altogether a call for an end to the search-
and-destroy missions. It made no reference to any necessity for
peaceful contact between the National Liberation Front and the
Saigon government but spoke vaguely of the period "when a cease
fire or truce between South and North Vietnam is achieved." It
talked of "an increased flow of American equipment" so that the
Southerners could take a larger share of the fighting, hardly a way
to lessen U.S. involvement in Southeast Asia. These and other

[2] Signed by Ernest W. Lefever and dated August 6, almost two weeks before
the Resolutions and Rules Committee opened its hearings.

stipulations not only made the peace talks meaningless but would have led to an intensification of the fighting. It was, in short, the old American solution of peace through military victory and much of it found its way into the language of the majority plank adopted by the 1968 Democratic Convention.[3]

Against the Administration were a variety of positions, from less hawkish to outright dove. Not only were few doves scheduled to testify, but their appearances seemed suspiciously arranged to fall in nonprime television time. The McCarthy forces threatened to hold separate hearings and were finally awarded more time. Again the Humphreyites had given evidence that they failed to grasp the depth of antiwar feeling.

The two key issues for the doves were the cessation of bombing in the North and the participation of the NLF in the peace talks. There was much talk that Humphrey was actually encouraging a halfway position between the hawks and doves offered by Clark Kerr, former President of the University of California and National Chairman of the National Committee for a Political Settlement in Vietnam (Negotiation Now!). It urged Humphrey to accept a bombing halt and McCarthy to give up his insistence on a coalition government and accept instead a standstill cease fire, leaving each side in *de facto* control of the territory it held, pending free elections. Another compromise, suggested by Senator Edmund S. Muskie, would have accepted NLF participation in the Saigon government once the war was ended but supplied no guarantees. There was the McCarthy position, which asked for

[3] The Democratic platform called for a halt in the bombing "when this action would not endanger the lives of our troops in the field; this action should take into account the response from Hanoi." A postwar Vietnam government should "encourage all parties and interests" to abide by "fair and safeguarded elections." There was no mention of the NLF: troop withdrawal was to be negotiated with "Hanoi." "Until the fighting stops, accelerate our efforts to train and equip the South Vietnamese army so that it can defend its own country" (again, a muddy road to peace). The plank also proposed "substantial U.S. contribution" to postwar reconstruction of South and North Vietnam—a commitment so vast that one doubts that any American government could carry it out.

both a bombing halt and a coalition government with "substantial participation by the NLF." "Any statement," it said, "of principle or intention—either in speeches or in party platforms—which does not deal with the future government of South Vietnam in specific terms is an evasion of responsibility."

There was still the Kennedy position—whether it was more or less dovish than McCarthy's was a question of one's viewpoint. It sought an immediate and unconditional bombing halt in the North, de-escalation in the South, and asked the U.S. "to seek an early end to the civil war" in the South with free and binding elections. In his first speech since his brother's assassination, Ted Kennedy called for "the mutual withdrawal" of all foreign forces from the South. That was dovish, since the Vietcong were clearly stronger than Saigon unaided, but the Kennedy stance did not specifically deal with the question of admitting the NLF into an interim coalition government and thus failed to satisfy the Mc-Carthyites. Some Kennedyites argued that the coalition government was no more than a device to protect the Saigon government.

The dove groups knew before they reached Chicago that to have any success they would have to fly together, in formation. Even before the Republican Convention a cabal had formed— Frank Mankiewicz, Fred Dutton, and Kenneth P. O'Donnell, former Kennedy advisers; Senators Wayne Morse, Oregon, and Claiborne Pell, Rhode Island; John Gilligan; and the Committee for a Democratic Convention, with George McGovern as chairman. Dutton was the guiding spirit. He had been the somewhat unwitting perpetrator of the 1964 Democratic Platform, which had made precisely one reference to the looming disaster in Vietnam, pledging "unflagging devotion to our commitments to freedom from Berlin to South Vietnam." He was convinced, as were the others, that this time the Democratic platform must be more specific and binding on the nominee.

Ironically, the cabal hoped to avoid a floor fight. The strategy had been to keep carpentering on specific planks, like gun control and the findings of the Kerner Commission, to fashion them to liberal specifications. There was even some hope that a peace plank could be planed smooth enough to permit the Vice-President to slide away from the President without too many splinters. One of the cabalists, Congressman Gilligan, was hoping to do for Humphrey on Vietnam what Humphrey had done for Truman on civil rights in 1948. He would take the peace plank to the floor, Humphrey to the White House, and himself to the Senate. "You can have twenty good years," a fellow cabalist told him, "and then fall on your face too."

Despite an impressive series of hearings before the Resolutions and Rules Committee, there was no peace plank in sight that could be agreed on—John Connally attacked McCarthy's and McGovern's positions, driving a wedge between hawks and doves still deeper, and the doves met to smooth out their differences on a peace plank of their own. There were more insurgents on the Platform Committee than on any other committee—over twenty-five of them. The group broke itself down into sections, with Theodore Sorensen given the responsibility of the Vietnam plank.

Goodwin, as McCarthy's peace-plank representative, was not pleased with this. The writer of an original draft, he reasoned, would have an advantage—in the fatigue and confusion, a draft might be hard to attack properly—and Goodwin was not quite certain where Sorensen was placed in the political web of Chicago. Goodwin called Pierre Salinger, now laboring for McGovern, and the two spent the night creating another minority plank. It was brought to the dove caucus the following day, and Sorensen confirmed Goodwin's suspicions by trying to exclude him from the caucus on the grounds that he was not a platform-committee delegate. Sorensen was now accused of fashioning a plank acceptable to Humphrey. Indeed, the Sorensen draft was less dovish than the McCarthy stand and might have isolated McCarthy still further at the convention. After an all-day-and-all-night drafting battle, the McCarthy, Kennedy, and McGovern groups reached a compromise, which Goodwin read to McCarthy over the phone. Later becoming the minority plank on Vietnam, it called for an unconditional end to the bombing while continuing to provide all necessary air and other support for American troops. It asked a negotiated mutual withdrawal of American and North Vietnamese troops from South Vietnam and it would "encourage" Saigon to negotiate with the NLF. South Vietnam would assume increasing responsibility for resolving the conflict. It stood for unilateral de-escalation, which had been missing from the original McCarthy proposal. It "resolved to have no more Vietnams." The document contained military guarantees for the safety of American troops, it was less than clear about the status of the NLF in negotiating the conflict. Because of a kind of deliberate vagueness, it would obviously have been easier for regular Democrats to accept than the McCarthy plank. McCarthy agreed to the compromise minority plank; the following week, as the minority forces neared a floor fight, he was to have doubts.

Chicago burned with rumors of every kind. The water system would be filled with LSD (some say that it was, but that chlorine neutralized the LSD) . . . Humphrey would become a dove . . . Daley was switching to the LBJ brand. "Chicago," said an airlines magazine, "is everyone's kind of town. It's a 'Take Me Along' kind of town, especially suitable for husbands and wives away from home for a spell of Fun. Chicago is dynamic, it's exciting, it's sprawling, yet it is not overwhelming. It is a city that easily can grow on you and it wears well." It had also been refurbished for the occasion. On the southside, around the convention hall, there was new curbing, new fences screened off can-filled vacant lots, unsightly small buildings, and other emoluments of poverty. A big painted sign said, MAYOR DALEY, A FAMILY MAN, WELCOMES YOU TO A FAMILY TOWN.

A family town ought to know how to deal with the young, but Chicago thus far had shown no special insights. It had become a symbol of oppression, a sort of Midwestern Bastille, through its stern suppression of peace demonstrators in the spring. Like an authoritarian personality, it could tolerate no dissidence and it displayed no humor, no appreciation of the high comedy, rebellious or not, in such gestures as nominating a Yippie pig for President. It was an easy city to taunt. A less arrogant place, if it could not forgo the Democratic green and suggest the convention be moved to a less controversial city (but could America, having taken its stand, back down in Vietnam?), might have tried at least to temper its response. But Chicago believed in, and all summer its Mayor promised the use of force, and the opposition could not and would not back down because it was exactly that spirit which it was most against. Chicago threatened, blustered, refused to grant permits for meetings and marchers or find sleeping accommodations, and still they came, the Yippies (Youth International Party), the National Student March, the War Mobilization League. The scenario read escalation.

Dramatically, the Chicago syndrome of action and overreaction seemed precisely what McCarthy and his campaigners had been saying for months caused America trouble. For them Chicago *was* Vietnam in many ways. But political considerations and caution dictated that the McCarthyites become noncombatants. The candididate, who could easily have brought screaming thousands to Chicago, asked them to stay home. He demanded that Al Lowenstein call off his Coalition for an Open Convention. Lowenstein had wanted ten thousand citizens—or a hundred thousand—to converge on the Democrats, to convince them through their sheer power of numbers to nominate McCarthy. For Lowenstein it was the only way, and he was certain now that the candidate was losing deliberately. But McCarthy was afraid of violence and demagoguery. His campaign would play it straight politically, although, oddly enough, the Mitchell strategy of confrontation at the convention hall paralleled the youth strategy on the streets.

As the weekend opened, the McCarthy camp seemed as ready as possible in the face of a bus strike, cab strike, phone strike, communications-worker strike, omnipresent police, shortage of hotel rooms, and faulty air conditioning at the Hilton. Lucey had arrived with a long checklist and was delighted to find all the items done. At the convention hall a command post had been set up for Mitchell, Gleason, Lucey, who would serve as floor manager (a position officially left open, though, in case Jesse Unruh agreed to take it), and Gans' deskmen. It was connected to the convention floor by telephone and walkie-talkie, and there was an elaborate radio hookup with the Hilton headquarters (which turned out to be less efficient than it looked). Between three and four thousand McCarthyites were manning the various parts of the operation. The transportation pool alone had several hundred cars, mini busses, and drivers. One kid, sitting behind the wheel of a new Cadillac, was asked whose car it was. "My father's," he said. "His chauffeur drives my old man in my Mustang." Another was told to pick up a VIP at the airport, the California labor leader, Paul Schrade, who had been shot during the Kennedy assassination and was now a McCarthy supporter. The driver was told to shave and put on a suit and tie for such a personage. He was bewildered to find Schrade in a beard and Hawaiian shirt.

Probably the most mysterious McCarthyite in Chicago went by the name of "Mr. Johnson." Mr. Johnson was a partisan of Jimmy Hoffa, and he had become a McCarthyite out of dislike for Robert Kennedy, who put Hoffa in jail. "Mr. Johnson is completely honest," one of the few campaigners who knew about his existence remarked. "He's been indicted over two hundred times and never been convicted once." Mr. Johnson was an electronics wizard, specializing in bugging or debugging phones. Although under constant surveillance by the FBI, he slipped into Chicago unseen to debug the McCarthy phone system. He also carried a device which could burn out the wires in the phones of the opposition, but his actions are shrouded in mystery. . . .

"I hear Pat Lucey's got quite an operation in Chicago, but I guess I'm happy about it," McCarthy had said, characteristically nonchalant. Lucey, a dark, quiet, straightforward man, was determined to keep clear of the McCarthy factiousness. "There is only one enemy and that's Humphrey," he said. "Everybody is for McCarthy who is with us and everybody who is not is a prospect." Lucey was, at this point, the most acceptable man in the McCarthy campaign to Democratic regulars. He spent long hours on the phone, courting party leaders, and his suggestion was that Humphrey coattails were not strong enough to carry Democratic candidates. McCarthy's were. But in the end, all roads seemed to lead back to a few leaders like Dick Daley.

Friday before the convention opened Lucey had a talk with Daley in the Mayor's office. He had sent Daley an advance copy of a *Chicago Sun-Times* poll which showed McCarthy beating Nixon and Nixon outpolling Humphrey by nine per cent in Illinois. "Humphrey can't win," Lucey said. "We've beaten polls before," Daley answered. "That's more than a twelve-point spread. It's a lot." Lucey said, Daley had no answer. His real choice seemed to be Lyndon Johnson. Lucey observed that Daley did not mention Humphrey's name.

On Saturday Daley had another visitation, this time from Ohio Congressmen John Gilligan and Charles Vannick. The two were concerned that Ohio Democrats, especially Gilligan running for the Senate, would be vulnerable with Humphrey on the ticket, especially if Humphrey campaigned as a hawk. Daley remarked that perhaps the convention ought to return to LBJ, and he was told that if it did Ted Kennedy would step in. Daley said, "Do you think Kennedy could do it in November?" and they told him it would be a landslide for Kennedy.

Saturday evening Lucey sent Goodwin to see Connally. It was true that Connally had attacked McCarthy harshly for his Vietnam stand and the Czech statement, but Connally was evidently extremely annoyed at Humphrey—"upset," as he put it to Goodwin. The Southern governors, who as a coalition of favorite sons, could make or break Humphrey, thought that Humphrey had committed himself to retain the unit rule, but that now he was backtracking and—stories were rife—moving doveward. If Connally had to choose between two doves, he might be angry enough to pick McCarthy, Lucey reasoned. So he had sent Goodwin to see Connally, a visit which lasted for two hours. They played cat-and-mouse on the question of a McCarthy-Connally ticket, and Connally did not say no. In politics, strange alliances have been fashioned, though this one was probably an apparition all along.

On Sunday Daley had another visitor, Jesse Unruh of California. Unruh, faced with divisions among the California Democrats, had still not come out explicitly for McCarthy, but he had made favorable sounds and told McCarthyites that he would endorse McCarthy at the California caucus on Tuesday. Daley now appeared to concur that Humphrey was a loser, but said that McCarthy was unacceptable. ("If Daley would have released the Illinois delegation, Unruh would have high-pressured the California delegation for McCarthy," says the California Democrat Gerald Hill.) Unruh reported this talk to Lucey, who said, "Maybe Daley will change his mind."

So there were, on Sunday and still on Monday, some small grounds for thinking that the long campaign might yet stagger on to victory. None of the evidence was impressive alone, but it added up to a possibly convincing picture. Daley surprised the delegates by holding Illinois uncommitted until Wednesday. What was in his mind (or why he had the right to such power and, yet, inscrutability) no one knew: it might have been the steady warnings of polls and politicians showing Humphrey's unpopularity; it might have been Kennedy, whose boomlet was yet to sound; it might have been Johnson, on whose five-foot-high sixty-fifth birthday cake the Hilton bakers were already slaving in secret parts of the kitchen. The Southern governors, like Buford Ellington of Tennessee, were holding to their position as favorite sons. Everyone knew that Humphrey had the requisite number to win, but would his side hold together? Could the Mitchell wedge break his forces in two? If Humphrey could be stopped on the first ballot another candidate might sneak in. As late as Monday afternoon, many McCarthyites believed that Humphrey had been halted.

There was another possibility, too. If Humphrey would change his Vietnam stand and his seeming vacillation on party reform, it might be possible to love him. Sunday night, at a party, one of Humphrey's principal aides talked to a man close to McCarthy and he said if McCarthy would move delegates to Humphrey the Vice-President would have mobility on the issues, and if he had mobility on the issues he would have greater latitude in his Vice-Presidential choice. If Humphrey came close to McCarthy on the issues would McCarthy be interested in the Vice-Presidency? "Gene has never said he would accept the Vice-Presidency, but I know he would if Humphrey can meet his conditions," McCarthy's associate said.

So the hunt for delegates went on. It was, said one lady brightly, like "rush week." There was a "Eugene's" downtown, and Peter and Mary (without Paul) could be heard there singing "Vote for Gene McCarthy"—maybe, after all, the delegates would.

The candidate arrived on Sunday with an entourage that included the Secret Service men (four of whom were named Gene), the maître d' of his favorite Washington restaurant, the Assembly, who supervised the cooking, and the Negro barber for the House of Representatives. McCarthy looked fresher than when he first set foot on the snows of New Hampshire, and he would take it fairly easy at Chicago, too. He was not eager to visit delegations, going to no more than a half dozen caucuses, and his contempt for what he plainly considered a rigged convention was made visible when he decided not to attend a delegate meeting and would have left John Bailey, Democratic National Chairman, waiting in the street if John Kenneth Galbraith had not stood in for him.

Sunday night McCarthy talked to a thousand delegates in Orchestra Hall about the rule of reason and the quality of American political life—he would be consistent in his utterances to the last—but on Monday he faced his own campaign. With the candidate, in his suite on the twenty-third floor of the Hilton, were Mitchell, Lucey, Finney, Rauh, Goodwin, Clark, and McCoy. McCarthy asked Rauh about the status of the credentials fights and Rauh made a report. Finney then asked if the Georgia challenge was advisable. Finney was sure the Bond challenge would fail; it would be better, he thought, to accept the compromise than upset the delegates and lose strength for the Vietnam-plank battle. Mitchell, who had not wanted Finney in Chicago, had thought him defeatist and tried to bar him from the McCarthy encampment, now flew at Finney, saying he had no right to talk to delegates. McCarthy decided to go ahead with the Georgia challenge, but, as Rauh—in a halfway position between Finney and Mitchell—said, "It was sad that on the Monday the convention opened we should still be without direction."

Mitchell was making progress with the challenges, but, on the other hand, what Finney had feared most was coming to pass: McCarthy had no more votes than a month before, and what additional votes he might be able to get all came from the same pool of perhaps a thousand delegates who were in some agreement on impending fights. McCarthy could not win unless he broke into the Humphrey strength and now, on Monday, that wafer of hope began to crumble. The Southern governors, one by one, were going to Humphrey. There was, too, advance word of the new Harris poll. McCarthy, whose popularity had been rising in a long, gradual curve, had fallen behind Nixon, and he was only slightly ahead of Humphrey. McCarthy was undoubtedly still far ahead in the key states, but the poll dealt a punishing blow to arguments that he was the popular choice. That day, too, the Democrats controlling the convention began to show their iron. Without warning, the Democratic leadership moved up the credentials challenges from Tuesday to Monday night.

"This is the damndest convention I ever saw," an old-time delegate remarked just before the convention opened Monday evening. "Everybody is so uncommunicative." They should have been happy, too. The delegates had spent the last fourteen hundred days waiting for these four (when the ladies could wear their diamond donkey pins and the men their donkey hats). A very sizable number had not lived up to their President's strictures on fitness—fat was the overwhelming impression of these eighteenth-century-British-landowner equivalents: the depletion-benefited oilmen, the subsidized wheat and cattlemen, the unionists and party regulars. Studying the faces on the dais, one wondered if double chins and jowls were grown on purpose so that their wearers could look like politicians, much as Bernard Shaw believed giraffes had grown long necks to reach the high fruits.

The seating plan of the delegations had been determined with an eye toward maximum efficiency. The party faithfuls, like the host Illinoisans and the porky Texans, ranged in front and the rebellious New Yorkers, Californians, Wisconsinites, New Hampshirites, and others—along with the beleaguered Southern regulars —in back, where they would least disrupt. The whole panorama had the atmosphere of the beginning of a class war—the barons around the throne; the professors and the students, the middle-class peace people and do-gooders, the Negroes, the Mexican-Americans, and migrant workers, all struggling to get in and cut their throats.

The barons would use force if it came to that, but they had subtler, Orwellian weapons at their disposal. The camps of the nominees had been limited to twelve floor passes each, but the regulars could evidently get all they wanted—"I saw every labor guy I knew in the country on the floor," Joe Rauh said. The microphones of dissident delegations could be stilled by a switch on the dais, or the band—its musical-comedy numbers and military marches glaringly inappropriate—could drop an acoustic perfume over the smelly sounds of protest. Even the boring speeches—"this we have done, . . ." "the challenge of, . . ." "the high calling of public office"—were a weapon: clichés dulled quickness and sensibility. It was not that the regulars seriously expected to lose. But they did not wish to take chances, and they wanted most of all to end the convention by Thursday night, with or without the issues aired.

There was a surprising keynote address by Senator Daniel K. Inouye of Hawaii, who spent more time on the nation's ills than extolling the Democratic Party, but, like all the speeches, his was unintelligible to the rebellious delegations in the back. There was the important vote for abolishing the unit rule, as a temporary rule. Texas rose to strenuously object. Texas had a letter from Hubert Humphrey which recommended retaining the unit rule for the 1968 convention—the first clear sign that Humphrey was backing away from positions acceptable to party reformers. Many delegates did not seem to understand what the balloting was about, which is probably why Texas was beaten as the convention, by voice vote, decided to do away with the unit rule for 1968. Now the credentials fights, and Jesse Unruh, Chairman of the California delegation, was on his feet calling for an adjournment.

Unruh argued that the challengers needed more time, that it was highhanded of the convention managers to change the schedule of battles. Perhaps Unruh thought the insurgents could gain strength by the delay, perhaps he was still hoping for lightning to strike on his own faint hopes for the Permanent Chairmanship—but his motive was considered bad tactics in the McCarthy control room, since the credentials challenges were ready. The adjournment vote would reveal the true strength of the insurgents earlier than the Mc-

Carthyites wished and dissipate momentum. Nonetheless, Unruh had to be backed, and the word went out to vote for the motion, which got only a predictable 875 votes.

There was the vote on the Texas challenge delegation. The challengers lost, although they got about 1000 votes. Then Georgia. The compromise plan—with one-half of each delegation to be seated—worked out in the Credentials Committee had not been observed at the convention. There were no seats on the floor for the members of the Georgia challenge delegation, who had been sitting in the balcony until their turn came, and they could get on the floor only by barricading the turnstiles. The Bond delegation made a passionate appeal—Bond displaying his calmness when he was rushed to the wall by two Georgia black regulars—and the voting began. "Massa*tu*setts?" cried the female recording secretary, and the challengers went down, with 1041 votes. Then the dissidents began to chant "Jul-yen Bond, Jul-yen Bond," Daley scowled and made a gesture, Bailey rushed to the foot of the podium, the chairman banged the gavel, and at two-thirty a.m. the first night was over.

Tuesday, the President's birthday, was unbelievable from start to finish.

At four a.m. Jerry Hill had a talk with Jesse Unruh, who had now decided, after seeing the strength of the Humphreyites at the convention, that it was the end for Gene McCarthy. Would the McCarthyites support Ted Kennedy? Unruh wanted to know. Hill said he would try to find out, using potential support for the minority peace plank as litmus paper. Unruh communicated his view to McCarthy before the candidate made an appearance at the California caucus. Perhaps reacting to Unruh's pessimism, McCarthy fairly outdid himself in unwillingness to press himself or his well-known ideas in the futile hope of influencing a few votes, which, were they sincere, would have come over by then anyhow. To summarize his campaign in a few minutes, he said, would be "like building a ship in a battle." No doubt he and his campaigners were furious at the regular Democrats for failing totally to recognize the McCarthyites' contribution in revitalizing the party; at George Mc-Govern for "faking around the edges"; at the Kennedys, who had *not* joined him but hurt him badly by whisperings of a Ted Kennedy candidacy, putting the Kennedy regulars on ice. But McCarthy's refusal to restate his Vietnam position was not important, nor was George McGovern's performance, though he stole the show and a few delegates. The vital thing at the California caucus was what Hubert Humphrey said about Vietnam.

McCarthy had given a final warning the day before that he regarded this issue in dead earnestness:

> The Vice-President's platform proposal on Vietnam is a reaffirmation of the policies of the present Administration and is in full accord with his statement of yesterday. He asks the Democratic Party to offer to the people four more years like the last three. He has adopted a position which has been overwhelmingly rejected in primary after primary. The policies we are asked to accept have proven themselves to be harmful to the welfare of the country and politically unacceptable. There is little escape from the conclusion that Secretary Rusk has won this stage of the platform fight. Now the lines are clearly drawn between those who want more of the same, and those who think it necessary to change our course in Vietnam. The Convention as a whole will decide.

Inside the McCarthy campaign the hope still was that Humphrey at the caucus would at least give just that small signal that the hawk pass was unguarded so that the irregulars could sneak through with their peace plank. That clue would have anticipated the break with Johnson and the shift in policy which was the McCarthy price for party unity. It would have permitted McCarthy to resolve his divergent interests: his loyalty to the party on the one hand and to his youthful supporters on the other. Humphrey needed this support to win in November. He could win at the convention even without the defections he might incur by permitting a victory for the minority plank. McCarthy would have had negotiating power and, perhaps, the Vice-Presidency.

Perhaps Humphrey had sincerely agreed with the President or believed only a hawk could beat Nixon. Perhaps he thought the dove plank would imperil secret negotiations. Perhaps he thought Johnson would repudiate him if he took a soft plank on Vietnam. The President—whose car waited at the airport—might come to deliver the rebuke in person. He had already given Humphrey and his staff an hour-and-a-quarter phone lashing on Sunday and indicated his displeasure at the prospect of a Humphrey shift; he even flew Hale Boggs of Louisiana, Majority Whip in the House and chairman of the Platform Committee, to Washington to drill in his message. He had forwarded messages from the generals that a bombing halt would cause American casualties; and he sent Charles Murphy, the former head of the Civil Aviation Board, to Chicago to make sure that the Democratic plank did not cast aspersions on the President's policy.

At the California caucus, then, Humphrey was caught, either way. A delegate asked, "Mr. Vice-President, specifically, in what ways, if at all, do you disagree with President Johnson's policy on Vietnam?"

"Would you mind if I just stated my position on Vietnam?"

"No! No! No! No!"

Humphrey talked about aggression from the North and Democracy in the South and about not imposing a military solution, and then he said; "The roadblock to peace, my dear friends, is not in Washington, D.C. It is in Hanoi, and we ought to recognize it as such."

The deed was done; had Humphrey made a critical decision that was to elect Richard Nixon President of the United States? Nothing was left to the doves but to fight in any way they could and damn the consequences.

The first concrete result of the Humphrey performance at the

California caucus was an interview given by McCarthy at three that afternoon in his hotel suite to the editors of the Knight newspaper chain. "MCCARTHY CONCEDES HE'S A LOSER," said the *Chicago Daily News* headline the next morning:

> In an exclusive interview Tuesday in his hotel suite overlooking Lake Michigan McCarthy put his long legs up on a coffee table and admitted:
> "I think it was probably settled more than twenty-four hours ago."
> "You mean it's wrapped up for Humphrey?" he was asked.
> "I think so," the Minnesota Senator said calmly.
>
> Q: Do you think Humphrey will have to take a different position [on Vietnam]?
> McCARTHY: Well it looks as though he's going to try to say that Nixon's position and mine [Humphrey's] on the war are the same, and try to neutralize that issue, and run on domestic issues. That was his pitch today. It looks to me that that's the way Humphrey's going to try to play it.
> Q: Well, if he doesn't change on the war, if he doesn't try to break away, what do you think you're going to do?
> McCARTHY: Well, I don't know. There's not going to be any third party. I just   I expect I'd probably, after a couple of weeks, say that there's not much choice, and I would recommend Humphrey and go out and see what I could do to elect the right kind of a Congress, Senate, probably. . . . The problem I have is with the young people. I've been more insistent than I really wanted to be about not supporting the ticket. Because they'd figure this is a sellout. They're ready to accuse you of a sellout, anyway.
>
> Q: Are you going to talk to the convention?
> McCARTHY: I will if Johnson comes in on his platform. I don't think he'll come.
>
> Q: . . . Is there any possibility of [Ted Kennedy's] being nominated?
> McCARTHY: Oh, they're working on it, I don't know.

Less than an hour after the reporters left, McCarthy would be talking with Ted Kennedy's brother-in-law Steve Smith in the same room. The Draft-Kennedy rumors had been sweeping Chicago since the weekend. Smith met with Daley on Friday, had been reassured that Daley was not attempting to trap Kennedy into a Vice-Presidential draft. Then Smith returned to Hyannis Port, reporting to Kennedy that all the makings for a serious draft were there, and the two decided that Kennedy would neither encourage nor discourage a draft. Saturday, Daley put the Kennedy bug in Gilligan's head and by Sunday, when Smith returned to Chicago, the Draft-Kennedy idea had substance. On Monday McCarthy asked Goodwin, "What about this Teddy thing?" Tuesday, McCarthy told Pat Lucey, "I want to see Steve Smith." Lucey could not remember where Smith was staying (at the Standard Club), and he walked back to his hotel to get the number. His memory may have been affected by his worries on whether such a meeting should take place. The possibilities of a news leak—which would kill Kennedy's chances—were too great. It had to be arranged some other way.

Goodwin, meantime, had also talked to McCarthy, who agreed to have Goodwin arrange a conference for him with Smith. Smith was now certain from his talks with delegates that Kennedy could get the nomination, with or without McCarthy, but he would need McCarthy's support to win in November against Nixon. (Before the California caucus, which revealed that there would be no compromise peace plan, the Kennedy forces had been certain McCarthy was a strong contender as Humphrey's Vice-President, but that possibility no longer existed.) Smith said that he would come, arriving on the twenty-third floor around four-thirty. The McCarthyites hurriedly sequestered Walter Reuther, who had an appointment with McCarthy a few minutes later—the Smith visit was top secret.

"The Senator is not a candidate," Smith was careful to say at once. McCarthy said that he wanted his own name in nomination; after that he would urge his people to vote for Ted Kennedy if he were willing to run. "While I'm willing to do this for Teddy, I never could have done it for Bobby," he said, irritating Smith with the gratuitous swipe. He did not go as far as Smith had hoped, which was to agree to put Kennedy's name in nomination at the convention himself.

Smith went back to the Standard Club and—with Pat Lucey, heretofore uncomfortable about talking with Smith because of his McCarthy commitment—went over the delegate situation, state by state. Lucey's tally now showed

Black caucus	200
Kennedy	500
McCarthy	650
McGovern	150
Humphrey	1120

The 500 Kennedy votes were new, not part of the same pool of delegates which had veen voting the minority line on the credentials fights. These were the "soft" Humphrey votes and Smith thought Kennedy could get them. Humphrey would then be stopped. Smith was making efforts to bring Daley in when, at eight-thirty, there was a news flash from CBS correspondent David Schoumacher saying that Smith, in a two-hour meeting with Mc-Carthy (it had lasted ten minutes), had solicited McCarthy's support for a Kennedy candidacy. According to Peter Maas in *New York* magazine, Smith exploded, "Who the hell is Schoumacher?"

There were no secrets in the McCarthy campaign, or few that could be kept. Schoumacher, a keen reporter, had been on the twenty-third floor and heard from one of McCarthy's young staffers that an important visitor was there. One of the Secret Service men told him the guest was a Kennedy person and Schoumacher, through one of McCarthy's adult aides, quickly established the facts. (He had not known what Smith looked like, but he now realized the identity of the slim, graying, snappily dressed man who had passed him in the hall.)

Furious, Smith got on the phone to Goodwin—Goodwin, reached already by Schoumacher, had stuck to the prearranged "cover" story, that Smith and McCarthy had only discussed the platform fights—and said, "What kind of a can of worms do you have over there?" Goodwin went on television to say that, though a Kennedy candidacy had been discussed, Smith had not sought McCarthy's support. That wasn't enough for Smith, who wanted a further denial from McCarthy or Goodwin in McCarthy's name. But Goodwin's second denial never got on because, by that time, McCarthy's concession to the Knight newspaper reporters was flooding the air. Kennedy called Smith to say that it was lost, and Smith told Daley. Daley agreed that Kennedy could not now have the nomination without clubbing and Kennedy was not willing to club. The next morning Kennedy removed his name, irreversibly, from nomination.

Anything could happen in 1968 and often did, and a Kennedy nomination may have been precluded by a simple news flash. McCarthy's offer had been direct and generous—he had asked nothing in return—but he was inevitably bound to his cause and tied to the strange world of political cause and effect. His chance for the nomination was almost certainly gone, but a Kennedy candidacy might help the peace plank. And if Kennedy tried and failed, Humphrey too might be stopped in the process. It was the palest of possibilities but not one which McCarthy could have overlooked.

The convention that began on Tuesday night was a creature quivering with uncertainty. Had McCarthy conceded? Was Hubert stopped? Was Kennedy running? Was Johnson going to come? Was war breaking out between the cops and the kids downtown? The creature staggered blindly.

"Massa*tu*setts"—the balloting came and went on the remaining credentials battles and the majority report. The Bond challenge lost, but the insurgents could console themselves—the states had been put on notice for 1972. Now commenced the serious business of the evening, the vote on the minority report on the unit rule. The McCarthyites were no longer alone: support had developed throughout the convention; many Humphreyites were tired of always opposing reform. Regular party leaders, like the New York upstate leader Joe Crangle, marshaled Humphrey support—and Crangle spoke for the minority report. Among the delegations there seemed to be deep confusion—state after state passed until, finally, someone asked what the vote was about and Carl Albert said it was on the minority report on unit rule. There were switches then, as the antiabolition forces collected themselves: the contest would be close. How would Missouri decide? Missouri was thought to be for unit rule, but Mitchell had done some dealing there—a lawsuit against the Missouri Democratic Party and a credentials fight had both been pending; they would be dropped if Missouri voted for abolition—and Missouri put its sixty votes for the minority.

There was jubilation behind the plasterboard walls of the McCarthy control room—"That resolution is a revolution," Curt Gans said, "and we did that." Governors Hoff and Hughes came in looking bushed, to huge applause. And, though many delegates apparently did not realize what they had voted for, it was, indeed, a revolution. The convention had just decreed that the hated unit rule was abolished down to the precinct level for future conventions and that every effort had to be made to insure that delegates were chosen in ways open to public participation and in the calendar year of the national convention.

Yet the flush of victory was brief, for now came a hail of developments. The first reaction to Schoumacher's news flash was confusion—were the McCarthyites Kennedyites now, or what? Before that was answered, a message arrived on the radio linking the command post with McCarthy headquarters at the Hilton: "The police have encircled the Hilton and anybody planning to take the McCarthy shuttle back, forget it." And then, from the teletype machine, one end at the convention hall and the other at the Hilton, impossible words tumbled out: McCarthy had admitted defeat.

Back at the Hilton, McCarthy's concession had brought despair even to his wife and daughter Mary, who burst into tears. The candidate said that his understanding had been that the story would not be released until after the convention was over. According to one of his chief aides, his real reasoning was somewhat different. He had been in politics long enough to know that news does not hold still, least of all at a national convention where a Presidential contender has said something of key importance. The clue lay in the kids toward whom he always felt ultimately responsible. He knew he could not win, and he wished often to soften their disappointment, to prepare them in advance for defeat.

However humane the motive, the concession caused serious difficulties for those, like Mitchell, who were laboring at the hall. When the news came Mitchell was discussing the following night's nomination speeches with two of the men who would put McCarthy's name before the convention, Harold Hughes and Julian Bond. The proposed speeches sounded like empty words, suddenly, and Mitchell was deeply upset and very tired. Mitchell went into a press conference which had been intended as a valedictory to the abolition of the unit rule—the third important rule change in the party in a hundred years—on which Mitchell had tirelessly labored, only to have the questions dominated by McCarthy's admission of defeat.

Nor was that quite the end of it, because a serious weakening in McCarthy strength that might follow his statements could have implications for the balloting on the other critical fight remaining: the peace plank. The party regulars wanted to get it over with that night. For some the dominant consideration was, in fact, the lateness of the hour, which would keep the arguments short and off the television screens. For a moment the McCarthyites in the control room did not want to adjourn—*their* energy always hit a zenith just before dawn—but Mitchell and Finney, astoundingly, were in agreement now that the delegates ought to be given one last chance to think about accepting the minority peace plank before condemning the Democratic Party to division and probable defeat. "Let's go home, let's go home," came the chant from the floor. Dalcy, not wanting to adjourn, his face contorted with anger, was forced to accept. The delegates had been in session seven and a half hours.

At the hotel McCarthy and friends had gone out to dinner. "It was a good McCarthy-type evening," one of the group remarked, "with everybody reciting poetry and chatting, and then Norman Mailer came along and spoiled it with his intensity." Mailer's description of McCarthy that night, in *Miami Beach and the Siege of Chicago*, is justly famous:

> This reporter looked across the table into one of the hardest, cleanest expressions he had ever seen, all the subtle hints of puffiness and doubt sometimes visible in the Senator's expression now gone, no, the face that looked back belonged to a tough man, tough as the harder alloys of steel, a merciless face and very just, the sort of black Irish face which could have belonged to one of the hanging judges in a true court of Heaven, or to the proper commissioner of a police force too honest ever to have existed.

The candidate returned to the hotel, and by this time there were skirmishes around the Hilton and the National Guard was on its way. Only one thing had not happened on Tuesday—the President, wisely, had not arrived.

Compared with Wednesday, Tuesday was a day of rest. The day's events included the great peace-plank battle, the nomination for President, McCarthy's attempt to withdraw his name, the madness on Michigan Avenue, followed by an early-Thursday-morning candle march of protesting delegates, and the appearance of Mr. J., the monkey.

The McCarthyites were now at odds with their candidate. Both Mitchell and Finney urged him to go to the convention floor and lead the fight for the dove plank in person, to deliver an impassioned address that would bring down the hall. It had been Mitchell's understanding all along that McCarthy would do this. "Why should we choose a President like a Pope, with a puff of smoke from the White House?" McCarthy had joked; no, the new politics demanded an end to anachronisms. A candidate *should* go to the floor if the situation demanded it, and Mitchell had itemized for McCarthy the various moments at which the candidate's appearance might make a difference—one of the credentials fights, the unit-rule battle on Tuesday, the peace plank. The last seemed appropriate.

Three times on Wednesday, Mitchell called McCarthy and asked him to come, but McCarthy didn't want to. "I've always been running against Johnson," he said; if Johnson showed up so would he. He complained about the minority peace plank, though he had previously approved it, for being too wordy, too argumentative, and skirting the issue of NLF participation in an interim government. The campaigners argued that an appearance would increase the vote for the peace plank and for McCarthy himself—in any case, the captain ought to go down with his ship. But McCarthy was concerned about heating up the convention still more. Already the non-Humphrey delegates were in fury: they had been pushed around strategically, buried acoustically, and sometimes roughed up physically. Who knew what a Periclean oration would lead them to? No, McCarthy would not come. Instead he and his brother Austin played mock baseball in his suite, using an orange for a ball. Sometimes he would glance down at the crowd in Grant Park across the street standing in silent vigil, like an accusation. "The worst thing about what's happening," he said, "is that it leaves those kids nowhere to go."

Just after one p.m., the convention was gaveled back into session and Hale Boggs began to read the minority plank and paused for a moment, as Murray Kempton says, "overcome possibly by the horror of what his wife and daughter would say to him at dinner." STOP THE WAR signs rose in the delegations. One hour—on the most decisive issue facing the nation since World War II, determining the present and future direction of the party and its fate in November—one hour was awarded to each side to state its case so that the really urgent goal, in the minds of the convention managers, be reached: that the convention be closed on time. Boggs read a letter from General Creighton W. Abrams warning that if the bombing in North Vietnam were to be suspended "unilaterally" the enemy would soon quintuple its capability in the DMZ. (The terms were, then, that North Vietnam must also cease its bombing?) Mrs. Geri Joseph, cochairman of the Humphrey campaign, put her finger squarely on majority opinion. "An imposed coalition government is nothing more than a stepping stone to a long-term Communist take-over," she said.

The doves, united at last, turned out as allies: Wayne Morse, Paul O'Dwyer, Kenneth O'Donnell, Ted Sorensen, John Gilligan, Albert Gore, and Pierre Salinger, who, invoking the name of Robert Kennedy, ignited the first spontaneous demonstration of the convention with signs and chants of "Stop the War." If the war were to be stopped—and the Administration, in its subsequent bombing halt, seemed to rely on many of the same arguments offered at Chicago by supporters of the minority plank—it would not be stopped here. The vote was a predictable 1567¾ to 1041½—the insurgents had picked up exactly one-half vote over the Georgia-challenge tally. The doves went into a mournful demonstration behind New York, wearing black arm bands. Black crepe was placed on the New York standard, which was carried on the delegates' shoulders like a martyr on a bier. Security forces stopped the funeral procession with a raised white glove.

If, in the streets, the punishment was meted out by the police, at the convention hall it was administered by the band. As the doves broke into their threnody, "We Shall Overcome," the oompahs struck up with "Off We Go Into the Wild Blue Yonder," "As the Caissons Go Rolling Along," and "Anchors Aweigh." In those two brands of music one heard the sound of division in America.

There was the most subdued of demonstrations that night when McCarthy's name was put in nomination. The fight had gone out of his forces and the elaborate security provisions made it impossible to get McCarthyites into the balconies. Even the upper-level press sections were strangely full of people furtively passing out Humphrey signs even as Governor Hoff was comparing McCarthy to Jefferson and Julian Bond was asking "whether the party that claims to be for the people can respond to the people." "We want Gene," chanted the faithful, holding up signs like BUCKS COUNTY, PA., FOR MCCARTHY or Ben Shahn's McCarthy dove posters. The band played "Mame" and the futile banners waved.

At the McCarthy command post the campaigners were as sleepwalkers, passing each other unseen and unseeing. The deep roars of the Humphrey demonstration told the story. The coffee was gone and the free Pepsi-Cola dispenser offered only a hiss.

There was a last-minute contretemps as Gans tried to switch the McCarthy vote to Ted Kennedy, but people were past caring, and even as the balloting began the audio on the television set covering the count at the hall was shut off. They were watching another network's account of the action on Michigan Avenue.

> Chicago, Chicago, the barbed wire town,
> Chicago, Chicago, where cops knock you down.
> If you try to walk on the street
> You're beat in Chicago, Chicago,
> Where Mayor Daley has no respect for the kids.
> Chicago's Dick Daley, he called out the troops,
> They did things that shame the U.S.A., Say,
> We had the time, the time of our lives,
> We watched the cops arresting our wives,
> In Chicago—damn this town!

It had started on Sunday evening when the Yippies were turned out of Lincoln Park on Chicago's North Shore. A group of them had come south carrying two flags which looked like, but were not quite, that of the NLF. Met on the north side of the Michigan Avenue bridge by police who acted as though the Yippies were vandals bent on the sack of Rome, about a dozen Yippies crossed the bridge, to be turned back by five busloads of cops, some two hundred in light-blue crash helmets with plastic visors, night sticks drawn, who pushed and prodded perfectly innocent bystanders, including a man with a bad leg and a cane unable to move fast enough for their taste. Blood pouring from his head, a Yippie was led away. YOU KNOW I CAN'T HEAR YOU WHEN THE WATER'S RUNNING, said a button worn by a plain-clothes grim-faced cop in a closed visor who carried the gas gun. This was the first encounter, and so the familiar and horrible history of the rioting went, escalating until, by Wednesday night, onlookers were pushed through the plate-glass windows of the Hilton by the police, beaten, and left bleeding. As the violence erupted, McCarthy wanted to remove his name from nomination. The first idea was to remove it while he still led in the balloting, as he did early on in the count, but the vote moved too fast, the McCarthyites could not get to the dais, and the plan was dropped. McCarthy got 601 votes (his strength had deteriorated in the last day, after it was clear he must lose) to Humphrey's 1761. Loud opposition to a motion to make it unanimous was drowned by the band.

"Look at them," McCarthy said, staring out his Hilton room window. "The police have cut them off. They told them they could march and they've surrounded them. It's the way we treated the Indians. We always told them we were taking them to a happier hunting ground and we surrounded them. The country is like that. Milling around, ready to march, and nowhere to go. I must tell them downstairs this movement will go on because it doesn't depend on structure or organization but just on what is in people themselves. It's like striking a hammer on the anvil, it rings forever. It's like infinity."

At their citadel on the fifteenth floor, the McCarthyites had created a hospital for the wounded, attended by nurses. (They had smuggled sheets to Michigan Avenue, where they were used as bandages and even gas masks. Bail money was being collected, too.) McCarthy came down to find the beaten and bloodied huddled on beds. "We're trying to heal the wounded," he said gently. "That's all we ever tried to do." A little later somebody turned, and down the hall, on roller skates, came a monkey, a live monkey whose trainer had left him there while he joined the demonstration on the street. The monkey's name, he was told, was Mr. J.

"Mr. J.," somebody said, "go to the infirmary and get me a bottle of aspirin." Obediently, Mr. J. skated off and returned with a bottle of aspirin.

"Well, now I've seen everything," another said. "We should have nominated Mr. J."

"You haven't seen *everything*," said the other. "In the next room, in the bathtub, there's a lion cub."

Seemingly, there wasn't much more that could happen in the 1968 Democratic Convention. The ex-candidate came to thank a large assemblage of his followers and he looked more like a President than ever. The McCarthyites were convinced they could have made mash of Richard Nixon, but the party had thrown them aside. A few would help Humphrey at once, but the bulk of those in that room were undecided about what to do.

The ex-candidate crossed the street, as usual over the strong objections of the Secret Service, to the kids in the park and there he said, a little bitterly, "I have a sense of history in spots. I thought a half million votes in Pennsylvania would get me more than twenty delegates. Well, we have broken the unit rule and

Ralph Yarborough says we have emancipated Texas. Now we are a government-in-exile."

The following morning, at five-fifteen, the government-in-exile was raided by the police. It was at a party for the older McCarthy staff workers, those of twenty-five or so, hosted by Tony Podesta, in the three-room suite on the fifteenth floor which had been used by John Kenneth Galbraith and the ADA. There was beer and liquor, but the guests hadn't the least desire to celebrate—they were rehearsing for the future, polishing as they went, the anecdotes of their political adventure. The windows were open, and from the park came the demonstrators' chants to partisans in the hotel. "Blink your lights! Blink your lights!" The sympathies of the Mc-Carthyites were for the demonstrators. They blinked their room lights.

According to the police, solid objects like ash trays, beer cans, and even human excrement had been raining down from the hotel, and by means of binoculars and rifle sights they determined that they came from Suite 1506-A, where the party was. The McCarthy-ites deny categorically that anything was thrown from the suite. But from another room on the fifteenth floor someone did loose a single, deadly smoked fish. Perhaps it was Mr. J.

There were signs that the raid was premeditated. At twelve-thirty p.m. a McCarthy staff member who was being held in the basement of the Hilton in a makeshift detention center heard the police talking about a raid on the fifteenth floor. At four-thirty a.m., two hotel security men arrived to request the party to close the windows—they mentioned the beer cans and the windows were closed. At four-forty-five, a McCarthy girl was told that the elevator operators had been ordered not to stop on the fifteenth floor.

The McCarthyites in the suite failed to realize that the floor was sealed off. About a dozen were there when a contingent of a half dozen police and security officers entered and told them to leave. Podesta and Steven Cohen told the group not to resist—Podesta and Cohen still had their walkie-talkies, which the police refused to believe weren't tape recorders until they saw a demonstration—and the group was herded to the elevators. More police had arrived by then, and people in the hall had begun to scream and shout. A young law student who was shoved into a small table, started to pick it up with the idea of striking but put it down again, the McCarthyites testified—the police insisted that he hit a cop with it. The student was knocked unconscious by a night stick, which broke on impact. One cop cried, "I've been maced!" He had apparently gotten a dose from another policeman. George Yumich, another McCarthyite, was protesting that the police had no right to force them to the lobby—instead he would lead a delegation to the twenty-third floor where McCarthy was. A hotel employee said they couldn't go up because "ninety per cent of these people don't work for McCarthy anyway." Yumich argued. He was pushed to the wall. A policeman, says the Walker Report, "struck a glancing blow at Yumich, who was knocked to the floor and struck on the head and shoulders by two or three policemen, suffering a two-inch gash requiring five stitches."

There was hysteria on the fifteenth floor now, with girls screaming—Marybeth McCarthy, the Senator's niece, who had campaigned hard, was sobbing uncontrollably—as the police began systematically, and without instructions, to clear rooms far back from the street until forty or fifty people had been prodded down to the lobby. Then Goodwin urged everyone to sit on the floor, but one young man, beside himself, started to curse the cops, who pummeled him until some of the girls threw themselves between the young man and the police to stop the blows. Yumich, meantime, though a bloody mess, had managed to make it to the twenty-third floor, and there he found McCarthy, who had been unable to sleep and was fully dressed. He came at once to the lobby, and it was the first time anyone could recall having seen the Senator express strong emotion. He was very angry. "I'm afraid," he told one of the campaigners, "it's going to be like this from now on."

The incident of the fifteenth floor lasted less than half an hour, but it would be of important effect and lasting memory. Ten members of the Presidential campaign staff had been hit, four requiring hospitalization, with neither apologies from Chicago nor recognition from the party regulars or its nominee of what McCarthy considered an affront. Without doubt, the McCarthyites would now find it harder to join with Humphrey. The long campaign ended as the Senator stood in the Hilton lobby. He was among those with whom he had begun, the youth.

11 | End or Beginning?

Shortly before the Wisconsin primary Eugene McCarthy made an astonishing statement. "In a democracy," he said, "any political structure can be made to yield to the popular will." One of the great accomplishments of the Minnesota Senator and his campaign of 1968 was to show that a reform movement could still wield influence on government, and in the salient least vulnerable to popular pressure, foreign and military policy.

Before the McCarthy campaign, the tendency appeared to be away from popular choice and citizen participation. The leadership might talk of an "open society" but to all the really critical decisions, about taxation, monetary policy, or trade imbalances, popular access was forbidden. The basic choices were not, and could not be, under the prevailing ideology, shared.

Foreign policy, in particular, was almost completely dominated by professional and technocratic cadres—academic theorists, career government officials, the RAND Corporation, the National Security Council, the CIA—which based their thinking on considerations and rationales hidden from public gaze. The elections through which the popular will was supposed to assert itself hardly offered any serious possibility of a referendum on foreign policy, but neither was a choice offered on domestic policy because the two were inseparably intertwined. There was no credible way for a citizen to oppose successfully the allocation of his tax dollar for, say, a missile site in his neighborhood or any neighborhood, or to demand that his dollar be used for other purposes. By the occasional act of voting the citizen did not so much exercise power as surrender it.

The examination of the war by McCarthy and Kennedy was followed by a consideration of other things. If one asked why we were in Vietnam, one went quickly to questions about "realism" in foreign policy, deterrence, counterinsurgency, the new military metaphysics. The older McCarthy and Kennedy liberals could recall that barely twenty years before Americans had a deep distaste and distrust for everything military, and in relatively no time at all an old American tradition had almost disappeared—now, Americans seemed to be reassured by, even to like, a military apparatus unrivaled in size and complexity in the history of the world. American judgment decreed that Polaris submarines come before housing, helicopters before day-care centers, howitzers before clean streets. The idea of free choice seemed to have been replaced by a kind of military determinism.

To those opposed, this ranking of priorities seemed illogical, and they were forced to ask how a social error of such dimensions could have happened. They found an explanation in what McCarthy called the "process" of government. As he put it, "the danger is that our objectives become simply a function of the power which we possess, or the purposes we pursue are simply a projection of the programing, and therefore not subject to any kind of reason or moral judgment, or moral control."

The McCarthy phenomenon, then, was not simply a reaction to the war in Vietnam, although both the war's sanguinary and budgetary implications made it a perfect prism for discontent. The dissidents went on to attract a following which would have been considered unbelievable before the "test," as McCarthy put it. In the primaries they both entered, McCarthy and Kennedy got about three-fourths of the vote of the majority (as the Democrats still are) party. McCarthy alone, at one point during the summer, could claim over forty per cent of the national vote and he had been, a few short months before, a virtual unknown. In retrospect, it seems probable that if Kennedy had lived he would have been nominated and elected President. McCarthy, if nominated, in the opinion of many observers, would have beaten Nixon, too. (Even a third party headed by McCarthy and New York's Republican Mayor John Lindsay might have been successful in the improbable year of 1968.) An astonishing portion—perhaps a majority—of the American people appeared ready to accept serious change.

Despite their defeat, it almost seemed that the dissidents had made their case. The people had been aroused and the government been forced to listen. Popular participation would rise, the political parties would be cleansed and modernized, community control would be established, and the liberal mentality would assert itself against government instrumentalities like the Department of Defense. The war in Vietnam would end with all due speed. The Nixon Administration appeared to accept many of the same ideas, like ending the war, greater public candor, and shared power for the Cabinet and Congress. The gloomy tendencies of the previous years looked on the way to being reversed.

Though that may be, another possible outcome should not be overlooked. The war in Vietnam might not end for some time. The Department of Defense budget (swollen by new weapons systems like the ABM, proposed new bombers, stationary underwater missiles, and so on) could continue to absorb almost ten per cent of the Gross National Product for years to come, taking precedence over other needs, national or international. (Unjustly, the McCarthyites were accused of isolationism. It was the military programs they balked at, not international aid.) The road to reform would continue to trickle out at the Department of Defense, for it is plain now that there is not enough American money for everything.

If this is to be the script, the consequences could be serious. The people, if they wanted the massive redirection suggested by

McCarthy and Kennedy, would have to return to the streets. Many would not go, for seeing no change they would retire to disillusionment and apathy. (What's the use of protesting?) Those who take their places, believing that quiet protest—even on the scale registered in 1968—has little effect, may have less respect for the rules. The already tenuous hold the two-party system has on a sizable portion of the young will be further weakened. The massive realignment of voters suggested by 1968 not being recognized by the major parties, a tough new radical party could emerge, further polarizing the country into liberals and conservatives. The divisions revealed in 1968 could become chasms; the recognition that the people *are,* in the long run, essentially powerless could undermine democracy as we know it. Thoughts like these are apocalyptic, but it is idle to believe that such events could not occur.

In pondering the significance of the McCarthy campaign of 1968, one should observe that such a movement was not unique. Periodically in our history movements of political reform have erupted in the United States. New clashes with old, the powerless (or those who experience a loss of power) with the powerful, until, in a rising cacophony of protest, opposition passes the threshold of tolerance and the dissidents begin to organize, coalesce, unite. Taking power is only one way to achieve the goals of the movement that results. The protesters can work, as a cabal, within a major party to influence policy. They can run, or threaten to run, as a new party if their demands are not met. They can withhold power in order to punish or to weaken a major party to make it susceptible to their views. (Millions of voters appear to have withheld power from Hubert Humphrey in 1968, either by not voting or voting but not working for or contributing to his candidacy as they might have for Eugene McCarthy or Robert Kennedy.) By such means reformers attempt to put their ideas, if not themselves, in power.

It may be useful here to look, even if cursorily, at the reform movements since the Civil War. Independents, Mugwumps, Populists, Progressives, New Dealers (to some extent, at least), Stevensonians, McCarthyites—despite the differences, the family resemblance is detectable. Radicals sometimes, they were revolutionaries never. They stood for good government run by "good men," emphasized morality, worried that society was threatened by disintegration and divisiveness, and had a high Jeffersonian regard for local democracy and popular participation.

In his *Autobiography,* William Allen White offered a description that could be used almost verbatim for the McCarthyites of 1968 when he remembered the Progressives at the turn of the century as "hundreds of thousands of young men in their twenties, thirties and early forties" whose "quickening sense of the inadequacies, injustices and fundamental wrong" of American society offered the impetus to act. The Progressives were dead against the political machines, for they wanted a system with no machines at all. They would have organized the country behind the high-minded efforts of enlightened liberal men whom they called the "New Citizen." "Progressivism," writes Richard Hofstadter in *The Age of Reform; From Bryan to F.D.R.,* ". . . was not nearly so much the movement of any social class or group . . . it was a rather widespread and remarkably good-natured effort of the greater part of society to achieve some not very clearly specified self-reformation."

But the liberals were also "visibly, palpably, almost pathetically respectable" in their social criticism and cries for change. Almost invariably they were contentious, disorganized, arrogant and had difficulty in communicating with the masses, though they believed in grass-roots politics. They tended to sentimentalize the people, feared professional leadership, preferring amateurs, and were inclined to moralize and preach. Their job was the articulation of ideas, the education of the citizens, the attempt to supply enlightened leadership and to have their ideas accepted in practice.

The hard business of ordinary politics—the getting and maintaining of power—they often considered sordid.

Adlai Stevenson and Eugene McCarthy sprang from the tradition of liberal reform, the Kennedys less so, and the McCarthy-Kennedy primary battles thus had a significance which transcended rivalry or differences of issues. The Kennedy concept of politics is essentially pragmatic and has to do with leadership by a small group, even an elite, commanding from the top down. McCarthy's politics stressed power flowing from the bottom up, with leadership emerging from the ranks. That was the essential idea of the new politics, and while it may have been a hundred years old, it was new for the politics of our day.

The liberal philosophy and issue-minded politics embodied by McCarthy, as shown by his campaign, have great attractiveness, but they also have apparent weaknesses. Because strong leadership was feared, the McCarthy effort sometimes seemed as though there were no leadership at all. The result was that the campaign broke into factions and feuds. The campaigners seemed innocent of the dangers of ego and self-interest. The McCarthy idealists, older and young alike, pursued personal power, and even misused it, just as they had accused the President of doing. A MAN YOU CAN TRUST IN THE WHITE HOUSE went a McCarthy slogan in New Hampshire, but of trust within the campaign there was little.

Inexperience, conspiratorial attitudes (on the part of the young, inherited perhaps from the National Student Association), a naïve idea about politics (politicians, unlike amateurs, make fetishes of trust and loyalty—e.g., Hubert Humphrey's fatal fealty to the President), all contributed to weakening an effort which might well have been successful. The McCarthy campaign's inability to discipline itself behind common principles, to temporarily abandon individualism for the sake of the cause, to articulate its goals and stick by them, ignoring discouragement, to be *serious* about what it stood for, all reflected those characteristics of liberal reform movements in general which doom them to lose elections. Like other liberal

movements, the McCarthy campaign was, in the end, almost provincial and insular, as revealed in its inability to deal with the regular Democrats who often were not as illiberal as the McCarthyites
made them out to be.

The Kennedy and McCarthy campaigns, then, both had defects
in terms of acceptability, the one in the narrow base of its leadership and its too aggressive pursuit of power, the other in its individualism, eccentricity, and unwillingness to come to grips with
the problems of organization and power. These two broad groups
must in the future work together if the reformers are to have any
chance of success. Their failure could seriously weaken, if not
demolish, the Democratic Party.

"It's no secret that we are in trouble," said Senator Harold
Hughes, a man deeply involved with party reform, "especially
with the significant groups that have traditionally identified with
the Democratic Party." The leftward young, the poor, the racial
minorities, the liberal suburbanites and academics—all, restlessly
and forlornly, prowl the political landscape in search of a home.
No doubt, the elimination of the unit rule and other procedural
changes will make the party more open to them, and so will the
decline in power of those who still dominate the party councils—
labor, big-city machines, and the South. There's no good reason,
many say, why "the wounds cannot be healed and unity forged
by 1972," as Bill Moyers put it. Indeed, there is a very good reason
why not: a great many Democrats have changed as a result of
1968 and are no longer interested in reconciliation, healing, unity,
and forging. What they want is a party whose program they believe
in, not one which vitiates their principles.

"The current political debate eludes familiar description," said
the National Committee for an Effective Congress in the fall of
1968, after a survey of the House of Representatives, "because the
old labels have lost relevance and new terminology is required.
One group of men operates in terms of specific tangible interests,
while the other is passionately committed to abstract values. Their

concerns have as much to do with each other as Railroad Retirement Pensions and the Bill of Rights. Their personalities are as similar as Speaker McCormack and Julian Bond." The report went on, trying to account for the chasm between Democrats which had opened in Chicago, "Two groups are crystallizing: the classic, orthodox labor liberals and the emerging political modernists. What separates them is personal style, choice of priorities, understanding or rejection of the contemporary revolutionary scene."

The report called the traditional older liberal "custodial" ("a trade-union oriented joiner and fraternal type"), displaying high party loyalty, pragmatism, a reliance on the numerical, quantitative aspects of legislation and a contempt for nonconformists and intellectuals. The custodial liberal draws a line between labor and the poor. His opposite liberal number was "humanistic." He is a civil libertarian, accepts social protest beyond strikes as a force for change and asks not merely how many schools will be built but what will be taught. "His focus is on *quality*—in education, conservation, urban design, with prime emphasis on innovation and the role and rights of the individual with less emphasis on the bread and butter aspects of the New Deal."

Other terminology could be used to describe this split. (The psychiatrists Erich Fromm and Malcolm Maccoby offered "life-loving" people vs. machine, bureaucracy or procedure worshipers.) However expressed, the division does seem to exist. Millions of Democrats—and Republicans, too—are disenchanted with their party. They want something qualitatively new.

The evidence of 1968 suggests that such change will occur only if the present party leaders are forced to accept it or give way to new leaders. Such a reform means a determined and sustained effort, which too few seem willing to give, from the man, as E. L. Godkin once wrote, "who keeps his place in line on the day of battle, has his turn of outpost duty, and is ready for the obscure and inglorious duties of the service."

The Kennedy and McCarthy reformers have organized in at

least half the states. Nation-wide, they exist as the New Democratic Coalition, an instrument with which they hope to prod the party to reform. The coalition they have in mind is between the minority groups and the poor on the one hand and the liberal reformers and peace people on the other, with organized labor somehow brought in. The difficulties facing these groups in synthesizing their objectives, finding the money to organize, and building a common front are enormous—not the least being the question of who in the coalition leads whom—but their success is vital to the future of reform.

"The statue was too small for the pedestal," remarked Gustave Flaubert in appraising one of his novels. The puzzling post-Chicago actions and nonactions of Eugene McCarthy have forced many of McCarthy's former followers to reach a similar conclusion about their candidate. He wasn't big enough, they now say, for the movement which sprang up under him and which almost carried him to the Presidency.

The man who may have altered the course of American politics in one short year is accused of pride, pique, laziness, and even mental instability. McCarthy's answer, if there is to be one, must await the publication of his book, the writing of which was a chief reason for McCarthy's own near invisibility after the election, he says.

In McCarthy's view, his campaign can take at least some credit for five accomplishments: 1) the Paris peace talks on Vietnam; 2) an investigation of the military influence on United States foreign policy by a Senate subcommittee headed by Senator Stuart Symington; 3) Democratic Party reform, under a commission headed by Senator George McGovern; 4) the depersonalization of the Presidency under Nixon; 5) a new style for Cabinet members, who feel freer to speak out. A sixth may yet be added: reform of the draft laws. "We should give the Nixon Administration some time with these mechanisms," McCarthy says; "then we can take up the new or old issues if they are not moving."

McCarthy and his campaigners are responsible, in part, for the large number of Congressmen who are now emboldened to vote against the Department of Defense on many issues. And the many reformist committees and organizations now functioning will be found staffed by former McCarthyites.

McCarthy feels he was consistent from the opening to the end. In his announcement of candidacy he said he would campaign on the issues, because personality had come to play too great a role in American politics, and in the main he stuck to that pledge. He said he wanted to give the system a test, but nowhere is it written that that which is tested must pass.

After Humphrey's nomination, McCarthy made his last speech of the campaign, to the assembled youth in Grant Park. There were two things, he said, that he wanted to do.

> One was to prove something about the people of the country. The other, I hoped to prove something about the political process of this nation. I think we proved something about the people of this country. . . . They made a judgment which the politicians were afraid even to face up to before we took it to the people: namely, that in the midst of this war they were willing to say that we were wrong and that the policy ought to be changed. That was the judgment of the people of this country. But we got stuck along the way in trying to put it through what we call the political process. Not all the way, but we are stalled right now. But we are really not stopped.

He said, "I will carry on as I did. I said no compromise at any point." McCarthy's unwillingness to compromise is at the heart of what is now said against him.

If he gave Hubert Humphrey a late, wan endorsement, it was because Humphrey's move toward the dove position was also late and wan. How could McCarthy have embraced him and been consistent with his own campaign? If McCarthy was willing, and he was, to accept the post as Richard Nixon's Ambassador to the United Nations he had, after all, presented his conditions in advance—not just that a Democrat be appointed to the Senate to replace him (McCarthy's choice was Minnesota Congressman John Blatnik) but that McCarthy have a strong role in making policy and be free to continue as a dissident Democratic politician. Nixon accepted the terms—it was Republican Governor Harold Levander of Minnesota who rejected them when he refused to appoint a Democrat. (Though Governor Nelson Rockefeller personally tried to persuade him, Levander didn't see why he had to. McCarthy, he said, had already announced that he would not run as a Democrat from Minnesota.)

McCarthy's resignation from the Senate Foreign Relations Committee was, perhaps, the closest he came to an eccentric step, and he has admitted, guardedly, that it may have been a mistake. He apparently reasoned that he was permitting the committee to become smaller in number, eventually; but more important was his own seniority, for in the committee he was far down and had to wait his turn to speak. As a world-famous spokesman for an important set of issues, perhaps he deserved a better forum; perhaps he thought the Foreign Relations Committee was lapsing into impotence. But he was also moving into another role which might be described as that of a "parapolitician."

For he was shifting outside the system and he would be no longer a party man. In his Foreign Relations resignation—in such acts as staying away from the traditional Jefferson-Jackson Democratic dinner—he was turning his back on the old forms. The most extreme example of his intransigence was his vote for Senator Russell Long for Democratic Whip or Assistant Majority Leader. It was this vote for Long against Edward Kennedy that roused the storm.

"You can't do this thing," McCarthy was told by a man who has been close to him. "Long belongs to the other team. He cheered Daley after Chicago." McCarthy answered that the Whip was "somebody who washes the underwear." It wasn't an important job. And where were those so-called liberal votes that went to Kennedy when Muskie, who deserved them, wanted them? Wasn't it the old politics all over again? "Russell never hurt me," he said. "Jack lied to me, Bobby smeared me, and Teddy never did anything to help."

To some, at any rate, this scale of dislikes—the Kennedys above Long's approval of Daley—is out of order, but McCarthy was not acting uncharacteristically. In the Senate he refused to vote for reforms when they came as small amendments to major legislation—he wanted substance, not shadow. Since he never credited the Kennedys in the role of reformers, the Ted Kennedy issue was for him exactly that kind of partial gesture people mistake for real change. And just as in his campaign he refused all entreaties to play the political game with the delegates, so now he was once more insisting that he would deal in essences, not forms.

McCarthy's iconoclasm toward forms and rituals may help to explain his strengths and weaknesses as a politician. He was clear-headed, proud, and perhaps a little self-righteous. He saw into things, and that which was revealed to him as synthetic or idolatrous he would not accept, regardless of its political utility. Moreover, his opinions on what was synthetic or wrong were entirely his own, and not greatly subject to the influence of others. His essential probity made him attractively different to millions of voters who had been lied to and misled so often that McCarthy's rugged honesty was something many believed they would never find on a platform again. His greatest triumph, perhaps, was that he seemed to embody all those old-fashioned virtues like courage, independence, self-reliance, and generosity of spirit that the country gave lip service to but which nobody really thought were much help as guides through the labyrinth of modern life. Yet in the end many perhaps empty forms and rituals do acquire a reality in the minds of men and a successful politician may have to deal with them as such. So for him his Foreign Relations step or his vote for Long were part of "a child's game," especially as compared to his challenge of the President. He seemed surprised that so many people took them seriously and judged him accordingly.

His ideas about leadership, too, were at variance with what many expected. He would not, and probably could not, portray himself, as Richard Nixon did, in the mold of a successful business executive. (Nixon's campaign posters showed him with an open attaché case—a "problem-solver," a "decision-maker.") Nor was McCarthy the general of a political army. "I'm not your leader. What do you need a leader for?" he said frequently after the campaign: Go organize yourselves. Only then will you be strong. Indeed, some of his acts seemed almost expressly calculated to free him from the demands of his former followers. He would be a spokesman, an articulator of ideas, not a messiah.

If there was a time for silence, as he believed, that time would one day end and he would begin speaking out on issues like the draft. His political base had been shaken, his credibility challenged but not, he judged, as much as pundits said. They had been wrong before, and so had the polls, which now showed him down in Minnesota. He had his options: he could get out of politics or he could rebuild his strength at home and run again, perhaps as a Democrat, despite his earlier disavowals, perhaps not. He could even run from a different state, like California or New York. As for 1972, so much depended on a long series of *ifs*. But a lively possibility in McCarthy's mind in the spring of 1969 was a third party.

On July 24, 1969, Eugene McCarthy ended speculation about his immediate political future by declaring that he would not run again for the Senate from Minnesota or from anywhere else. An aide insisted that McCarthy, despite earlier disclaimers, could have had the Minnesota Democratic nomination if he wanted it, and been re-elected. His withdrawal, rather, lay in a complex of reasons —his feeling that he had done all he could, or wished to do, in the Senate, his pessimism about reform within the Democratic party, and, perhaps, personal considerations as well. But the door remained slightly ajar for a McCarthy Presidential candidacy as an independent in 1972. That would depend on circumstances—on student unrest on the campuses, on Vietnam, on the performance of the President, on whether third-party candidates for state offices in 1970 built up sufficient support and leverage for the effort in 1972. McCarthy himself was not optimistic about the country. "We're back where we were in 1967," he remarked in a depressed moment.

Though Act III, cannot yet be written, Eugene McCarthy made 1968 a year Americans will long remember. A man met his times and there were certain incalculable results. Whether the man and his times will collide again no one can be sure.

Index

Index

Abrams, Creighton W., 275
Abzug, Bella, 20
ACT; *see* Alternative Candidate
Task Force
ADA; *see* Americans for Democratic Action
Albee, Edward, 217
Albert, Carl, 215, 229, 271
Albert, Eddie, 178
Allman, Joseph, 147
Ally, Carl, 132
Alternative Candidate Task Force
(ACT), 24
Americans for Democratic Action
(ADA), 22, 50, 153, 160;
World, 22
Anderson, Eugenie, 52–53
Anti McCarthy allegations, 60, 62–
64

Bachman, Eve, 172
Bailey, John, 261
Baldwin, James, 223
Bassett, Grace, 59
Biossat, Bruce, 235
Blatnik, John, 292
Boggs, Hale, 266, 274–75
Bond, Julian, 224, 261; at national
convention, 248–49, 264, 272

Bornstein, Matty, 92
"Bossism," 203–204
Boutin, Bernard, 89–90
Boyle, John, 117
Branigin, Roger, 128, 130, 136,
142, 146
Brown, Robert McAfee, 52
Brown, Samuel, 24, 91, 248
Bruner, Wally, 177
Burroughs, William, 241

California: campaigning in, 174–
89, conflicts between in-state
and out-of-state workers, 175;
Kennedy assassination, 189–90;
McCarthy forces in ghettos,
182–83; McCarthy-Kennedy debate, 184–87
California Democratic Council
(CDC), 23
Callahan, John, 147
Callanan, Charles, 12, 138, 152
Campaign Consultants, Inc., 9
Campaign expenditures, 3–4, 9, 80,
97, 132–33, 143, 169, 206–207,
211, 225
Campaigns: in California, 174–89;
conflicts between campaign
workers, 111–14, 129, 132, 150,

Campaigns (cont'd)
175, 212, 215–16, 226–30, 232–
33; disorganization of, 111–14;
financial contributions to, 79,
81, 134, 153, 195–96, 219; financial problems of, 132–36, 139,
142, 145, 147, 150–51, 175, 177,
206, 212, 216; in Indiana, 129–
41; in Nebraska, 142–43; in New
Hampshire, 3–13, 85–98; in New
York, 197; in Oregon, 144–71;
reorganization of, 151ff.; volunteer workers in, 3, 6–7, 10–11,
91–96, 110–12, 117–18, 216–19;
in Wisconsin, 110–24; Women
for McCarthy, 54, 95, 149, 218;
see also Pre-convention campaign
Campaigns, organized: as discounted by McCarthy, 53–55,
79–83, 114
Carlson, Bill, 67
CDA; see Coalition for a Democratic Alternative
CDC; see California Democratic
Council
Central Intelligence Agency
(CIA); Eugene McCarthy and,
51, 61
Chicago: Democratic National
Convention in, 240–79; violence
in, during convention, 276–81;
and Yippies, 256, 277; see also
Daley, Richard J.
Church, Frank, 25, 32, 77
CIA; see Central Intelligence
Agency
Citizens for Kennedy, 140
Citizens for McCarthy, 195–96;
and conflict with CDA, 195–96
Clark, Blair, 82–83, 86, 107, 135,
152–54, 175, 205, 231, 233, 261
Clark, Joseph, 31, 77
Clark, Robert, 184

Cleaver, Eldridge, 175
Clifford, Clark, 59, 104, 151–52,
154, 208, 210, 229
Coalition for a Democratic Alter-
native (CDA), 5, 24, 195–98,
207–208, 226; and conflict with
Citizens for McCarthy, 195–96
Coalition for an Open Convention,
256
Cogley, John, 82, 141
Cohen, Steve, 156, 279–80
Cole, Jack, 163
Comden, Betty, 115
Commission on the Democratic Se-
lection of Presidential Nominees,
230
Committee for a Democratic Con-
vention, 230, 253
Conference of Concerned Demo-
crats, 24, 76
Connally, John, 65, 204, 210, 241,
250, 254, 259
Connecticut primary, 145
Cooper, John Sherman, 78
Costikyan, Edward N., 153, 209,
226–27
Crangle, Joe, 271
Credentials Committee of Demo-
cratic National Convention,
242–49; Julian Bond and, 248–
49; sessions of, 245–51
Criswell, John, 216, 229
Culver, Nan, 150
Curtis, Kenneth, 221
Czechoslovakia: McCarthy's com-
ments on Soviet invasion of,
236–37

Daley, Richard J., 65, 121, 214,
216, 255–56, 258–59, 264, 268–
70, 273, 293
Davis, Sammy, 142
Degnan, June, 79

Delord, Jean F., 147
Democratic-Farmer-Labor Party, 47
Democratic National Convention, 240–79; Credentials Committee of, 242–49; and "Draft-Kennedy" idea, 268; and Humphrey's position on Vietnam, 266; irregularities in selection of delegates to, 242–49; Julian Bond at, 248–49, 264, 272; and Kennedy's decision to remove name from nomination, 268–70; keynote address of, 263; McCarthy's admission of defeat in, 271–72; peace-plank battle in, 251–55, 274–76; Rules Committee at, 249–51; unit-rule question at, 250, 263, 271; violence in Chicago during, 276–81
Dillon, Douglas, 78
Dirksen, Everett, 236
Dissenting Democrats (California), 24
Dodd, Thomas, 67
"Dump Johnson" movement, 23–24, 31, 77
Dutton, Fred, 145, 253

Edwards, Don, 25, 35
Eldridge, Ronnie, 23
Eller, Jerome, 33, 108, 110, 137, 144, 152–53, 227, 237
Ellington, Buford, 260
Epstein, Jason, 176
Evans, Rowland, 211
Expenditures, campaign, 3–4, 9, 80, 97, 132–33, 143, 169, 206–207, 211, 225

Farmer-Labor Party, 47
Feiffer, Jules, 176

Feigenbaum, Joel, 92
Ferency, Zoltan, 24
Fife, Martin, 134
Financial contributions to campaigns, 79, 81, 134, 153, 195–96, 219
Financial problems of campaigns, 132–36, 139, 142, 145, 147, 150–51, 175, 177, 206, 212, 216
Finletter, Thomas K., 15 16, 195
Finney, Thomas, 151–55, 177–79, 185–88, 194, 207–213, 215–16, 225–30, 237, 261, 272–73
Ford, Gerald, 236
Freeman, Orville, 48, 56, 57
French, Eleanor Clark, 195
Friedan, Betty, 219
Friedman, Bruce Jay, 217
Fromm, Erich, 83, 176, 289
Fulbright, J. William, 65

Gabler, Joe, 67
Galbraith, John K., 25, 261
Gans, Curtis, 7–8, 22–24, 80, 91, 94, 107, 109, 116, 131–32, 141, 150, 153–55, 175, 196, 205–206, 212, 226, 228, 232, 248
Garth, David, 153–54, 177–80
Gavin, James, 25
Genêt, Jean, 241
Georgia Democratic Forum, 247–48
Gilligan, John, 231, 253–54, 258, 268, 275
Gleason, Martin, 201–205, 257
Goldberg, Arthur, 17
Goodwin, Richard, 5, 28, 95–96, 106–109, 122, 213–15, 225, 232–33, 241, 254–55, 259, 261, 268, 270
Gore, Albert, 275
Gore, Jack, 24
Gorman, Paul, 165–66

"Grass roots" campaign, 3, 9, 248
Green, Adolph, 115
Green, Diana, 148
Green, Don, 212
Grey, James, 248
Grossman, Jerome, 84–85
Gruening, Ernest, 65
Gulf of Tonkin resolution, 29, 65, 103

Haley, Alex, 223
Harrington, Michael, 219
Harris, Fred, 229
Hart, Philip, 221–22
Hartke, Vance, 25, 31, 32, 221
Hearnes, Warren, 122
Hemenway, Russell, 15–17, 60, 153, 208
Henkart, Maryanna, 148
Hershey, Louis B., 114
Herzog, Arthur, 4–13, 116, 144–49, 156–61, 172
Herzog, Mrs. Arthur, 5, 148
Hiatt, Arnold, 81, 133, 135, 153, 208
Hill, Gerald N., 23–24, 32, 175, 210, 259, 264
Hills, L. Rust, 8
Hoeh, David, 12, 24, 86
Hoff, Philip, 221, 230–31, 271
Hoffa, James, 257
Hoffman, Dustin, 139
Hogan, Gene, 147
Holsinger, G. W., 175, 209
Hoosiers for a Democratic Alternative, 24
Hoover, J. Edgar, 114
Hornsby, Jeremy, 237
Hughes, Harold, 214, 230–31, 272, 288
Hughes, Richard J., 242, 245–46, 249
Humphrey, Hubert H., 16–17, 26–27, 47–49, 54–56, 59, 65–68, 75, 116, 131, 145, 154, 157, 159, 163–66, 178–79, 188, 193, 197–99, 202–205, 208–211, 214, 224–25, 228–31, 234–35, 237–40, 243, 245, 248, 252, 254, 258–61, 263, 265–70, 276, 280, 285, 287, 291; McCarthy statement on, 163–65; at national convention, 248, 266; position on Vietnam of, 266; winning the nomination, 277
Huntley-Brinkley, 97
Hurtado, Dolores, 150
Hynes, Emerson, 67

Ickes, Harold, 7, 23, 195, 207
Indiana: campaigning in, 129–41; conflicts between in-state and out-of-state workers, 129, 132; hostility between McCarthy forces and Kennedy forces, 140–41; Indianapolis Star, 139–40; McCarthy attack on Kennedy, 141; primary election, 142
Innouye, Daniel K., keynote address of, 263

Jackson, Jesse, 223–24
Janeway, Eliot, 60, 82, 211, 221
Javits, Jacob, 198
Jenkins, Walter, 67
Johnson, Lyndon B., 6, 13, 16–17, 22, 26, 30–31, 33–36, 56, 60, 65–71, 75–78, 84–86, 89–91, 101, 103, 116, 128, 203–204, 208, 210–211, 236, 250, 258, 260, 266, 277; "Dump Johnson" movement, 23–24, 31, 77; McCarthy on, 26, 36, 56, 77, 78; on McCarthy's withdrawal from

1964 Vice-Presidential race, 67; out of Presidential race, 120; public disapproval of handling of Vietnam War by, 26
Johnson, Mrs. Lyndon B., 35, 65
Jones, Clarence, 195
Joseph, Geri, 275

Karenga, Ron, 182
Katzenbach, Nicholas deB., 62; before Senate Foreign Relations Committee, 29, 32
Keating, Kenneth, 157–58
Kefauver, Estes, 26
Kelly, Harry, 163
Kempton, Murray, 214, 226
Kennedy, Edward, 62, 84–85, 107–109, 145, 253, 258–59, 264–65, 267–70, 292–93; "Draft-Kennedy" idea, 268; removes name from nomination, 268–70
Kennedy, John F., 53, 55–56, 104, 293; animosity of McCarthy toward, 53, 55–56; elegy written by McCarthy after assassination of, 58; McCarthy campaign for, 57
Kennedy, Robert F., 17–18, 21, 25, 30 31, 35, 55, 70, 75, 84–86, 96, 98, 118, 120–21, 127–28, 138–43, 145 46, 148, 152, 157, 160, 163–72, 178, 182–83, 188, 202, 204–205, 213, 257, 283–85, 293; assassination of, 189–90; attacks on McCarthy's voting record, 157–60; debate with McCarthy, 184–87; entry into Presidential race of, 102–109, 139; McCarthy on noncandidacy of, 103–104
Kennedy, Roger, 52
Kennedys: animosity of McCarthy toward, 53, 55–56, 292–93; attempts by, to have McCarthy

withdraw from Massachusetts primary, 84–85
Kenworthy, E. W. (Ned), 34, 98, 163
Kerner Report, 62
Kerr, Clark, 252
King, John W., 86, 88–90, 97
King, Martin Luther, 138, 185
King, Mrs. Martin Luther, 138
Knudson, Coya, 53
Kopkind, Andrew, 63
Kovner, Sarah, 5, 195, 196, 207
Kraft, Joseph, 34
Kramarsky, Werner H., 133–34, 177
Kuchel, Thomas, 147
Kupferman, Theodore R., 20

Larner, Jeremy, 62, 141, 165 66, 236
Lausche, Frank, 231
Lawrence, William, 184
Lefever, Ernest W., 251n.
Levander, Harold, 292
Levine, Laurence, 33, 153, 195
Lewin, Leonard, 176
Lindsay, John V., 20, 134, 284
Lipsitz, Richard, 195
Loeb, William, 85, 100–101
Lomax, Louis, 182–83, 223
Long, Russell, 292–94
Lowell, Robert, 19, 95, 167–68, 176, 186
Lowenstein, Allard K., 21–25, 32, 77, 91, 109, 237, 256; formation of a national stop-the-war, dump-Johnson-if-necessary organization, 22–24; "shopping" for a candidate, 25–26
Loy, Myrna, 139
Lucey, Patrick, 131, 215, 230–31, 240–41, 257–59, 261, 268–69
Lynch, Thomas C., 188

Macdonald, Dwight, 219
MacLaren, David, 148
Maddox, Lester, 238, 247–48
Mailer, Norman, 57, 217, 273
Mankiewicz, Frank, 253
Mansfield, Mike, 78, 159
Martin, Richard, 99
Massachusetts primary, 96; attempts to have McCarthy withdraw from, 84–85
McCarthy, Eugene J., 15–19, 26–31, 282–94; admission of defeat, 271–72; animosity toward the Kennedys, 53, 55–56, 292–93; announcement of his future cabinet, 235–36; anti-McCarthy allegations, 60, 62–64; attempts of, to get Democrats to run against Johnson, 30–31; as a Benedictine novice, 42–44; in Berkeley, 31; birthplace and ancestors of, 37–39; break with Johnson Administration, 70; in California, 180–83, 185–90; campaigning for John F. Kennedy, 57; on the CIA, 51, 61; concern about increase in Presidential power, 17, 29; conflicting observations on, 59–61; Congressional legislative and voting record of, 50–52, 59–64, 140, 158–60; criticism of American participation in Vietnam War by, 70, 77–78; debate with Joseph McCarthy, 51; debate with Robert Kennedy, 184–87; decision to enter Indiana primary, 127–28; decision to enter New Hampshire primary, 86–87; decision to reorganize campaign, 151ff.; decision to run for Presidency, 32ff.; doubts of people as to his willingness to become President, 219ff.; as an econom-

ics teacher, 46; education of, 39–40, 42; effect of Robert Kennedy's assassination upon, 193–94; elegy written after John F. Kennedy's assassination, 58; as an employee in the War Department, 44; first speech after entering Presidential race, 76–77; in his view, accomplishments of campaign, 290; in the House of Representatives, 49–52; in Indiana, 129, 136–38, 141; irreverence for political personages of, 15–16; on John F. Kennedy, 55; Kennedy's attack on voting record of, 140–41, 157–60; lack of connection with black community, 137–38, 181–83; lack of financial support, 34; lack of support for, by nationally known Democrats, 35; low-keyed approach to blacks and civil rights, 31–32; on Lyndon B. Johnson, 17, 26, 36, 56, 77, 78; on Lyndon Johnson's withdrawal from race, 121; name of, placed in nomination, 276; at national convention, 240–41, 260–61, 264–65, 267–69, 271–74, 277–81; in New Hampshire, 12–14, 87–88, 96–98; nominating speech for Adlai Stevenson by, 17, 57; in Oregon, 161–65, 167–68, 170–71; organized campaigns discounted by, 53–55, 79–83, 114; pre-convention campaign of, 219–39; pre-convention political mistakes of, 235–37; press comments on, 34–35, 62–63, 78–79, 88–89, 100–101, 137, 139–40, 229; refusal to withdraw from Massachusetts primary, 84–85; reluctance of Stevensonians to support, 19, 33–34; resignation from Senate Foreign Relations Committee, 292; on Robert Kennedy's decision to run, 105–106, 108–109; on Robert Kennedy's noncandidacy, 103–104; on Senate seniority system, 59; as a Senator, 55–71; on Soviet invasion of Czechoslovakia, 236–37; speeches on Vietnam War by, 166–67; statement of, about supporting Humphrey if he changed position on Vietnam, 163–65; support of "Operation Breadbasket," 223–24; on a third party, 17; thoughts of, on being first Catholic President, 55; Vietnam plan of, 78; vote for Russell Long by, 292–94; willingness to run as Johnson's Vice-President, 65; in Wisconsin, 114–16, 118–23; withdrawal from 1964 Vice-Presidential race, 66–67; see also Campaigns, Pre-convention campaign, Primary elections

McCarthy, Mrs. Eugene, 27, 40–42, 44, 54, 138, 155

McCarthy, Joseph: debate with Eugene McCarthy, 51

McCarthy report on unemployment problems, 62

"McCarthy Summer," 216–19

McCarthy's Marauders or Mavericks, 52

McCoy, Thomas, 151–53, 155, 208, 227, 261

McGovern, George, 25, 31, 32, 230–31, 238, 353–54, 265

McGrory, Mary, 104, 189

McIntyre, Thomas, 89–90

McNamara, Robert, 103

Melnick, Daniel, 178

Michelson, Arthur, 232–33

Miglautsch, Tom, 117

Miller, Arthur, 176

Miller, Mayne, 209

Mills, Michael, 148

Minnesota: Democratic-Farmer-Labor Party in, 47–48; McCarthy's birthplace and education in, 37–45; McCarthy's first Congressional campaign in, 49; McCarthy's Senatorial campaign in, 53–55, 68

Mitau, G. Theodore, 47

Mitchell, Stephen A., 201–205, 214–16, 227–28, 237, 244, 250, 257, 260–61, 272–74

Mixner, Dave, 212, 248

Moore, Garry, 139

Morgan, Howard, 147, 246

Morgan, Thomas B., 184

Morgenthau, Hans, 235

Morse, Wayne, 65, 253, 275

Mott, Stewart, 134

Moyers, Bill, 288

Murphy, Charles, 266

Murphy, Philip, 141

Muskie, Edmund, 238, 252, 293

National Association for the Advancement of Colored People (NAACP), 137

National Committee for an Effective Congress (NCEC), 15, 28, 60, 160, 288

National Committee for a Political Settlement in Vietnam, 252

National Committee for a Sane Nuclear Policy (SANE), 19

National Conference on the New Politics, 20

National Student Association (NSA), 24, 229

National Student March, 256

NCEC; see National Committee for an Effective Congress

Nebraska: campaigning in, 142–43; primary election, 143

Nee, William (and wife), 54, 87, 122, 132, 170, 179, 232–33

Negaro, Charles, 248

Negro meetings and rallies, complications of, 222–23

New England Peace Action Committee, 85

New Hampshire: campaigning in, 3–13, 85–98; Manchester *Union-Leader,* 85–86, 100–101; primary election, 14, 98–99; Salem campaign, 7–14; student volunteers in, 91–94

"New politics," 8

New York: campaigning in, 197; fight for delegate votes, 198; primary election, 197–98

New York Coalition for a Democratic Alternative; *see* Coalition for a Democratic Alternative

Newfield, Jack, 78

Newman, Paul, 117, 139

Newman, Phyllis, 116, 117

Nixon, Richard M., 11, 60, 105, 118, 145, 199, 214, 224–25, 258, 266, 267, 284, 291–92, 294

Novak, Robert, 211

NSA; *see* National Student Association

O'Brien, Lawrence, 104, 145, 230, 237–38

O'Connell, Patricia, 148

O'Donnell, Kenneth, 214, 230, 253, 275

O'Dwyer, Paul, 195, 198, 275

"Oklahoma Octopus," 229

"Operation Breadbasket," 223–24

Oregon: campaigning in, 144–71; primary election, 172

Oregonians for McCarthy, 144*ff.*

Organized campaigns discounted by McCarthy, 53–55, 79–83, 114

Packard, Vance, 176

Painter, John, 147

Peace Action Committee, 20

Peace and Freedom Party, 175

Peace movement, 19*ff.*

Pearson, Drew, 63–64

Pell, Claiborne, 253

Pennsylvania primary, 145

People for McCarthy, 218

"People Power," 200, 205

Peretz, Martin, 134, 153–54

Perry, Eleanor, 169–70

Perry, Frank, 170

Perry, James M., 8

Peter, Paul, and Mary, 168

Peterson, Don, 24–25, 112

Pirie, Robert, 133, 208

Podesta, Tony, 279–80

Polls: disparity among, 234; predictions of, 13, 36, 94, 97, 100, 103, 116, 142, 145, 160, 171, 180, 189, 209, 223, 224–25, 234–35, 258, 261

Poor People's Campaign, 197

Pre-convention campaign, 219–39; at Boston's Fenway Park, 225; complications caused by presence of Secret Service during, 222; dissension within, 232–33; doubts of people as to McCarthy's willingness to become President, 219*ff.*; McCarthy before state delegations during, 220–21; "McCarthy Summer," 216–19; McCarthy's comments on Soviet invasion of Czechoslovakia, 236–37; McCarthy's political mistakes during, 235–37; split leadership of, 226–29; support of "Operation Breadbasket," 223–24; *see also* Campaigns

Press comments on Eugene McCarthy, 34–35, 62–63, 78–79, 88–89, 100–101, 137, 139–40, 229

Primary elections, 84, 283–84; in Connecticut, 145; fight for delegate votes in New York after, 198; in Indiana, 142; in Massachusetts, 84–85, 96; in Nebraska, 143; in New Hampshire, 14, 98–99; in New York, 197–98; in Oregon, 172; in Pennsylvania, 145; in Wisconsin, 124

Pueblo, capture of the, 91, 103

Pulliam, Eugene C., 140

Quigley, Abigail; *see* McCarthy, Mrs. Eugene

Quigley, Stephen, 132–36, 153, 205–206

Rafferty, Max, 147

Randall, Tony, 8, 10

Raskin, Hy, 251

Rauh, Joseph, 21, 225, 244, 247–48, 261, 263

Rayburn, Sam, 50

Reece, Norval, 155, 161–62, 222

Reed, Herbert, 113–14, 182, 244

Reston, James, 167–68

Reuther, Walter, 66, 268

Reynolds, Frank, 184

Rockefeller, Nelson A., 145, 162, 224, 292

Romney, George, 9, 25, 85; withdrawal from race, 96

Roosevelt, Eleanor, 21

Roosevelt, Franklin D., 47

Rosenberg, Alex, 23

Rosenblatt, Maurice, 31, 67, 152, 153, 206, 208

Rosetti, Frank, 218

Rusk, Dean, 29, 32, 105, 114, 265

Ryan, Robert, 10

Safer, John, 33, 67, 152–53, 208

Salem, New Hampshire, 7–14; McCarthy in, 12–13; Nixon in, 11

Salinger, Pierre, 140, 143, 171, 214, 254, 275

Saltonstall, John, 217

SANE; *see* National Committee for a Sane Nuclear Policy

Sayre, Francis, 32

Schauinger, Herman, 46, 67, 212

Scheer, Robert, 20

Schmidt, John, 242

Schoumacher, David, 98, 107–109, 189, 269 70

Schrade, Paul, 257

Scott, Lael; *see* Herzog, Mrs. Arthur

SDS; *see* Students for a Democratic Society

Secret Service: complications caused by presence of, 222

Serling, Rod, 139

Shaick, Harry, 150

Shapiro, Samuel, 251

Shea, John, 15–16, 33, 195

Shivers, Alan, 203

Shmerz, Herbert, 157

Simon and Garfunkel, 139

Singal, Dan, 116–17, 148

Smaby, Alpha, 25

Smith, Margaret Chase, 59

Smith, Stephen, 157, 231, 268–70

Sorensen, Theodore, 109, 143, 145, 198–99, 214, 230, 254, 275

Southern Christian Leadership Conference, 223

Southern, Terry, 217, 241
Stassen, Harold, 47
Stavis, Ben, 92
Stein, Howard, 81–82, 95, 97, 133, 135–36, 153–54, 226
Steingut, Stanley, 214, 226–27
Stevenson, Adlai, 15, 18, 26–27, 56, 287; McCarthy's nominating speech for, 17, 57
Stevensonians, 195; belief of, that McCarthy could become successor to the liberal leadership, 17–18; reluctance of, to support McCarthy, 19, 33–34
Stone, I. F., 78
Stone, Martin, 154
"Stop the war" movement, 19ff.
Strauss, Lewis B., 61
Student volunteers, 10–11, 91–94, 110–111, 117–18, 132; confused by Kennedy entrance into Presidential race, 131; film about, 169–70
Students for a Democratic Society (SDS), 20
Styron, William, 176, 217
Svourc, Claire, 148
Sykes, Jay, 112

Terry, Robert, 156
Teuber, Andy, 148
Theater people campaigning for McCarthy, 8, 10, 115–16, 117, 139, 168, 176
Third party idea, 21; McCarthy opposed to, 17
Thye, Edward, 52–53, 55
Thomas, Piri, 223
Thomas, Steve, 148
Travers, Mary, 95
Truman, Harry S., 55, 254
Tuchman, Jessica, 8, 107, 242

Unemployment Problems, Special Committee on, 61–62
Unit-rule question, 204–205; at Democratic National Convention, 250, 263, 271
Unruh, Jesse, 212, 214–15, 220, 230, 257, 259, 263–64

Vanden Heuvel, William, 109, 157, 160
Vannick, Charles, 258
Vaughn, Robert, 24
Vietnam War: disapproval of Johnson's handling of, 26; Humphrey's position on, 266; McCarthy's criticism of American participation in, 70, 77–78; McCarthy's plans for, 78; McCarthy's speeches on, 166–67; national convention fight about plank on, 251–55, 274–76; President urged to continue bombing suspension, 70; "stop the war" movement, 19ff.
Volunteer workers, 3, 6–7, 10–11, 91–96, 110–12, 117–18, 216–219

Wallace, Henry A., 48
War Mobilization League, 256
Warren, Earl, 17
Warshafsky, Ted, 112
Watkins, Minnesota, 37–39
Watson, James, 147
Weinstein, Hannah, 219
Weisl, Ed, 23
Westmoreland, William, 5, 14
Whelan, Wayne, 242
Whipple, Blaine, 147, 155–56
White, Paul Dudley, 217
White, William S., 34

Wicker, Tom, 69, 142
Wiesner, Jerome, 217
Wilkins, Roy, 137
Wilson, Jerome, 20
Wisconsin: campaigning in, 110–124; conflicts between in-state and out-of-state workers, 111–114; election eve speech, 122–23; primary election, 124; *Waukesha Freeman*, 118

Wisconsin Concerned Democrats, 24
Women for McCarthy, 54, 95, 149, 218; "Operation Penetration," 95

Yarborough, Ralph, 203, 279
Yippies (Youth International Party), 256, 277
Yumich, George, 280